New Horizons in Periodontology

Proceedings of the 25th Scientific Congress
of the
Turkish Society of Periodontology
Antalya, Turkey
21 - 27 May 1995

Edited by
Serdar Mutlu
Istanbul University, Faculty of Dentistry, Capa, Istanbul, Turkey
Stephen Porter
Eastman Dental Institute, University of London, 256 Gray's Inn Road, London, UK
Selçuk Yılmaz
Marmara University, Faculty of Dentistry, Nisantasi, Istanbul, Turkey
Crispian Scully
Eastman Dental Institute, University of London, 256 Gray's Inn Road, London, UK

SCIENCE REVIEWS

British Library Cataloguing in Publication Data

New Horizons in Periodontology
Proceedings of the 25th Scientific Congress of the Turkish Society of
Periodontology

A catalogue record of this book is available from the British Library
ISBN 1-900814-20-X

Production editor: Sara Nash
Typeset by DL Technology, PO Box 9, Buckhurst Hill, Essex IG9 5BE, UK
Printed in the UK by Cambrian Printers, Aberystwyth, Wales

In the USA, Henchek & Associates, 155 North Michigan Ave, Suite 500, Chicago,
IL 60601, USA.
Fax: +1 312 913 1404
e-mail: vchenchek@worldnet.att.net

Contents

Introduction

The Turkish Society of Periodontology (TSP) was founded in 1970 by Professor Peker Sandallı and his colleagues. Over the 25 years TSP has served Turkish dentists and patients, in the area of periodontology, by providing symposiums, courses and scientific meetings. The TSP now has more than 200 members and continues to grow. TSP works closely with the International Academy of Periodontology and European Federation of Periodontology. Many internationally renowned speakers participate in our meetings.

At the silver anniversary of TSP, the 25th scientific meeting, we were fortunate to include excellent speakers from all over the world. These Proceedings we believe are an excellent way to celebrate the past 25 years. We hope that they will provide periodontists with a new window in their search for excellence in both patient care and in the science of periodontology.

Serdar Mutlu BDS, MSc, PhD
Stephen Porter PhD, MD, FDSRCS, FDSRSCE
Selcuk Yılmaz BDS, MSc, Dr Med Dent, PhD
Crispian Scully PhD, MD, MDS, FDSRCS, FDSRCPS, FFDRCSI, FRCPath

Acknowledgements

We are grateful to the organisers of the meeting and to the main sponsor Turkish Airlines.

We would like to thank the organising committee of the 25th meeting of the TSP:

Dr Elvan Efeoğlu, Dr Ülkü Noyan, Dr Ali Riza Kılıç, Dr Bahar Kuru,
Dr Tevhide Oktay, Dr Okan Acar, Dr Erengül Kıraç, Dr Murat Özveri,
Dr Sinem Kayrak and Dr Bora Yıldıran.

We are also grateful to our colleagues Dr Aslan Gökbuget and Dr Uluc Yılmaz for their help in the organisation of the scientific program of the meeting. Our special thanks go the contributors of the Proceedings; without them this book would not have been possible. Finally we would like to thank Science Reviews for their work in the preparation of these Proceedings.

1   Local and systemic medications: adjuncts to periodontal therapy

Seb Ciancio

Department of Periodontics, School of Dental Medicine, University of Buffalo, State University of New York, New York 14214, USA

A variety of chemical agents have been evaluated in a number of studies relative to their abilities to either reduce plaque already formed or to retard its formation. The role of these chemical agents as part of a treatment plan for patients with periodontal disease has increased in importance in recent years as our knowledge of the characteristics of supragingival plaque has increased. The value of topically applied agents in the alteration of plaque has been clarified. The various available agents are summarized below.

Fluorides

A number of short-term studies indicate that stannous fluoride is an effective anti-plaque agent with activity related in part, to the presence of the tin ion.[1,2] A 28-month study in 12-year old children who rinsed daily with either 0.05% sodium fluoride or 0.1% stannous fluoride showed efficacy at the end of an initial 4-month period. However, no difference was apparent after 16 and 28 months.[3]

Most recent studies have evaluated a 0.4% stannous fluoride gel. Several studies have reported significant reductions in plaque and/or gingival inflammation. One study reported significantly less plaque in abutment teeth with SnF2 gel.[4] While another study in orthodontic patients found no reductions in plaque.[5] One of the problems with stannous fluoride is that is has been difficult to develop a formula which is stable for long time periods but newer formulations such as stabilized stannous fluoride(6,7) may correct this problem. The only adverse effect associated with stannous fluoride is the development of a black stain on some teeth which can be removed by a routine prophylaxis.

Bisbiguanides

Chlorhexidine gluconate, a cationic bisbiguanide, is the best known and most widely used member of this class.

The efficacy of chlorhexidine in significantly reducing plaque and gingivitis (compared to placebos) when used twice daily as a supplement to toothbrushing is now well established. Early studies employed 10mL of a 0.2% solution for a total of 20mg chlorhexidine per use. Studies supporting the effectiveness of 0.12% chlorhexidine, used 15mL of a 0.12% solution.[8,9] The total amount of chlorhexidine per use was essentially the same, and the clinical findings with the two formulations were similar-plaque reductions in the 50 to 55% range and reduction in gingivitis of about 45%. The major side effects of chlorhexidine are a brown staining of teeth and tongue, formation of supragingival calculus, taste alteration, and oral desquamation in children.[10,11] Additionally, allergic reactions have been reported in some patients, particularly Asians.[12,13,14]

Its mechanism of action is due mainly to rupture of the bacterial cell wall and precipitation of the cytoplasmic content.

When used following brushing one should allow at least 30 minutes between toothbrushing and rinsing with this chemical because of an interaction (and possible inactivation) between various positive charged dentifrice detergents, and the cationic chlorhexidine [15] Also, an antagonistic interaction can also occur with the anionic fluoride ion in mouthrinses, toothpastes and stannous fluoride products. The 30-minute interval is intended to minimize diminution in activity of chlorhexidine.

Essential oils

Listerine is the main product found in this category and is neutral in electrical charge. It is a combination of the phenol-related essential oils, thymol and eucalyptol, mixed with menthol and methylsalicylate. Efficacy has been seen in both short and long term studies regardless of the level of oral hygiene.

Recent studies have been 6 months in duration. Plaque reduction has ranged from 20 to 34% and gingivitis reduction from 28 to 34% when Listerine was used twice daily following toothbrushing.[16,17,18] Microbiologic studies demonstrated that there was no emergence of opportunistic, potential or presumptive pathogens.

The only adverse effects have been an initial burning sensation and bitter taste. The mechanism of action of phenolics is by cell wall disruption and inhibition of bacterial enzymes. Also, there is some evidence that it may extract the lipopolysaccharide derived endotoxin from Gram negative bacteria.[19]

Quaternary ammonium compounds

The agent most commonly used in this category is cetylpyridium chloride in a concentration of 0.05%. This group of chemical agents is cationic and binds to oral tissues but not as strongly as the bisbiguanides. When used orally, they bind strongly to plaque and tooth surfaces but are released from these binding sites at a more rapid rate than chlorhexidine. This rapid release is one of the reasons why they are not as effective as chlorhexidine. This agent has been evaluated in a number of short-term studies with efficacy on plaque reduction of 25-35%. However, its use in a six-month study has only been reported once with a reduction in plaque of 14% reported.[20]

The quaternary ammonium compounds exhibit some of the same side effects as chlorhexidine. These include some staining and enhanced calculus formation, especially when used at higher concentrations. Burning sensation and occasional desquamation have also been reported.

Their mechanism of action is related to their ability to rupture the cell wall and alter cytoplasmic contents.

Sanguinarine

Sanguinarine is currently used in both a mouthrinse and toothpaste as an anti-plaque/gingivitis agent (Viadent). It is an alkaloid extract from the blood root plant *Sanguinaria canadensis*. It contains the extract at 0.03% (equivalent to 0.01% sanguinarine) and 0.2% zinc chloride. The findings on the use of the mouthrinse and dentifrice used singly have been equivocal. Some studies report a significant reduction in plaque and gingivitis.[21,22] Others suggest minimal effect.[23]

When mouthrinse and dentifrice usage were combined, however, significant reductions in plaque and gingivitis were reported in three 6-month studies with plaque reductions of 17 to 42% and reduction in gingivitis of 18 to 57%.[24,25] The only adverse effect reported with this agent has been a burning sensation when used initially. Although this product has been shown to have a strong affinity for plaque, its mechanism of action has not been clarified.

Triclosan

This chemical is available in dentifrices and mouthrinses under a variety of names in many countries outside of the United States and is now available in the United States as Colgate Total Toothpaste. Triclosan is both a bisphenol and a nonionic germicide with low toxicity and a broad spectrum of antibacterial activity. It is widely used in soaps, antiperspirants, and cosmetic toiletries. Since it does not bind well to oral sites due to its lack of a strong positive charge, formulations have been developed to enhance its ability to bind to plaque and teeth. These formulations include:
_combination with zinc citrate to take advantage of the potential anti-plaque and
    anti-calculus properties of the latter
_incorporation of triclosan in a copolymer of methoxyethylene and maleic acid to
    increase its retention time (Colgate Total); and
_combination with pyrophosphates to enhance its calculus reducing properties.

These products also contain 0.243% sodium fluoride/silica base to provide an anti-caries effect. Triclosan in concentrations of 0.2 to 0.5% and zinc citrate from 0.5 to 1% have resulted in a significant reduction in plaque and gingivitis. They also have been shown to produce a significant reduction in calculus when it was part of the study.[26,27]

Significant reductions in plaque, gingivitis, and calculus have also been found with a dentifrice containing 0.3% triclosan and 0.25% of the copolymer of

Table 1 *Oral antimicrobials - data from six-month or longer studies.*

	% plaque reduction	% gingivitis reduction	Anti-Candida effect
Chlorhexidine (Peridex PerioGard	45-61	27-67	+
Essential oils (Listerine)	19-35	15-37	+
Cetylpyridinium chloride (Cepacol, Scope)	14	24	+
Sanguinaria (Viadent)	0[a]	0[a] +	
	[b]17-42[b]	[b]18-57[b]	
Stannous fluoride	0	0	-
	0-77	45-72	
Triclosan	12-30	20-75	-

[a]. Use of dentifrice
[b]. Use of both dentifrice and mouthrinse

methoxyethylene and maleic acid.[28,29] Short-term studies with a mouthrinse formulation (0.3% triclosan and 0.25% copolymer) have also shown significant reduction in plaque and as a pre-brushing rinse.[30,31]

The most often studied agents with the potential for value in control of supragingival plaque are summarized in Table 1.

Pre-brushing rinses

A prebrushing rinse which appears to be of value is one containing triclosan and a copolymer of maleic acid. It is available outside the United States with efficacy reported in both short and long term studies.[30] Plax is a pre-brushing rinse available with different agents in different countries. In the United States it is a detergent-sodium benzonate mixture which has shown some plaque reduction in a few short-term studies[32,33] but, in most short and long-term studies, it appears to be similar to a placebo.[34-38]

Oxygenating agents

Peroxide and peroxide releasing agents have been shown to be of value in short-term usage in the treatment of acute necrotizing ulcerative gingivitis and periodontitis. When hydrogen peroxide containing products have been used as part of an oral hygiene program, most long-term studies have shown no benefit over control groups.[39,40] However, some benefits have been reported in short-term studies.[41,42]

Long term usage of hydrogen peroxide has altered normal healing,[43] produced soft tissue lesions,[44] and served as a co-carcinogen in an animal model.[45,46]

Antibiotics

Numerous investigators have evaluated the use of antibiotics to halt the progression of periodontitis, with some benefit demonstrated when these medications are incorporated into the treatment protocol.[47,48,49] Although the value of antibiotics as adjuncts to periodontal disease has not been clearly established, recent studies support their use as adjunctive agents for some forms of periodontal disease.[50,51] Continued refinement of local delivery systems for antimicrobials and the recent acceptance by the US Food & Drug Administration of tetracycline containing fibers (Actisite®) may eventually allow controlled and predictable use at refractory sites including furcations.[52]

Increased knowledge about the infectious nature of periodontal diseases has prompted the use of adjunctive antibiotics in the treatment of periodontitis patients. Since a specific plaque hypothesis was proposed, there have been several studies on plaque infection. It has been shown that the anaerobic portion of the complex microflora associated with advanced periodontitis comprised 90% of cultivable bacteria. In active periodontal lesions, investigators have isolated higher proportions of *Campylobacter rectus*, *Prevotella intermedia*, *Bacteroides forsythus*. *Porphyromonas gingivalis* has been found to be the most prevalent microorganism in localized active disease, and *Peptostreptococcus micros* and C. rectus in generalized active disease. On the other hand, facultative anaerobic or capnophilic microorganisms such as *A. actinomycetemcomitans* or *Eikenella corrodens* may play an important role in the pathogenesis of localized juvenile periodontitis and aggressive adult forms of periodontitis.[53]

Systemic versus crevicular administration of antibiotics in the treatment of periodontal disease is still a matter for further study. The systemic route has been used in a number of studies because it could allow the antibiotic to enter the periodontal pocket via the gingival crevicular fluid to affect microorganisms within the diseased crevice. Also, an oral dose that is effective in inhibiting the growth of

Table 2 *Recommended dosages of antibiotics commonly used as adjuncts to non-surgical mechanical periodontal therapy.*

Name	Dose	Duration in days	Present in GCF
Tetracycline HCl	250 mg four times daily	14-21	Higher than serum levels
Minocycline	50 mg AM 100 mg PM	14-21	Higher than serum levels
Doxycycline	100 mg daily	14-21	Higher than serum levels
Clindamycin	150 mg three times daily	10	Similar to serum levels
Metronidazole	250 mg three times daily	10	Similar to serum levels
Augmentin	250 mg three times daily	10	Lower than serum levels
Amoxcillin plus metronidazole	375 mg three times daily	7	Minimal Similar to serum levels
Actisite®	Varies with fiber length	10	High GCF concentration, not detectable in serum

5

most periodontal bacterial species is readily achieved by systemic administration in all periodontal pockets for the entire treatment period. On the other hand, crevicular administration through an appropriate delivery system has the potential advantage of producing subgingival concentrations which significantly exceed those achievable by systemic administration. These higher concentrations minimize the development of resistance by bacteria. The various antibiotics which have been found to be useful as adjuncts to mechanical periodontal therapy and their recommended dosages are summarized in Table 2.

Tetracyclines

Tetracyclines have an excellent profile of activity against bacteria associated with periodontal disease progression and have been most often studied in the treatment of various types of periodontal disease. Additionally, since collagen destruction occurs in periodontal disease, reduction of host-derived collagenase activity may increase their therapeutic value beyond that of antibacterial activity.

The tetracyclines are the only class of antibiotics tested to date that achieve gingival fluid levels higher than blood levels. Tetracycline and doxycycline[54] concentrate in the gingival fluid at 2 to 4 times blood levels following multiple doses. Minocycline, a more lipid soluble compound, achieves gingival fluid levels 5 times that of blood levels.[55] At the concentrations achieved in gingival fluid, it has been shown that 90 to 95% of the subgingival flora are susceptible in vitro. Also, most periodontal isolates are more susceptible in vitro to minocycline and doxycycline than tetracycline hydrochloride.[56]

In addition to their antibacterial properties, tetracyclines may strengthen host factors by their ability to inhibit collagenase activity.[57,58] It has also been noted that topically applied tetracyclines have the ability to demineralize root surfaces.[59] This may "condition" these surfaces so that endotoxins are removed and the attachment of fibroblasts is enhanced. Because of this, root surface modification may become a valuable adjunct to various forms of periodontal therapy.

Clindamycin

Clindamycin is effective against most periodontal pathogens with the exception of *A. actinomycetemcomitans* and *E. Corrodens*.[60] Also, it appears in crevicular fluid at concentrations which are antibacterial. This antibiotic has been found to be of value in patients who are refractory to most forms of periodontal therapy including surgery and use of other antibiotics.

The major adverse effect of clindamycin therapy is the possible development of pseudomembranous colitis. Therefore, it is contraindicated in patients with a history of this condition or severe gastro-intestinal problems. Since diarrhea and abdominal cramping are early signs of this disorder, therapy should be terminated when these symptoms arise. Oral vancomycin has been found to be most effective in treating antibiotic associated colitis which can occur not only with clindamycin, but also with other broad spectrum antibiotics.

Metronidazole

Metronidazole is effective against a number of anaerobic bacteria but is only minimally effective against *A. actinomycetemcomitans*. Following oral administration, it is found in crevicular fluid in levels high enough to inhibit anaerobic periodontal organisms.[61] Studies with metronidazole have been mainly in cases of adult periodontitis and findings have been mixed.[62,63,64]

Because it is mainly effective against various Bacteroides and spirochetes but not most other periodontal pathogens, the value of metronidazole is limited. In addition, compliance is a problem since alcohol intake is totally contra-indicated while taking this medication. Also, some patients stop medication because of a complaint of taste aberration, and a "metallic" taste in their mouth.

Penicillins

The various penicillins are of minimal value in treating periodontal disease since periodontal pockets often contain bacteria which produce an enzyme (*i.e.* beta lactamase) which inactivates penicillin. One method to overcome the effect of beta-lactamases is to combine a beta-lactamase inhibitor such as clavulanic acid with the penicillin compound. One such commercially available combination, Augmentin (SmithKline Beecham Pharmaceuticals, Philadelphia, PA, USA) has been investigated for use in treating periodontal disease. It consists of amoxicillin and potassium clavulanate, the potassium salt of clavulanic acid. Clavulanic acid inhibits most beta-lactamases.

One study described the results of treatment in 10 patients with adult periodontitis who had not responded to surgery and the adjunctive use of tetracyclines.[65] These patients responded well to Augmentin therapy.

Combination therapy

A combination of 250 mg of metronidazole and 375 mg of amoxicillin, each three times daily for seven days has been found to be effective in eliminating *A. actinomycetemcomitans*[66] Since this microorganism is not susceptible to either antibiotic alone, the synergistic effect of this drug is of interest, although its' mechanism is not well understood.

Major problems with this form of therapy are that it includes a drug which is highly allergenic (*i.e.* penicillin) and that diarrhea is a significant occurrence, the latter resulting in non-compliance.

Local delivery of antimicrobials
Tetracycline HCl periodontal fibers: The recent availability of Actisite® (tetracycline hydrochloride) fibers in the United States and Europe for use as an adjunct to scaling and root planing for the reduction of probing pocket depth and bleeding on probing in patients with adult periodontitis offers much promise for future therapy. Studies in over 1,300 patients have shown that treatment with scaling and root planing plus fibers can reduce periodontal pockets better than scaling and

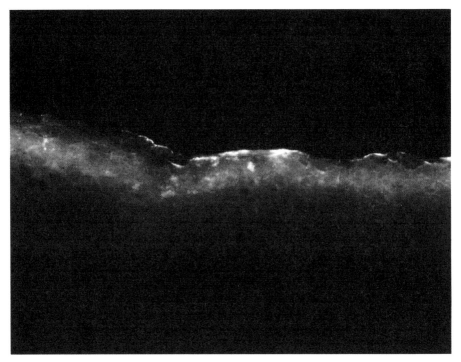

Figure 1 *Fluorescence of tetracycline in epithelium adjacent to placement of a tetracycline containing fiber. Reprinted with permission from Ciancio SG, Cobb CM, and Leung M. Tissue concentration and localization of tetracycline following site-specific tetracycline fiber therapy.* J Periodontol 1992; **63,** 849-853.

root planing alone, and that these fibers are extremely safe for use with minimal side effects.[67,68,69] When the fibers are left in place for 10 days, they result in gingival crevicular fluid levels of antibiotic in excess of 1500 mg/mL,[70] a concentration which is effective against periodontal pathogens and high enough to minimize the development of resistance.

Local delivery of tetracyclines
Recently we evaluated the concentration in gingival tissue adjacent to periodontal pockets packed with these fibers.[71] The study population consisted of 10 patients with at least 2 pockets in both maxillary quadrants of 5mm in depth and exhibiting bleeding on probing. After an initial scaling and root planing, placebo or tetracycline fibers were randomly assigned by quadrant and placed in 2 non-adjacent pockets. Fibers were removed at the time of surgery (*i.e.*, day 8). Periodontal surgery was performed utilizing a flap incision that allowed biopsy of an interdental papilla from each of the 2 test sites in each quadrant. One biopsy was analysed for tetracycline concentrations by high performance liquid chromatography. The second biopsy was examined by both light and ultraviolet fluorescence microscopy to determine the

location of residual tetracycline and the intensity of inflammatory cell infiltrates. The results showed that the tissue concentration of the antibiotic in tetracycline-treated sites was 64.4 ng/mg (ng of tetracycline/mg tissue weight) which corresponded to 43 mg/mL of tetracycline and was below levels of accurate measurement in placebo-treated sites. Tetracycline tissue concentrations corresponded to the ultraviolet fluorescence microscopy with a Pearson correlation coefficient of r = 0.92. Tetracycline fluorescence was noted in the soft tissue wall ranging from 1 to 20 mm (Figure 1). This study showed that these fibers could deliver levels of antibiotic into tissue adjacent to a periodontal pocket at concentrations which could kill all suspected periodontal pathogens. It is noteworthy that in another study similar tissue concentrations of this antibiotic could also reduce host derived collagenase activity.[72]

Metronidazole gel

A gel containing 25% metronidazole (Elyzol®, Dumex, Denmark) has recently been developed for local application into periodontal pockets and is commercially available in Europe. The gel is formulated in a mixture of mono and triglycerides and produces a mean crevicular peak concentration of antibiotic of 128 µg/mL at 8 hours, and becomes less than 1 µg/mL after 36 hours in 92% of patients studied.

The results of the clinical studies for this metronidazole-containing gel for subgingival application suggest that use of this product produces results both clinically and microbiologically similar to scaling and root planing.[73] The data also demonstrate that, as has been previously reported, metronidazole is not effective against *A. actinomycetemcomitans*, and would, therefore, not be of value in periodontal pockets containing this microorganism, such as in localized juvenile periodontitis.

Minocycline paste

A subgingival delivery system of 2% minocycline hydrochloride marketed as Dentomycin® (Lederle Laboratories, Pearl River, NY, USA) was recently approved in Great Britain for use as an adjunct to subgingival debridement. Approval was based on a series of laboratory and clinical studies demonstrating safety and efficacy.[74,75] Initial clinical and laboratory studies carried out in Japan prior to 1990 led to approval of the formulation in that country under the name Periocline® (Sunstar, Tokoyo, Japan).

The results of these studies suggest that subgingival delivery of minocycline gel may be a valuable adjunct to subgingival debridement, particularly in patients with pockets deeper than 7 mm.

Conclusion

In view of our understanding of periodontal diseases as infections, the use of antibiotics and non-antibiotic antimicrobials as adjuncts to traditional therapy has become increasingly important in daily practice. However, due to the overprescribing of antibiotics by health practitioners dentistry must develop careful guidelines so that this abuse does not increase. The advent of effective local delivery systems for antimicrobials and the ;use of non-antibiotic antimicrobial agents in dentifrices, rinses, and irrigants may decrease this abuse potential, minimize adverse effects seen with systemic therapy, and improve the results and predictability of periodontal therapy.

The dental practitioner must monitor this rapidly change knowledge base and select those chemical agents which are abest for an individual patient so that optimal periodontal health is obtained and sustained.

References

1. Camosci DA and Tinaoff N. Antibacterial determination of stannous fluoride. *J Dent Res* 1984;**63**, 1121.
2. Tinaoff N, Weeks DB. Current status of SnF$_2$ as an antiplaque agent. *Pediatr Dent* 1979;**1**, 199.
3. Leverett DH, McHugh WD, Jensen OE. Effect of daily rinsing with stannous fluoride on plaque and gingivitis. *J Dent Res* 1984;**63**, 1083.
4. Tinaoff N, Manwell MA, Zamerck RL, *et al.* Clinical and mirobiological effects of daily brushing with either NaF or SnF$_2$ gels in subjects with fixed or removal dental prostheses. *J Clin Periodontol* 1989;**16**, 284.
5. Boyd RL, Legott PJ, Robertson PB. Effect on gingivitis of two different 0.4% SnF$_2$ gels. *J Dent Res* 1988;**67**, 503.
6. Perlich MA, Bacca LA, Bollmer BW, Lanzalaco AC, McClanahan SF, Sewak LK. The clinical effect of a stabilized stannous fluoride dentifrice on plaque formation, gingivitis and gingival bleeding, A six-month study. *J Clin Dent* 1995;**6**[Spec Issue], 54-58.
7. Beiswanger BB, Doyle PM,. Jackson RD, Mallatt ME, Mau MS. The clinical effect of dentifrices containing stabilized stannous fluoride on plaque formation and gingivitis: A six-month study with *Ad libitum* brushing. *J Clin Dent* 1995,6[Spec. Issue], 46-53.
8. Segreto VA, Collins EM, Beiswanger BB, *et al.* A comparison of mouthrinses containing two concentrations of chlorhexidine. *J Periodont Res* 1986;**21**(Suppl), 23.
9. Grossman E, Reiter G, Sturzenberger OP, *et al.* Six month study on the effects of a chlorhexidine mouthrinse on gingivitis in adults. *J Periodont Res* 1986;**21**(Suppl), 33.
10. Brecx M, Borwnstone E, MacDonald L, Gelskey S, Cheang M. Efficacy of Listerine®, Meridol® and chlorhexidine mouthrinses as supplements to regular tooth-cleaning measures. J Clin Periodontol 1992, **19**, 202-207.
11. Gjermo P. Chlorhexidine and related compounds. *J Dent Res* 1989;**68**(Spec. Issue), 1602.
12. Okano M *et al.* Anaphylactic symptoms due to chlorhexidine gluconate. *Arch Dermatol* 1989;125, 50-52.
13. The Japanese Ministry of Public Welfare, *Information About Adverse Reactions of Drugs for Clinical Use: 1975-1988.* Tokyo, Japanese Ministry of Public Welfare, 1975;**1**(9),1978;**2**(26),1980;3(37),1981;**4**(42);5(46),1985;**8**(67), in Japanese.
14. Ljunggren B, Moller H. Eczematous contact allergy to chlorhexidine. *Acta Derm Venereol (Stockh)* 1972;**52**, 308-310.
15. Barkvoll P, Rolla G, Svendsen AK. Interaction between chlorhexidine digluconate and sodium lauryl sulfate *in vivo*. *J Clin Periodontol* 1989;**16**, 593.

16. DePaola LG, Overholser CD, Meiller TF, *et al.* Chemotherapeutic inhibition of supragingival dental plaque and gingivitis development. *J Clin Periodontol* 1989;**16**, 311.

17. Gordon JM, Lamster IB, Seiger MC. Efficacy of Listerine antiseptic in inhibiting the development of plaque and gingivitis. *J Clin Periodontol* 1985;**12**, 697.

18. Lamster IB, Alfano MC, Seiger MC, *et al.* The effect of Listerine antiseptic on reduction of existing plaque and gingivitis. *Clin Preven Dent* 1983;**5**, 12.

19. Fine DH, Letizia J, Mandel ID. The effect of rinsing with Listerine antiseptic on the properties of developing plaque. *J Clin Periodontol* 1985;**12**, 660.

20. Lobene RR, Lobene S, Soparker PM. The effect of cetylpyridinium chloride mouthwash on plaque and gingivitis. *J Dent Res* 1977;**56**, 595(Abstr).

21. Wennstrom J, Lindhe J. Some effects of a sanguinarine -containing mouthrinse on developing plaque and gingivitis. *J Clin Periodontol* 1985;**12**, 867.

22. Abbas DK, Thrane P, Othman SJ. Effectiveness of Viadent as a plaque inhibiting mouthwash. *Scan J Dent Res* 1985;**93**, 494.

23. Siegrist BE, Gusberti FA, Brec ME, *et al.* Efficacy of supervised rinsing with chlorhexidine digluconate in comparison to phenolic and plant alkaloid compounds. *J Periodontol Res* 1986;**21**(Suppl), 60.

24. Hanna JJ, Johnson JD, Kuftinec MM. Long term clinical evaluation of toothpaste and oral rinse containing sanguinaria in controlling plaque, gingival inflammation, and sulcular bleeding during orthodontic treatment. *Am J Orthod Dentofacial Orthop* 1989;**96**, 199.

25. Kopczyk RA, Abrams H, Brown A, *et al.* clinical and microbiological effects of a sanguinaria-containing mouthrinse and dentifrice with and without fluoride during 6 months of use. *J Periodontol* 1991;**62**, 617.

26. Stephen KW, Saxton CA, Jones CL *et al.* Control of gingivitis and calculus by a dentifrice containing a zinc salt and triclosan. *J Periodontol* 1990;**61**, 674-679.

27. Svatun B, Saxton CA, Rolla G. Six-month study of the effect of a dentifrice containing zinc citrate and triclosan on plaque, gingival health, and calculus. *Scand J Dent Res* 1990;**98**, 301.

28. Cubells AB, Dalman LB, Petrone ME, Chaknis P, Volpe AR. The effect of a triclosan/copyolymer/fluoride dentifrice on plaque formation and gingivitis, a six-month clinical study. *J Clin Dent* 1991;**2**, 63-68

29. Deasy MJ, Singh SM, Rustogi KN, Petrone DM, Battista G, Petrone ME, Volpe AR. Effect of a dentifrice containing triclosan and a copolymer on plaque formation and gingivitis. *Clin Prev Dent* 1991;**13**, 12-19.

30. Rustogi KW, Petrone DM, Singh SM *et al.* Clinical study of a pre-brush rinse and a triclosan/copolymer mouthrinse, effect on plaque formation. *Am J Dent* 1990;**3**(Spec. Issue), S67.

31. Singh SM, Rustogi KW, Volpe AR *et al.* Effect of a mouthrinse containing triclosan and a copolymer on plaque formation in a normal oral hygiene regimen. *Am J Dent* 1990;**3**(Spec Issue), S63.

32. Bailey L. Direct plaque removal by a pre-brushing dental rinse. *Clin Prev Dent* 1989;**11**, 21.

33. Emling RC, Yankell SC. First clinical studies of a new pre-brushing mouthrinse. *Compendium Contin Educ Dent* 1985;**6**, 636.

34. Balaynk T, Sharma N, Galustains J. Antiplaque efficacy of Plax pre-brushing rinse. Plaque mass/area analysis. *J Dent Res* 1991;**70**, (Spec. Issue), 374(Abstr. 869).

35. Cronin MJ, Kohut BE. A two-phase clinical efficacy study of Plax pre-brushing rinse. *J Clin Dent* 1991;**3**, 20.
36. Chung L, Smith SR, Joyston-Bechals. The effect of a pre-brushing mouthwash (Plax) on oral hygiene in man. *J Clin Periodontol* 1992;**19**, 679.
37. Frietas Bastos L, Collaert B, Attstrom R. Plaque removing efficacy of the pre-brushing rinse Plax. *J Dent Res* 1991;**70**, 768.
38. Singh SM. Efficacy of Plax pre-brushing rinse in reducing dental plaque. *Am J Dent* 1990;**3**, 15.
39. Wolff CF, Philstrom BL, Bakdash MB *et al.* Four-year investigation of salt and peroxide regimen compared with conventional oral hygiene. *J Am Dent Asoc* 1989;**118**, 67-72.
40. Jones CM, Blinkhorn AS, White E. Hydrogen peroxide, the effect on plaque and gingivitis when used in an oral irrigator. *Clin Prevent Dent* 1990;**12**, 15.
41. Gomes BC, Shakun ML, Ripa LW. Effect of rinsing with 1.5% hydrogen peroxide (Peroxyl) on gingivitis and plaque. *Clin Prevent Dent* 1984;**6**, 21.
42. Wennstrom J, Lindhe J. Effect of hydrogen peroxide on developing plaque and gingivitis in man. *J Clin Periodontol* 1979;**6**, 115.
43. Branemark P-I, Ekholm R. Tissue injury caused by wound disinfectanta. *J Bone Joint Surg*, 1967,**49**(A), 48-52.
44. Rees TD, Orth CF. Oral ulcerations with use of hydrogen peroxide. *J Periodontol*, 1986, **57**, 689.
45. Weitzman SA, Weitberg AB, Stossel TP, Schwartz J, Shklar G. Effects of hydrogen peroxide on oral carcinogenesis in hamsters. *J Periodontol*, 1986, **57**, 685-688.
46. Weitzman SA, Weitberg AB, Niederman R, Stossel TP. Chronic treatment with hydrogen peroxide - Is it safe? *J Periodontol*, 1984, **55**, 510-514.
47. Kornman KS. Karl EH. The effect of long-term low-dose tetracycline therapy on subgingival microflora in refractory adult periodontitis. *J Periodontol* 1982;**53**, 604-610.
48. Soder PO, Frithiof L, Wikner S, Wouters F, Engstrom P, Rubin B, Nedlich U, and Soder B. The effect of systemic metronidazole after non-surgical treatment in moderate and advanced periodontitis in young adults. *J Periodontol* 1990;**61**, 281-288.
49. Okuda K, Wolff L, Oliver R, Osborn J, Stoltenberg J, Bereuter J, Anderson L, Foster P, Hardie N, Aeppli D, and Hara K. Minocycline slow-release formulation effect on subgingival bacteria. *J Periodontol* 1992;**63**, 73-78.
50. Novak MJ, Stamatelakys C, Adair SM. Resolution of early lesions of juvenile periodontitis with tetracycline therapy alone: Long-term observation of four cases. *J Periodontol* 1991;**62**, 628-633.
51. Walker CB, Gordon JM, Magnusson I, Clark WB. A role for antibiotics in the treatment of refractory periodontitis. *J Periodontol* 1993;**8**, 772-778.
52. Newman MG, Kornman KS, Doherty FM. A 6-month multi-center evaluation of adjunctive tetracycline fiber therapy used in conjunction with scaling and root planing in maintenance patients: Clinical results. *J Periodontol* 1994;**7**, 685-691.
53. Slots J. The predominant cultivable microflora of advanced periodontitis. *Scand J Dent Res* 1977;**85**, 114-120.
54. Pascale D, Gordon J, Lamster I, Mann P, Seiger M, Arndt W. Concentration of doxycycline in human gingival fluid. *J Clin Periodontol* 1986;**13**, 841-844.
55. Ciancio SG, Slots J, Reynolds HS, Zambon JJ, McKenna Judy Dorsheimer. The effect of short-term administration of minocycline HCl on gingival inflammation and subgingival microflora. *J Periodontol* 1982;**53**, 557-561.

56. Gordon JM, Walker Cindy Bragg. Current status of systemic antibiotic usage in destructive periodontal disease. *J Periodontol* 1993, **64**, 760-771.
57. Golub LM, Ramamurthy SN, McNamara TF, Gomes B, Wolff M, Casino A, Kapoor A, Zambon J, Ciancio S, Schneir M, Perry H. Tetracyclines inhibit tissue collagenase activity: a new mechanism in the treatment of periodontal disease. *J Periodont Res* 1994;**19**, 651-655.
58. Golub LM, Goodson JM, Lee HM, Vidal AM, McNamara TF, Ramamurthy NS. Tetracyclines inhibit tissue collagenase. *J Periodontol* 1985, **56**(suppl), 93-97.
59. Terranova VP, Franzetti LC, Hic S, DiFlorio R, Lyall R, Wikesjo U, Baker P, Christersson L, and Genco R. A biochemical approach to periodontal regeneration: Tetracycline treatment of dentin promotes fibroblast adhesion and growth. *J Periodont Res* 1986;**21**, 330-337.
60. Walker CB, Gordon JM, Cornwall HA, Murphy JC, Socransky SS. Gingival crevicular fluid levels of clindamycin compared with its minimal inhibitory concentrations for periodontal bacteria. *Antimicrob Agents Chemother* 1981;**19**, 867-871.
61. Notten F, Oosten AK-V, Mikx F. Capillary agar diffusion assay for measuring metronidazole in human gingival crevice fluid. *Antimicrob Agents Chemother* 1982;**21**, 836-837.
62. Van Oosten MAC, Mikx FHM, Renggli HH. Microbial and clinical measurements of periodontal pockets during sequential periods of non-treatment, mechanical debridement and metronidazole therapy. *J Clin Periodontol* 1987;**14**, 197-204.
63. Jenkins WMM, MacFarlane TW, Gilmour WH, Ramsay I, MacKenzie D. Systemic metronidazole in the treatment of periodontitis. *J Clin Periodontol* 1989;**16**, 433-450.
64. van Winkelhoff AJ, Rodenberg JP, Groene RJ, Abbas F, Winkel EG, DeGraaff J. Metronidazole plus amoxicillin in the treatment of *Actinobacillus actinomycetemcomitans* associated periodontitis. *J Clin Periodontol* 1989;**16**, 128-131.
65. Walker Cindy Bragg, Gordon JM, Magnusson I, Clark WB. A role for antibiotics in the treatment of refractory periodontitis. *J Periodontol* 1993;**8**, 772-778.
66. van Winkelhoff AJ, Rodenbert JP, Groene RJ, Abbas F, Winkel EG, DeGraaff J. Metronidazole plus amoxicillin in the treatment of *Actinobacillus actinomycetemcomitans* associated periodontitis. *J Clin Periodontol* 1989;16, 128-131.
67. Goodson JM, Cugini MAKent RL, Artmitage GC, Cobb CM, Fine D, Fritz ME, Green E, Imoberforf MJ, Killoy WJ, Mendieta C, Niederman R, Offenbacher S, Taggart EJ, Tonetti M. Multi-center evaluation of tetracycline fiber therapy. I. Experimental design. *J Periodont Res* 1991;**26**, 361-379.
68. Goodson JM, Cugini MA, Kent RL, Armitage GC, Cobb CM, Fine D, Fritz ME, Green E, Imoberforf MJ, Killoy WJ, Mendieta C, Niederman R, Offenbacher S, Taggart EJ, Tonetti M. Multi-center evaluation of tetracycline fiber therapy: II. Clinical response. *J Periodont Res* 1991;**26**, 371-379.
69. Goodson JM, Offenbacher S, Farr DH, Hogan PE. Periodontal disease treatment by local drug delivery. *J Periodontol* 1985;**56**, 265-268.
70. Tonetti M, Cugini MA, Goodson JM. Zero-order delivery with periodontal placement of tetracycline-loaded ethylene vinyl acetate fibers. *J Periodont Res* 1990;**25**, 243-249.
71. Ciancio SG, Cobb CM, Leung M. Tissue concentration and localization of tetracycline following site-specific tetracycline fiber therapy. *J Periodontol* 1992;**63**, 849-853.
72. Golub LM, Ramamurthy SN, McNamara TF, Greenwald RA, Rifkin BR. Tetracyclines inhibit connective tissue breakdown: new therapeutic implications for an old family of drugs. Crit Rev Oral Biol Med 1991;**2**, 297-305.

73. Pedrazzoli V, Kilian M, Karring T. Comparable clinical and microbiological effects of topical subgingival application of metronidazole 25% dental gel and scaling and root planing in the treatment of adult periodontitis. *J Clin Periodontol* 1992;**19**, 715-722.
74. Kurimoto K, Ishoshima O, Naora Y, Anada T, Kobayashi Y, Kobayashi M, Arai H, Takashiba S, Nanba H, and Yokoyama M. Periodontal therapy by local delivery of minocycline. Clinical study on optimum concentration of LS-007. *J Jpn Assoc Periodontol* 1987;**29**, 930-936.
75. van Steenberghe D, Bercy P, Kohl J, DeBoever J, Adriaens P, Vanderfacillic A, Andrianenssen C, Rompen E, DeVree H, McCarthy EF, and Vandenhove G. Subgingival minocycline hydrochloride ointment in moderate to severe chronic adult periodontitis: A randomized, double-blind, vehicle-controlled, multi-center study. *J Periodontol* 1993;**64**, 637-644.

2   Ecology of the plaque–host interface

Hubert N. Newman

Eastman Dental Institute, 256 Gray's Inn Road, London WC1X 8LD, UK

There is currently no evidence to suggest that the chronic inflammatory periodontal diseases are classical specific infections, or due to invasive processes. There is considerable evidence to indicate that they are due to shifts in the proportions of individual organisms in dental plaque, although it is not yet clear whether these are only at species, or at sub-species level. In relation to these shifts, there have been many studies of plaque microbiology and of putative host response factors, but relatively few of the actual plaque itself in situ on the tooth root surface nearest to the bottom of the periodontal pocket, the apical border plaque. A series of investigations of this plaque has established some of the principal characteristics of this disease-associated microbial biofilm in various forms of chronic periodontitis: moderate and advanced adult, juvenile and post-juvenile, idiopathic rapidly progressive adult, and in forms with defined underlying systemic factors, such as chronic neutropenia and Papillon-Lefèvre Syndrome. The apical border plaque features are surprisingly similar in all these forms of chronic periodontitis. The organisms are mainly Gram-negative cocci, but include Gram-positive cells. They often show abundant intracellular polysaccharide granules, and there is amorphous or fibrillar matrix between the cells. Immunogold electron microscopy shows that the Gram-negative forms include Porphyromonas gingivalis and Actinobacillus actinomycetemcomitans, and their surface-associated materials or SAMs include elements not only directly related to the producer cell but in the plaque matrix away from the cells and even in the underlying dental cuticle. These substances are often more toxic to periodontal tissue components than lipopolysaccharides or endotoxins commonly associated with disease. Coronal to the most apical organisms, at the bulk plaque border, zonation is evident in the microflora of the plaque, with spirochaetes often abundant in the outer layers, especially in routine chronic adult periodontitis. Bacteria do occur in the underlying periodontal soft tissues, but they are sparse, and their frequency does not increase with more severe disease. Organisms may be found in intact as well as in damaged areas, while the cells most likely to be associated with tissue damage in the cases of periodontitis studied are polymorphonuclear neutrophil leucocytes and plasma cells. It may be concluded that the relationship between plaque and chronic inflammatory periodontal diseases is a question of ecology, and that direct study of the plaque-host interface has already and is likely to continue to contribute significantly to our understanding of the aetiology and pathology of these diseases, and to improved, ecologically-based methods for their control and prevention.

Introduction

It is conventional to describe chronic periodontitis as the destructive phase of the chronic inflammatory periodontal diseases. In spite of many advances in our knowledge of the microbiology and host response elements that result in chronic periodontitis, our understanding of the actual destructive mechanisms in this group of conditions remains limited. In molecular biology terms, as each new class or sub-class of possible reagents and receptors emerges, we are faced with an increasing number of putative disease mechanisms. Most of the findings do not indicate more than that a very wide range of possible destructive mechanisms may be adduced to explain the aetiology, pathogenesis and progression of chronic periodontitis in its different forms. The detailed microbiology and host response have been considered elsewhere in this symposium. The present review concentrates on the ecology of the plaque-host interface, because it is critical in relation to all stages in the disease process, and especially the destructive phase, chronic periodontitis.

It is axiomatic in microbial ecology that microorganisms function very differently in their natural habitat than can be deduced from pure culture studies. Similarly, however we dissect out the multitude of cellular and humoral elements of the host response, systemic and local periodontal, it is essential to establish their significance *in situ* in the affected tissues. Only a synthesis of microbial and host factors *in situ* is likely to clarify the situation. That is why it is vital to establish the ecology of the plaque-host interface, from the apical border of the plaque to the affected connective tissues. As in this review, it is especially pertinent to use human material, with the obvious limitations of such biopsies clearly in mind. (The reader is asked to note that the Editors have requested that only literature from 1990 be cited, and this request has been respected where possible.)

An ecologic view of chronic periodontitis

In relation to the plaque-host imbalance that leads to chronic periodontitis, several pertinent facts rarely receive mention, even though they may be considered fundamental to the disease process:

1. Except in the most susceptible patients, who usually have demonstrable systemic host defence deficiencies, the disease usually takes decades to destroy the periodontal ligament, even around a single tooth. Often the dentist may intervene exodontically before this stage. As a corollary, it is therefore probably no longer correct to consider periodontitis directly as the major cause of adult tooth loss.
2. The pathological entity that constitutes chronic periodontitis may be regarded as a protective system or mechanism. Just as in other successfully controlled

infections, the body is protected at the cost of relatively minor local tissue loss. This needs clarification:

(a) The bacterial mass represented by dental plaque is enormous in infection potential terms, yet the disease process is very slow, and the tissue complex of the periodontium, epithelium, ligament and bone, retreats in good order and with the same basic structure throughout the entire disease process[1,2]. This is evident even in the most extreme cases of susceptibility, as in chronic neutropenia[3] when the rate of disease progression is more rapid.

(b) Despite the prolonged nature of the disease process, the residual periodontal tissues deep to the zone of the lesion remain unaffected[4].

(c) The downgrowth of epithelium that is a predominant feature of periodontal pocket formation in pathophysiological terms in fact reflects merely the protective, covering function of epithelium when a tissue surface is breached. Failure to appreciate this point can lead to misinterpretation of the significance of root surface exposure in the mouth in older people, where it is at least as likely, if not more likely, to represent continued adult tooth eruption[5] as chronic periodontitis. We must be more careful not to equate cementum exposure in the mouth in older patients with attachment loss due to periodontitis.

(d) The basic pathology of chronic periodontitis is not unique. The zones of the lesion of chronic periodontitis provide an example of the infectious inflammatory lesion in general. Thus, there is a central zone of infection, the plaque, with humoral and cellular (polymorphonuclear neutrophil leucocyte -PMN) components overlying it, an underlying connective tissue zone of PMN and plasma cells, an underlying zone of fibrosis (the re-formed transseptal and possibly other fibre systems) and, as in bone infections elsewhere, a deeper layer of resorption, central to which the marrow spaces contain a focus of inflammatory cells[4,6]. While somewhat more disordered in the more rapidly progressive forms of chronic periodontitis, this zonation walling off the infection focus is representative of such lesions in general. This has major treatment implications. We should always bear in mind the nature of the lesion of chronic periodontitis, and attempt to enhance the protective and minimise the destructive elements of the host response. Apart from conventional antimicrobial attempts to control plaque, therefore, a range of factors are currently under consideration as potential protective modifiers of the host response[7].

(e) Although bacteria plainly do enter the periodontal tissues, even with toothbrushing and other routine oral hygiene activities, and while rare microabscesses occur around equally rare microbial groupings in soft connective tissues, there is no evidence that the process is invasive. Organisms when present are sparse, and as likely to be found in intact tissue as at sites of tissue breakdown, again regardless of the rate of progression of the disease[3,4,8,9]. Microbial products are far more likely to penetrate, although to what depth has not been established.

(f) As a corollary, plaque bacteria usually tend to be absent from sites of breakdown, which are, however, generally associated with the presence of plasma cells and PMN[10]. In fact, in rapidly progressive forms of periodontitis, such as juvenile periodontitis (for classification see Newman[11]), more degenerate plasma cells are present, which is indicative of more antibody response and defective local polymorphonuclear neutrophil leucocyte (PMN) function. In JP, this includes lysosomal granule loss in PMN within the local blood vessels. The greater numbers of plasma cells in JP connective tissue may reflect a response to higher levels of penetrating plaque bacterial antigens, but also an increase in antibodies to types I and II collagens[10].

Plaque bacteria are generally absent from sites of breakdown regardless of the rate of disease progression, even in the most rapidly progressive forms of periodontitis, as in chronic neutropenia[3].

In a previous review of the fundamental importance of an ecological approach to understanding the relationship between plaque and chronic inflammatory periodontal disease[12], it was made clear that natural diet did not permit the build-up of plaque at the subcontact area approximal site that is the locus of initiation, and in most cases of progression, of CIPD. Given modern soft diet, which allows such excessive plaque accumulation at this site of greatest risk, the basically protective nature of the host response is reflected in the fact that it usually takes decades for extensive tissue loss to occur, and in the rarity with which tooth loss is a consequence of that process, without dental intervention.

Given such elements, it is possible to view chronic periodontitis as an infection, resembling others, but differing in that there is usually a very slow progression given the size of the bacterial load represented by dental plaque.

It is not in dispute that dental plaque is the direct cause of chronic periodontitis, nor that certain plaque species, and probably adapting biovars of those species (although whether serotype, ribotype, plasmid or bacteriophage-modified biovars are most relevant to disease aetiology is not yet established), are more disease-relevant than others. It is, however, also clear that the question of the relationship between plaque and the chronic inflammatory periodontal diseases is primarily one of ecology[12]. Further, given the wide range of organisms implicated in chronic periodontitis, and given the general understanding of what is meant by specific infection, care should be exercised in the use of the word specific in relation to any form of chronic periodontitis, and much greater consideration should be given to the term 'mixed anaerobe infection', in view of the obvious analogy between periodontal anaerobic infections and infections affecting other parts of the alimentary tract.

It is probable that metabolites rather than whole cells mediate the tissue destruction of the lesion of chronic periodontitis. It is evident that the disease is episodic, and unpredictable as to its episodes, and it seems likely that disturbances at the plaque-host interface as far as whole bacterial cells are concerned, or in the deeper tissues in relation to bacterial metabolites, underlie these episodes.

At least two possible scenarios come to mind concerning explanations for episodes of tissue loss in chronic periodontitis. Both would involve a disruption of the basically protective leucocyte layer, mainly PMN and plasma cell, allowing ingress of noxious bacterial products. In this connection it is also possible, although not proven, that junctional or attachment epithelium is more penetrable in rapidly progressive forms of periodontitis. The other scenario, additionally, would result in limited proliferation of penetrating organisms, resulting in microabscess formation and, in common with other abscesses in collagenous connective tissues, including bone, in tissue breakdown.

Of mixed anaerobe infections

Clarification of the bacterial aetiology of chronic periodontitis will require understanding as to whether the essential bacterial factor is the species, a serotype, ribotype, or plasmid- or bacteriophage-modified biovar, or particular bacterial products, for each incriminated organism. As so many microbial factors have been implicated, it is probably a mixture, reminiscent of the mixed anaerobe infections so well known to gastroenterology. This connection has rarely been made[13]. Yet the analogies are plain. In many gastrointestinal tract infections, the problem does not derive from an extraneous species acting as a specific pathogen, but from a disturbance in the balance of the commensal microflora.

The mere presence of a periodontitis-related species or sub-species in a diseased patient, or at a diseased site in that patient, does not necessarily prove other than an association, chance or otherwise, not least when there is no clear evidence of any such exogenous infection in periodontitis, and when critical levels of plaque anaerobes and their products, or of host response elements, are more likely to result in an episode of tissue loss. Even if a given species may change in proportion *before* an episode of tissue loss, that would be more likely to be due to a shift in host response stimulating that overgrowth. Any subsequent tissue breakdown, of course, would then merely represent the protective host response to that overgrowth, suppressing it and walling it off (reformed transseptal fibres, for example).

Notwithstanding efforts to alter basic postulates of specific infection, and a blurring by some of the understanding of the differences between commensalism and infection, there are currently no sound grounds to consider any organism implicated in chronic periodontitis as a classical specific pathogen. It should be possible to grasp the concept of a mixed anaerobe infection due to host-commensal microflora imbalance, without feeling obliged to describe chronic periodontitis as a classical specific infection due to an exogenous primary pathogen. The concept to grasp is as follows: which of the oral commensals manages to survive the unfavourable environmental conditions at the host-plaque interface, so that tissue breakdown supervenes. albeit at a slow, intermittent overall rate?

Of incidence and rate

Chronic inflammatory periodontal diseases, unlike most infections, are primarily not conditions one "gets," but diseases of *rate*. All humans (and other mammals) appear subject to chronic gingivitis, in one form or another, and the prevalence of chronic periodontitis is high, and probably underestimated given the inadequacy of probing methodology and instrumentation until recently[14,15], and use of crude instrumentation, as for CPITN[16]. Also, prevalence and incidence studies should ideally be whole mouth based, and should concentrate on the high risk site, namely, the approximal, which is generally where CIPD begins, and progresses most. Data which purport to establish the epidemiology of routine periodontitis (chronic, adult onset, slowly progressive - Newman[11]) should not include other than approximal surface data, should be whole mouth, use a probe with tip diameter 0.5 mm and a tine as parallel as possible[15], and provide data indicating satisfactory intra- and inter-examiner consistency in recording pocket probing depth. Further, as mentioned before, care should be exercised in assessing so-called attachment loss in older subject groups, as this may merely reflect continued tooth eruption. Even given the limitations of studies that do not take such factors into account, such a prevalence for other diseases would excite considerable interest and, indeed, may explain the considerable developments in recent years in industry-based anti-plaque research and development[7,17,18].

The importance of understanding that we are dealing with diseases of rate is that as a consequence our treatment should be directed at controlling the condition so as to maximise tooth retention and function. There is a clear need in this context to bear the patient's needs and wishes in mind, for example. appearance. speech, comfort, ability to enjoy eating, rather than professional concepts of pocket reduction/elimination or even tissue regeneration. Ideally, of course, we hope to attain the capacity to prevent the unfavourable shift in plaque-host imbalance reaching clinical or patient significance.

The interface plaque biofilm

An individual species may be disease-associated for a variety of reasons, including numbers present at an affected site, animal studies indicating such a relationship, and host response factors to that organism. It is not sufficient to mention mixed infections[19]: the analogy needs to be drawn with mixed anaerobe infections in other locations. Nor do paradoxes help: disease-related species such as *P.gingivalis* and *Treponema denticola* may be found at higher levels in relation to healthy sites[20]. While in general the frequency of isolation and the count of disease-related plaque species are higher at diseased loci, the prevalence of the species is at variance with accepted notions of classical infectious disease. For example, black pigmented anaerobes occur in the subgingival plaque of young children and on the oral mucosa of neonates, albeit in low numbers. In a study of the prevalence of *P. gingivalis, Prevotella intermedia* and *A. actinomycetemcomitans,* three of the current major "periodontopathogens"[21], 15 0f 21 prepubertal and 11 of 15 postpubertal subcontact area gingival margin plaque samples were positive for *P. intermedia*, corresponding positive tongue dorsum samples being 17 and 12 respectively. 4 of 8 subcontact and 3 of 8 tongue samples contained *A. actinomycetemcomitans* in the prepubertal group, with 6 of 9 and 3 of 9 being positive respectively in the postpubertal group. 3 of 21 plaque and 2 of 21 tongue samples were positive for *P. gingivalis* prepubertally, while 5 of 15 plaque and also 5 of 15 tongue samples were *P. gingivalis* positive in the postpubertal children. These groups were selected to avoid changes associated with puberty, and only Caucasian male children were studied, and routine radiographs scrutinised, to obviate the likelihood of juvenile periodontitis (for modern classification of periodontitis see Newman[11]). At the other extreme, enteric organisms have been found in the plaque of 14% of a large group (3000) of adult periodontitis patients[22].

In another adult periodontitis population examined by Slots and co-workers[19], comprising only 24 patients, enteric bacteria were found in two thirds of the plaques, averaging about one quarter of the cultivable plaque organisms. Further, previously unrelated species, such as staphylococci, have been associated with periodontitis[23,24].

While not considering chronic periodontitis as an example of a typical gut mixed anaerobe infection, Haffajee and Socransky[19] have summarised a number of microbial associations in chronic periodontitis-associated plaque, which are clearly analogous to such mixed infection. They cite the combinations *F. nucleatum/ Bacteroides forsythus/Campylobacter rectus, Streptococcus intermedius/ P.gingivalis/ P.melaninogenicus, S.intermedius/F.nucleatum/P.gingivalis, P.gingivalis/ A.actino- mycetemcomitans/B.forsythus* and *T.denticola*. There would appear to be an inverse relationship between levels of *P.gingivalis* and *P.intermedia*, although the clinical significance of this is not clear[25].

The mere association of increased numbers of one or more species or subgroups with an increased diseased activity or severity may be misleading, given the slow rate of disease progression, compared with the potential ability of microorganisms to proliferate, even *in vivo*. One may note the failure to date to demonstrate a causative role for fusiform bacilli and spirochaetes in acute necrotizing ulcerative gingivitis, in spite of the known rapid onset and progression of the latter. The direct causative factor in ANUG is almost certainly a host deficiency. It seems likely that variations in the destructive:protective elements of host response also relate to the time of onset and progression of chronic gingivitis to periodontitis and progression (episode onset and duration) of the different forms of chronic periodontitis. Thus, the increased levels of "periodontopathogens" detected at progressing compared with non-progressing sites may reflect adaptation to host change rather than direct causation.   That said, of course, plaque remains the direct cause of chronic periodontitis, which cannot occur in the absence of bacteria. As a corollary, if the host factors that predispose to these critical times of disease onset and of episodic progression could be identified, this would lead to more direct methods of controlling and, ultimately, of preventing the various forms of CIPD, and especially of chronic periodontitis.

It has been suggested that truly virulent pathogens, such as *Mycobacterium tuberculosis* and *Salmonella typhi* may colonise an individual for protracted periods without disease supervening, the inference being that periodontitis-related species are analogous in their behaviour to such classical specific pathogens[19]. This is to unnecessarily obfuscate the issue. The prevalence to date of all chronic periodontitis-related plaque species in populations of different ages and types, with and without any form of chronic periodontitis, makes it clear beyond rational doubt that chronic periodontitis is due to overgrowth of commensal species which adapt to unfavourable subgingival environmental growth conditions. There is the additional complication that it is unlikely that all strains or biovars of a given disease-related species are equally pathogenic[26]. Further, although the flora is varied, with many commensal, symbiotic and antagonistic relationships between its constituent organisms, plaque is generally remarkably stable in a given individual. Thus the periodontal flora of twin children was significantly more similar than those of unrelated children of the same ages, and those of identical twins were even more similar than those of fraternal twins, indicating some element of host genetic control of flora composition[27]. This in turn may also have relevance in relation to systemic predisposition to infection. Moore *et al.*[27] point out distribution differences, many periodontitis-related species occurring in focal infections elsewhere in the body[28,29,30]. It may be observed that the number of individual species so far identified in plaque is very large: 509 according to Moore and Moore[30]. Of these, 28 bacterial, 5 treponemal and at least one mycoplasmal species have been associated with periodontal tissue destruction. Hardly what one would classify as a specific infection, but not so difficult to correlate to mixed anaerobe infections elsewhere in the alimentary tract.

At the same time it is clear that disease-related species can be transmitted through intimate contact, as between spouses[31] and mother and child[32]. In the former study the spouses of two couples showed the same sero- and ribotypes of *A. actinomycetemcomitans* and identical *P. gingivalis* ribotypes. Ribotype variation was more obvious between spouses. In the latter study, *Prevotella melaninogenica* ribotypes were only partly shared in 11 mother-child pairs, indicating that in young children (4 - 32 months) at least, sources additional to the mother influence colonization, and that Gram-negative anaerobes appear in the mouth even in pre-dentate children.

On apical border plaque.

There has been the suggestion that the count of a putative chronic periodontitis-related species may be so low for emphasis on it not to be justified[30]. However, the predominant species at an actual disease site may not be that deduced from relatively gross samples. In chronic periodontitis, it may be more relevant to note the proportion at a given locus in relation to the advancing front of the lesion, with particular emphasis on the apical plaque border, and on the unattached flora between the border and the bottom of the periodontal pocket. Such studies have shown that there is a limited range of organisms in the apical border plaque. Plainly, it is most relevant to concentrate on the latter, since its removal above all is associated with significant inflammation resolution in periodontitis. Also, failure to sample from the border may lead one to conclude that a species is absent from that site (Newman, unpublished observation).

The morphotypes at the actual border are mainly Gram-negative, but include Gram-positive coccoid forms. Many are polysaccharide-producing, intracellularly as well as extracellularly, which one would expect in sub-contact area gingival margin plaque in children[12], but not in this location, and they include *P. gingivalis* and *A. actinomycetemcomitans* as identified *in situ* by immunoelectron-microscopy[13]. The flora morphotypes are similar, it may be observed, regardless of whether the chronic periodontitis is routine adult, or rapidly progressive, juvenile or adult onset[33,34,35].

In chronic periodontitis, unlike health or gingivitis, the apical border plaque terminates in several ways along the cementum surface, ranging from a long, extremely thin, acute-angled wedge to a series of bacterial islands of mainly Gram-negative but also Gram-positive cocci and short rods. The most apical intact cells are usually Gram-negative cocci and short rods. The actual most apical microorganisms are almost always lysed. PMN were noted frequently in the superficial plaque, underlining their protective role in this location[33].

The cell walls and matrix of the apical border plaque contained much polyanionic material, probably mucopolysaccharide and glycoprotein. Spirochaetes as well as cocci and rods had demonstrable glycocalyces[34]. The deep plaque near the apical border contained abundant intracellular polysaccharide in the predominant Gram-positive coccoid bacteria. The overlying mixed bacterial layer in this location also comprised Gram-positive and negative intracellular polysaccharide-containing cocci and rods, IPS granules being larger in Gram-positive than Gram-negative cells. Spirochaetes also contained IPS.

It is surprising that the plaque literature so seldom considers the ecological significance of these polymers, both extracellular and intracellular. For example, apart from attachment to other cells and host surfaces, glycocalyces or "fuzzy" coats may serve as an antiphagocytic shield by being highly hydrophilic, and thereby not readily surrounded by the more hydrophobic phagocytes[34]. Similarly, IPS of the glycogen-amylopectin type are generally synthesized from dietary sugar, and it is conventional to assume that in the absence of simple sugars, stored IPS is used for energy purposes. However, IPS production in plaque is associated with unbalanced growth rather than storage, as indicated by the cell ghosts in the most apical plaque. Further, the presence of apparently intact IPS-containing cells in the apical border plaque makes it clear that such bacteria can form such polymers in an environment well below the gingival margin, but hitherto assumed to be relatively alkaline. As root caries can also occur in this location, near the bottom of the periodontal pocket, even in rapidly progressive periodontitis[35], it may be concluded that acidic milieus predisposing to caries can occur in such an unforeseen location.

Concerning the variable size of IPS granules, this, too, may relate to growth phase, as small IPS granules have been observed during stationary, and large during late stationary phases of growth of rumen bacteria subjected to excess fermentable carbohydrate[36].

The morphotypes of the apical border plaque, as stated, appear similar, even in different forms of severe or rapidly progressive periodontitis. Cocci, short rods, cocco-bacilli and variously sized spirochaetes were dominant in middle and apical thirds of root plaques in juvenile periodontitis patients[37]. However, the zonation observed in adult periodontitis specimens of root plaque is absent[35]. Given the similarities in morphotypes present, at the apical border, and while identification *in situ* is progressing[13], and remains a major objective of current research into aetiology, pathogenesis and progression of the different forms of periodontitis, there is no doubt that a limited range of organisms locates in the apical border plaque, regardless of the rate or severity of periodontal destruction[35], even in cases as severe as chronic neutropenia[3]. This fact has probably been obscured by the variation even a short distance coronal to the actual border. The maximum spirochaete and mycoplasma counts also occurred most frequently apically, and coccal counts tended to increase also the more apical the sample[38,39], probably due to the Gram-negative disease-associated anaerobes noted ultrastructurally in this location.

Damage mechanisms at the plaque-host interface

While there is no doubt that plaque, probably through tissue penetration by microbial metabolites rather than whole cells, is the direct cause of chronic inflammatory periodontal diseases in all their stages, there is also no doubt that the periodontally-targeted host defence system, while basically protective of the host, contributes to the pathology, or that variability in that response determines the extent and rate of tissue destruction in periodontitis[12]. As Loesche[40] has observed, slow and intermittent destruction of the periodontium is the price paid for protection against subgingival plaque microorganisms. Without this basically protective response, however, the damaging effects of commensal plaque species would be unlikely to be limited for many decades, as is actually the case, to the peripheral (periodontal) tissues[12]. Indeed, when such organisms are not contained locally, the result is systemic spread with focal infection, often with serious, even fatal consequences[28,29].

As the tissue damage in periodontitis can therefore be considered a by-product of the immune reaction[4,41], some of the more likely plaque-host reactions will be considered here. Toxic elements include directly injurious substances such as ammonia, urea, indole, skatole, hydrogen sulphide and methyl mercaptans, and a range of enzymes capable of degrading collagen and ground substance. Whole bacteria may activate complement, neutrophils and macrophages, while cell surface-associated materials (SAMs) may act as polyclonal B-cell activators, as may exopolysaccharides of the plaque matrix[4,42]. Immune complexes can activate complement, and can induce periodontitis experimentally[43]. Lipopolysaccharide from Gram-negative plaque organisms can activate macrophages with resultant secretion of such molecules as IL-1β, TNF-α, prostaglandins and a range of hydrolytic enzymes[44]. Plaque factors may also activate IL-2 and lymphotoxin production by T-lymphocytes, contributing to inflammation and tissue breakdown. Osteoclast activation may result from T-cell cytokine activity[45].

While whole cell bacterial entry may be relatively uncommon, bacterial products are likely to be more frequent in the disease-affected tissues. One possible damage mechanism is by LPS promotion of adhesion of PMN to fibroblasts, which would relate to damage to the latter mediated by PMN[46]. In reverse, there may be host deficiencies, rendering the subject more susceptible. For example, in localised juvenile periodontitis, there is an abnormal PMN phagosome-lysosome fusion, but only for the disease-related species *A.actinomycetemcomitans*[47,48].

Recent studies have demonstrated that the fuzzy material around putative periodontopathogens has potent disease-related biochemical activities. Purified capsular material from *A.actinomycetemcomitans* has bone-resorbing activity[49,50], and can inhibit fibroblast proliferation and collagen synthesis[51,52,53]. Similar behaviour has been shown for surface-associated material (SAM) from other major periodontitis-related species, *P.gingivalis*[54] and *Eikenella corrodens*[55].

Bacterial bone-resorbing factors listed by Hopps[56] included lipopolysaccharides (LPS), lipoteichoic acids, *Actinomyces* factor, peptidoglycans, muramyl dipeptide, bacterial lipoprotein and capsular material, the latter including SAMs. *P.gingivalis* LPS appears to be more active than those of *A.actinomycetemcomitans* or *C.ochracea* at low concentrations[57]. As Hopps[56] noted, LPS can act synergistically with host-produced bone resorbing factors such as PGE_2 and so-called osteoclast activating factor[58]. The resorptive capacity of LPS has been attributed to the lipid A portion of the molecule, since the activity can be blocked by polymyxin B, which binds selectively to this region[59]. In her review of possible mechanisms of bone resorption in chronic periodontitis, Hopps[56] noted that *P.gingivalis* LPS induced collagenase[60] and plasminogen activator[61] release from osteoblasts, and that activation of preformed osteoblasts by this LPS was osteoblast-mediated. Part of the activity was attributed by Hopps[56] to Il-1 and PGE_2 from fibroblasts. LPS may also act through inhibition. For example *A.actinomycetemcomitans* LPS has been shown to be capable of inhibiting bone collagen sythesis[62]. Of course, at present we do not know the depth of penetration of periodontitis-affected tissues by microbial products. But, as Hopps[56] points out, if products such as LPS, lipoteichoic acid, muramyl dipeptide and peptidoglycan do reach the alveolar bone surface, they are likely to bring about bone loss. Hopps and Sismey-Durrant[61] concluded that *P.gingivalis* LPS also induces osteoblast release of collagenase, and that LPS-stimulated fibroblasts release such bone-resorbing factors as IL-1 and PGE_2. Apart from direct or indirect effects on bone resorption, LPS may affect the periodontal tissues by inhibition of bone collagen synthesis.

Meikle *et al.*[63] observe that Il-1-like molecules can be produced by many cell types in periodontal tissues, including fibroblasts, osteoblasts, endothelial cells and macrophages. They considered that periodontitis-related plaque organisms mediated connective tissue breakdown in periodontitis through the ability of their cell wall antigens to stimulate IL-1 and TNF-α production by circulating mononuclear cells. These in turn induce the synthesis of the matrix metalloproteinases collagenase, gelatinase and stromelysin. They emphasised that tissue damage is more likely to result from the side-effects of these cytokine mediators on the constituent cells of the periodontium, than from the direct actions of bacteria or their products. In this connection, one again needs to be reminded of the fundamentally protective nature of the host response. Only when it is defective is the resultant periodontitis likely to progress more rapidly. At the same time, one also needs to be reminded of the potent tissue-damaging potential of the SAMs produced by some periodonto-pathogens[52,53,55,64]. It is equally evident that the SAMs greatly increase the antigenic load, especially in rapidly progressive forms of periodontitis, whether juvenile or adult onset, and evident as high titres of serum IgG antibodies, for example, to *A.actinmycetemcomitans* in localised juvenile periodontitis, to *P.gingivalis* in rapidly progressive periodontitis, adult onset, and to *E.corrodens* in both[42]. Meghji *et al.*[42] consider that, at least for *A.actinomycetemcomitans*, the antibody may be responsible for inhibiting the bone resorption-related SAM protein from this organism.

Conclusions

The relationship between plaque and chronic periodontitis is ecological. Shifts in proportions of species, or possibly at a sub-species level, lead to the supervention of microbial groupings that are disease-related. Damage can be direct or indirect. It seems likely that host factors influence these configurations, and it is clear that host response deficiencies often relate to more rapidly progressive periodontitis. Research as close as possible to the host-plaque interface, preferably directly on affected tissues and plaque, is essential if we are to unravel the precise aetiology, pathogenesis and varying rates of progression of the different forms of chronic periodontitis. That in turn is likely to provide the most practical basis for disease control and prevention, targeted as appropriate at plaque and/or host factors.

References.

1. Friedman MT, Barber PM, Mordan NJ, Newman HN. The "plaque-free" zone in health and disease: a scanning electron microscope study. *J Periodontol* 1992, **63**, 890-896.
2. Friedman MT, Barber P, Newman HN. Ultrastructure and histochemistry of the dental cuticle in adult periodontitis. *J Periodontol* 1993, **64**, 520-528.
3. Vaughan AG, Vrahopoulos TP, Joachim F, Sati K, Barber P, Newman HN. A case report of chronic neutropenia, clinical and ultrastructural findings. *J Clin Periodont* 1990, **17**, 435-445.
4. Newman HN, Challacombe SJ. Infection and the periodontal ligament. In: Berkovitz BKB, Moxham BJ, Newman HN, eds. *The Periodontal Ligament in Health and Disease.* London, Mosby-Wolfe, 1995, 293-313.
5. Newman HN. On passive eruption. *Periodont Abstr* 1994, **42**, 41-44.
6. Moskow BS, Polson AM. Histologic studies on the extension of the inflammatory infiltrate in human periodontitis. *J Clin Periodont* 1991, **18**, 534-542.
7. Newman HN, Wilson M, Henderson B. Chemical control of dental plaque. In: Scully C, Porter S, eds. *Innovations and Developments in Orofacial Health Care.* Northwood, Science Reviews, 1995, 155-185.
8. Liakoni H, Barber P, Newman HN. Bacterial penetration of pocket soft tissues in chronic adult and juvenile periodontitis cases. An ultrastructural study. *J Clin Periodont* 1987; 14, 22-28.
9. Liakoni H, Barber PM, Newman HN. Bacterial penetration of the pocket tissues in juvenile/postjuvenile periodontitis after the presurgical oral hygiene phase. *J Periodontol* 1987; **58**, 847-855.
10. Joachim F, Barber P, Newman HN, Osborn J. The plasma cell at the advancing front of the lesion in chronic periodontitis. *J Periodont Res* 1990; **25**, 49-59.
11. Newman HN. The classification of periodontal diseases. In: Newman HN, Rees TD, Kinane DF, eds. *Diseases of the Periodontium.* Northwood, Science Reviews, 1993, 1-26.

12. Newman HN. Plaque and chronic inflammatory periodontal disease - a question of ecology. *J Clin Periodont* 1990; **17**, 533-541.
13. Newman HN, Barber PM. Dental plaque structure *in vivo*. In: Wimpenny J, Handley P, Gilbert P, Lappin-Scott H, eds. *The life and dealth of biofilms*. Cardiff, Bioline, 1995, 27-32.
14. Van der Zee E, Davies EH, Newman HN. Marking width, calibration from tip and tine diameter of periodontal probes. *J Clin Periodont* 1991; **18**, 516-520.
15. Atassi F, Newman HN, Bulman JS. Probe tine diameter and probing depth. *J Clin Periodont* 1992; **19**, 301-304.
16. Almas K, Bulman JS, Newman HN. Assessment of periodontal status with CPITN and conventional periodontal indices. *J Clin Periodont* 1991; **18**, 654-659.
17. Newman HN. Chemical agents in the management of chronic inflammatory periodontal disease. In: Newman HN, Williams DW, eds. *Inflammation and immunology in chronic inflammatory periodontal disease*. Northwood, Science Reviews, 1992, 141-167.
18. Newman HN. Irrigation based systems in plaque control in chronic periodontitis. *J Parodont 1995;* **14**, 381-397.
19. Haffajee AD, Socransky SS. Microbial etiologic agents of destructive periodontal diseases. *Periodontology 2000* 1994; **5**, 78-111.
20. Wilson M, Lopatin D, Osborne G, Kieser JB. Prevalence of *Treponema denticola* and *Porphyromonas gingivalis* in plaque from periodontally healthy and periodontally diseased sites. *J Med Microbiol* 1993; **38**, 406-410.
21. Zimmer W, Wilson M, Marsh PD, Newman HN, Bulman JS. *Porphyromonas gingivalis, Prevotella intermedia* and *Actinobacillus actinomycetemcomitans* in the plaque of children without periodontitis. *Microb Ecol Hlth Dis* 1991; **4**, 329-336.
22. Slots J, Feik D, Rams TE. Prevalence and antimicrobial susceptibility of *Enterobacteriaceae, Pseudomonadaceae* and *Acinetobacter* in human periodontitis. *Oral Microbiol Immunol* 1990; **5**, 149-154.
23. Rams TE, Feik D, Young V, Hammond BF, Slots J. Enterococci in human periodontitis. *Oral Microbiol Immunol* 1992; **7**, 249-252.
24. Rams TE, Feik D, Slots J. Staphylococci in human periodontal diseases. *Oral Microbiol Immunol* 1990; **5**, 29-32.
25. Torkko H, Asikainen S. Occurrence of *Porphyromonas gingivalis* with *Prevotella intermedia* in periodontal samples. *FEMS Immunol Med Microbiol* 1993; **6**, 195-198.
26 Sundqvist G, Figdor D, Hanström L, Sorlin S, Sandström G. Phagocytosis and virulence of different strains of *Porphyromonas gingivalis. Scand J dent Res* 1991; **99**, 117-129.
27. Moore WEC, Burmeister JA, Brooks CN *et al.* Investigation of the influences of puberty, genetics, and environment on the composition of subgingival periodontal floras. *Infect Immun* 1993; **61**, 2891-2898.
28. Newman HN. Guest editorial, focal infection revisited - the dentist as physician. *J dent Res* 1992; **71**, 1854.
29. Newman HN. Focal infection revisited. *Periodont Abstr* 1993; **41**, 73-77.
30. Moore WEC, Moore LVH. The bacteria of periodontal diseases. *Periodontology 2000* 1994; **5**, 68-77.
31. Saarela M, von Troil-Lindén B, Torkko H, Stucki A-M *et al.* Transmission of oral bacterial species between spouses. *Oral Microbiol Immunol* 1993; **8**, 349-354.
32. Könönen E, Saarela M, Karjalainen J, Jousimies-Somer H, Alaluusua S, Asikainen S. Transmission of oral *Prevotella melaninogenica* between a mother and her young child. *Oral Microbiol Immunol* 1994; **9**, 310-314.

33. Vrahopoulos TP, Barber PM, Newman HN. The apical border plaque in chronic adult periodontitis. An ultrastructural study. I. Morphology, structure, and cell content. *J Perioontol* 1992; **63**, 243-252.
34 Vrahopoulos TP, Barber PM, Newman HN. The apical border plaque in chronic adult periodontitis. An ultrastructural study.II. adhesion, matrix, and carbohydrate metabolism. *J Periodontol* 1992; **63**, 253-261.
35. Vrahopoulos TP, Barber PM, Newman HN. The apical border plaque in severe periodontitis. An ultrastructural study. *J Periodontol* 1995; **66**, 113-124.
36. Cheng K-J, Kironaka R, Roberts DWA, Costerton JW. Cytoplasmic glycogen inclusions in cells of anaerobic Gram-negative rumen bacteria. *Canad J Microbiol* 1973; **19**, 1501-1506.
37. Douglass KD, Cobb CM, Berkstein S, Killoy WJ. Microscopic characterization of root surface-associated microbial plaque in juvenile periodontitis. *J Periodontol* 1990; **61**, 475-484.
38. Omar AA, Newman HN, Bulman J, Osborn J. Darkground microscopy of subgingival plaque from the top to the bottom of the periodontal pocket. *J Clin Periodont* 1990; **17**, 364-370.
39. Kwek HSN, Wilson M, Newman HN. Mycoplasma in relation to gingivitis and periodontitis. *J Clin Periodont* 1990; **17**, 119-122.
40. Loesche WJ. Bacterial mediators in periodontal disease. *Clin Infect Dis* 1993; **16** suppl 4, S203-S210.
41. Page RC. The role of inflammatory mediators in the pathogenesis of periodontal disease. *J Periodont Res* 1991; **26**, 23-42.
42. Meghji S, Henderson B, Kirby A, Newman HN, Wilson M. Serum antibody response to surface-associated material from periodontopathogenic bacteria. *FEMS Immunol Med Microbiol* 1995; **10**, 101-108.
43. Nisengard RJ, Beutner EH, Neugeboren NJ, Neider M, Asaro J. Experimental induction of periodontal disease with Arthus-type reactions. *Clin Immunol Immunopathol* 1977; **8**, 97-104.
44. Meikle MD, Heath JK, Reynolds JJ. Advances in understanding cell interactions in tissue resorption, relevance to the pathogenesis of periodontal diseases and a new hupothesis. *J Oral Pathol* 1986; **15**, 239-250.
45. Stashenko P, Jandinski JJ, Fujiyoshi P, Rynar J, Socransky SS. Tissue levels of bone resorptive cytokines in periodontal disease. *J Periodontol* 1991; **62**, 504-509.
46. Deguchi S, Hori T, Creamer H, Gabler W. Neutrophil=mediated damage to human periodontal ligament-derived fibroblasts, role of lipopolysaccharide. *J Periodont Res* 1990; **25**, 293-299.
47. Christersson LA, Albini B, Zambon JJ, Wikesjö UME, Genco RJ. Tissue localization of *Actinobacillus actinomycetemcomitans* in human periodontitis. 1. Light, immunofluorescence and electron microscopic studies. *J Periodontol* 1987; **58**, 529-539.
48. Van Dyke TE, Lester MA, Shapira L. The role of the host response in periodontal disease progression: implications for future treatment strategies. *J Periodontol* 1993; **64**, 792-806.
49. Wilson M, Kamin S, Harvey W. Bone resorbing activity of purified capsular material from *Actinobacillus actinomycetemcomitans. J Periodont Res* 1985; **20**, 484-491.
50. Wilson M, Meghji S, Harvey W. The effect of capsular material from *Haemophilus actinomycetemcomitans* on bone collagen synthesis *in vitro. Microbios* 1988; **54**, 181-185.

51. Kamin S, Harvey W, Wilson M, Scutt A. Inhibition of fibroblast proliferation and collagen synthesis by capsular material from *Actinobacillus actinomycetemcomitans. J Med Microbiol* 1986; **22**, 245-249.

52. Meghji S, Wilson M, Henderson B. Anti-proliferative and cytotoxic activity of surface-associated material from periodontopathogenic bacteria. *Arch oral Biol* 1992; **37**, 637-644.

53. Meghji S, Henderson B, Nair S, Wilson M. Inhibition of bone DNA and collagen production by surface-associated material from bacteria implicated in the pathology of periodontal disease. *J Periodontol* 1992; **63**, 736-742.

54. Wilson M, Meghji S, Barber P, Henderson B. Biological activities of surface-associated material from *Porphyromonas gingivalis. FEMS Immunol Med Microbiol* 1993; **6**, 147-155.

55. Meghji S, Wilson M, Barber P, Henderson B. Bone resorbing activity of surface-associated material from *Actinobacillus actinomycetemcomitans* and *Eikenella corrodens. J Med Microbiol* 1994; **41**, 197-203.

56. Hopps RM. Mechanisms of bone resorption in chronic inflammatory periodontal disease. In: Newman HN, Williams DW, eds. *Inflammation and immunology in chronic inflammatory periodontal disease.* Northwood, Science Reviews, 1992, 107-126.

57. Lino Y, Hopps RM. The bone-resorbing activities in tissue culture of lipopolysaccharides from the bacteria *Actinobacillus actinomycetemcomitans, Bacteroides gingivalis* and *Capnocytophaga ochracea* isolated from human mouths. *Archs Oral Biol* 1984; **29**, 59-63.

58. Raisz LG, Nuki K, Alander CB, Craig RG. Interactions between bacterial endotoxins and other stimulators of bone resorption in organ culture. *J Periodont Res* 1981; **16**, 1-7.

59. Harvey W, Kamin S, Meghji S, Wilson M. Interleukin 1-like activity in capsular material from *Haemophilus actinomycetemcomitans. Immunol* 1986; **60**, 415-418.

60. Sismey-Durrant HJ, Atkinson SJ, Hopps RM, Heath JK. The effect of lipopolysaccharide from *Bacteroides gingivalis* and muramyl dipeptide on osteoblast collagenase release. *Calcif Tiss Int* 1989; **44**, 361-363.

61. Hopps RM, Sismey-Durrant HJ. Mechanisms of alveolar bone loss in periodontal disease. In: Hamada S *et al.*, eds. *Periodontal disease, pathogens and host immune responses. Tokyo, Quintessence,* 1991; 307-320.

62. Wilson M, Meghji S, Harvey W. *Inhibition of bone collagen synthesis* in vitro by lipopolysaccharide from *Actinobacillus actinomycetemcomitans. IRCS Med Sci* 1986; **14**, 536-537.

63. Meikle MC, McFarland CG, Newman HN, Reynolds JJ. Cytokines and connective tissue degradation in chronic inflammatory periodontal disease. In: Newman HN, Williams DW, eds. *Inflammation and immunology in chronic inflammatory periodontal disease.* Northwood, Science Reviews, 1992; 87-106.

64. Kirby AC. Identification of a 64kDa osteolytic protein from *Actinobacillus actinomycetemcomitans* surface-associated material. *J dent res* 1994; **73**, 787.

3 Periodontal manifestations of systemic diseases

Stephen R. Porter and Crispian Scully

Department of Oral Medicine,Eastman Dental Institute for Oral Health Care Sciences, University of London, 256 Gray's Inn Road, London WC1X 8LD, UK

Introduction

Rapid destruction of the periodontium can be a feature of a wide range of systemic disorders, particularly HIV disease and also primary immunodeficiencies of neutrophil number and/or function (Porter and Scully, 1990; Wilton *et al.*, 1991; Porter and Scully, 1994; Winkler *et al.*, 1988, 1989). Rarely periodontal destruction may be secondary to structural anomalies of the periodontal ligament associated with congenital disease.

This chapter will review the more well-characterised disorders likely to give rise to destruction of the periodontium (Table 1)

Congenital causes of periodontal destruction

Genetic risk factors
Family studies indicate that susceptibility to early onset forms of periodontitis, particularly prepubertal and juvenile periodontitis may be, at least in part, influenced by the host genotype (Michalowicz, 1994).   The prevalence and distribution of juvenile periodontitis in affected families may follow an autosomal recessive mode of inheritance, but there is considerable heterozygosity in any pattern of inheritance of this disorder.   The genetic basis to adult (chronic) peridontitis is less clear.   A detailed review of this subject can be found elsewhere (Michalowicz, 1994).

Disorders of phagocyte number or function

Neutropenias
Destructive periodontitis giving rise to prepubertal, juvenile-like or rapidly progressive periodontitis can arise in cyclic neutropenia (Prichard *et al.*, 1984; Scully *et al.*, 1985), benign familial neutropenia (Stabholz *et al.*, 1990; Porter *et al.*, 1995) and other less well defined neutropenias (Baehni *et al.*, 1983).

Table 1 *Systemic causes of enhanced gingival/periodontal destruction.*

(1) Primary immunodeficiencies
    (a) Reduced neutrophil number
        Cyclic neutropenia
        Benign familial neutropenia
        Other primary neutropenias

    (b) Defective neutrophil function
        Hyperimmunoglobulinaemia E
        Kartagener's syndrome
        Chronic granulomatous disease
        Chediak-Higashi syndrome
        Acatalasia
        Leukocyte adhesion deficiency

    (c) Other immunodeficiencies
        Fanconi's anaemia
        Down's syndrome
        Severe combined immunodeficiency (SCID)

(2) Other congenital disorders
    Hypophosphatasia
    Ehlers-Danlos syndrome type VIII
    Acrosteolysis (Hajdu-Cheney syndrome)
    Type 1b glycogen storage disease
    Oxalosis
    Dyskeratosis benigna intrapeithelialis mucosae et cutis hereditara

(3) Secondary immunodeficiencies
    Malnutrition
    HIV disease
    Psychological stress
    Pregnancy
    Diabetes mellitus
    Crohn's disease

(4) Other acquired causes
    Vitamin C deficiency
    Tobacco smoking
    Smokeless tobacco smoking

Table 2 Possible mechanisms of periodontal destruction in insulin dependent diabetes mellitus (IDDM)

Mechanism	Comments
Periodontopathic microflora	Some conflicting data (Tervonen *et al.,* 1994) (*e.g. Porphyromonas gingivalis, Prevotella intermedia, Capnocytophaga, Campylobacter rectus, Fusobacterium nucleatum*
Impaired neutrophil function	Chemotaxis is the most likely defect; it may not correct with good glycaemic control. The chemotactic defect may occur in first degree non-diabetic relatives.
Excessive inflammatory response	Little evidence (*e.g.* genetically determined (MHC?) polysaccharide hyperesponsiveness of monocytes)
Defective collagen metabolism	Little human data (Oliver *et al.,* 1993) (*e.g.* decreased collagen production, decreased collagen degradation, reduced collagen in diabetic rats)
Impaired wound healing	No data on periodontal function (*e.g.* decreased collagen, poor tensile strength of collagen, reduced growth factors (*e.g.*platelet-derived growth factor, epidermal growth factor, TGF-β), increased collagenase activity)

Defective neutrophil function

Defective neutrophil function in hyperimmunoglobulin E syndrome (Hill-Quie syndrome, Job's syndrome) (Charon *et al.,* 1985), Kartagener's syndrome, chronic granulomatous disease (Cohen *et al.,* 1985), Chediak-Higashi syndrome (Weary and Bender, 1967), acatalasia (Delgado and Calderson, 1979), leukocyte adhesion deficiency (Roberts and Atkinson, 1990, Meyle, 1994) and Actin dysfunction syndrome can give rise to profound gingival inflammation and/or ulceration, sometimes with periodontal destruction (Hart and Shapira, 1994). The precise cause of the periodontal destruction associated with Papillon-Lefevre syndrome (periodontitis with palmoplantar keratosis) (Efeoglu *et al.,* 1990; Hart and Shapira, 1994) is unclear. It may be due to accompanying defective neutrophil chemotaxis or phagocytosis, increased superoxide production, myeloperoxidase deficiency, or reduced monocyte chemotaxis, or defective lymphocyte blastogenesis (Stadler *et al.,* 1989; Bimstein *et al.,* 1990; D'Angelo *et al.,* 1992; Bullon *et al.,* 1993) but there are few detailed studies of large numbers of affected patients, hence other causes of the periodontal destruction have been suggested (Vrahopoulos *et al.,* 1988).

There are many defects of cell mediated and humoral immunity in Down's syndrome but, from the little attention that has been paid, the phagocytic system may also be deficient (Reuland-Bosma *et al.*, 1988) and hence probably accounts for the increased liability to periodontal disease in this congenital disorder.

Aside from defective neutrophil number or function there are very few other primary immunodeficiencies that are known to give rise to severe gingivitis and/or periodontitis. Accelerated periodontal destruction in a patient with very poorly described Fanconi's anaemia has been documented (Opinya *et al.*, 1988). Complement deficiencies are not associated with periodontal destruction and there is little evidence that humoral immunodeficiencies increase liability to periodontal disease (Dahlen *et al.*, 1993; Porter and Scully, 1993 a,b), although some children with IgA deficiency may have gingivitis as a consequence of mouth breathing (Robertson and Cooper, 1974) and one study did find that patients with common variable immunodeficiency (CVID) had higher periodontal indices than immunocompetent individuals and patients with selective IgA deficiency (Norhagen-Engstrom *et al.*, 1992). Polar cell mediated immunodeficiencies do not give rise to enhanced gingival or peridontal destruction (Porter and Scully, 1994), although necrotising gingivitis has been reported in a small number of children with a variant of severe combined immunodeficiency syndrome (SCID) (Rotbart *et al.*, 1986) and occasional children can have periodontal destruction associated with subtle lymphocyte defects (Yoshida-Mindni *et al.*, 1995).

Congenital connective tissue disorders
Premature loss of deciduous teeth in childhood and spontaneous loss of permanent teeth in adulthood due to a deficiency or absence of cementum, are characteristic of hypophosphatasia and, may be the only signs of disease (odontohypophosphatasia) (MacFarlane and Swart, 1989; Chapple *et al.*, 1992; Plagmann *et al.*, 1994; Watanabe *et al.*, 1993). Cemental hypoplasia has also been implicated in the periodontal destruction of some children with early-onset periodontal disease.

Enhanced periodontal disease may be associated with Ehlers Danlos syndrome type VIII (Stewart *et al.*, 1977; Hartsfield and Kousseff, 1990) and may be a feature of acroosteolysis (Hajdu-Cheney syndrome) (Allen *et al.*, 1984), the periodontal destruction of the latter disorder possibly being due to lack of periodontal attachment and/or occlusal trauma.

Glycogen storage disease
Gingivitis (Ambruso *et al.*, 1985) or rapidly progressive periodontitis may be seen in some, but not all patients with type 1b glycogen storage disease (Beaudet and Anderson, 1987; Hara *et al.*, 1987), the periodontal disease possibly secondary to accompanying neutropenia and defective neutrophil chemotaxis and bacteriocidal activity (Beaudet *et al.*, 1980).

Oxalosis
Oxalosis causes external root resorption and subsequent mobility and early loss of teeth as a result of oxalate crystal deposition and inflammatory reactions within the gingiva and periodontal ligament (Wysocki *et al.*, 1982; Moskow, 1989).

A prepubertal periodontitis-like disorder has been reported in one patient with acrodynia (Obura, 1965).

Familial dysautonomia

Gingivitis and periodontitis may be common (but not severe) in familial dysautonomia (Riley-Day syndrome), a disorder characterised by autonomic, sensory and motor nerve dysfunction. The periodontal disease may be due to poor oral hygiene but interestingly, affected patients do not have excessive levels of dental caries (Boraz, 1984; Mass *et al.*, 1992).

Dyskeratosis benigna intraepithelialis mucosae et cutis hereditaria

Early loss of deciduous and permanent teeth with associated gingival inflammation has been noted in two patients with dyskeratosis benigna intraepithelialis mucosae et cutis hereditaria (From *et al.*, 1978).

Acquired disorders

Human immunodeficiency virus (HIV) disease

Although relatively few critical studies of the periodontal status of HIV-infected individuals have been undertaken, cross-sectional studies suggest that up to 50% of HIV-infected individuals may have gingival lesions, while under 10% have possibly HIV-specific periodontal lesions. The gingival and periodontal disease of HIV-infected persons can comprise:

(1) Non specific gingivitis indistinguishable from plaque-related gingivitis affecting non-HIV infected individuals

(2) HIV gingivitis (linear gingivitis, previously termed generalised atypical gingivitis) - gingivitis with associated erythema and oedema that does not respond to improved oral hygiene. The erythema can manifest as an intense linear band at the gingival margin, as petechiae-like red patches on the attached and/or non-attached gingivae, or as a generalised redness affecting the attached and/or unattached gingivae. Spontaneous gingival bleeding is common (Winkler *et al.*, 1988; Zambon, 1988; Robinson, 1992). While some workers believe that no similar condition occurs in non-HIV-infected individuals, neutropenic persons can have profound gingival erythema (Porter *et al.*, 1995).

(3) Acute necrotising gingivitis (ANG) essentially indistinguishable from that in non-HIV-nfected patients, causing gingival pain, ulceration, bleeding and interdental gingival cratering (Winkler *et al.*, 1988; Rowland *et al.*, 1993).

(4) Adult periodontitis/rapidly progressive periodontitis - plaque associated periodontitis indistinguishable from that seen immunocompetent individuals (Reichart *et al.*, 1987; Rosenstcin *et al.*, 1989).

(5) HIV-associated periodontitis (acute necrotising periodontitis) characterised by rapid localised or generalised periodontal destruction giving rise to pain, tooth mobility and infrabony pocketing (San Giacomo *et al.*, 1990; Thomas *et al.*, 1990).

(6) Acute necrotising stomatitis characterised by extensive and rapid destruction of the gingiva extending into adjacent mucosa and bone causing massive destruction of the oral soft tissues and underlying bone (Akula *et al.*, 1989; Winkler *et al.*, 1989; Williams *et al.*, 1990).

The precise aetiology of these periodontal lesions is still unclear, but data from selective cultural and indirect immunofluorescence studies of American HIV-infected patients indicates that *Porphyromonas (Bacteroides) gingivalis, Prevotella (Bacteroides) intermedia, Eikenella corrodens, Actinobacillus actinomycetem-comitans, Fusobacterium nucleatum* and *Peptostreptococcus micros* are frequently present in some but not all HIV-G or HIV-P lesions (Murray *et al.*, 1988; Gornitsky *et al.*, 1991; Murray *et al.*, 1991; Rams *et al.*, 1991). Detailed cultural analysis of the microflora of the periodontal lesions of AIDS patients found that *Streptococcus sanguis II, Lactobacillus acidophilus, Porphyromonas (Bacteroides) gingivalis, Fusobacterium nucleatum, Staphylococcus epidermids, Actinomyces naeslundii* and *Actinomyces viscosus* were the most frequently isolated subgingival bacteria (Zambon *et al.*, 1990). An investigation of Swedish HIV patients with clinically healthy gingivae, however, found no significant differences in selected bacteria in saliva or gingival crevices between individuals at different stages of HIV infection, and healthy control subjects (Lucht *et al.*, 1990). Enteric bacteria and Candida species may have some aetiological significance. There can also be some (but not consistent) directly proportional relationship between the severity of periodontal disease and degree of immunodeficiency in HIV disease (Barr *et al.*, 1992). Results of longitudinal studies are awaited to determine the precise associations between periodontal destruction, microflora and immunocompetence in HIV disease.

Diet
Malnutrition is probably still the most common cause of acquired immunodeficiency; there are no specific periodontal manifestations but severe protein-energy malnutrition can predispose to cancrum oris. The effect of diet of periodontal disease is reviewed in detail elsewhere (Genco and Loe, 1993). Despite similar levels of plaque, persons consuming a higher sugar diet develop more experimental gingivitis than controls but there is little evidence that a hard or fibrous diet influences periodontal disease (Sidi and Ashley, 1984; Egelberg, 1981). There is no apparent association between iron deficiency anaemia and increased susceptibility to periodontitis despite occasional suggestive clinical reports (Pack, 1984). Similarly, there is no relation between periodontal disease and folate or vitamin B6 deficiency, but oral supplements and topical folic acid appear to reduce gingivitis (Pack and Thomson, 1980; Thomson and Pack, 1982), and folate deficiency predisposes to periodontal disease in non-human primates (Dreizen *et al.*, 1970).

Gingival swelling, bleeding and ulceration, and periodontal destruction is a feature of profound vitamin C deficiency (Woolfe *et al.*, 1980). Vitamin C therapy can improve the periodontal status of patients with vitamin C deficiency but does not significantly affect otherwise healthy persons (Ismail *et al.*, 1983a) despite claims to the contrary and despite the improvement in monocyte chemotaxis in severe periodontitis (Johnson *et al.*, 1983). Nevertheless, one study has suggested that gingival health can be modulated by vitamin C (Leggott *et al.*, 1986).

Psychological stress
Psychological stress may increase susceptibility to acute necrotising gingivitis and perhaps adult periodontitis (Baker *et al.*, 1967) and some studies have suggested that

patients with these periodontal disorders may have had greater need of psychiatric counselling for stressful life events (Green *et al.,* 1986). Poor patient compliance with maintenance therapy may correlate with a high frequency of stressful life-events and poor personal relationships (Becker *et al.,* 1988).

Sex steroids
Sex steroids may influence gingival and periodontal inflammation (Sooriyamoorthy and Gower, 1989). Menstruation, pregnancy and oral contraceptive and androgen therapy (Michaelides, 1981) cause a temporary predisposition to gingivitis, but no notable increased liability to periodontal destruction (Amar and Chung, 1994).

Diabetes mellitus
The association between diabetes mellitus and periodontal disease is well reviewed elsewhere (Seymour and Heasman, 1992; Yalda *et al.,* 1994). In general there remains disagreement as to the likely susceptibility of patients with diabetes mellitus to the development of gingivitis and periodontitis. The cross-sectional nature of most earlier studies may account for the conflicting data, but the results of recent investigations that take account of duration of diabetes mellitus, degree of metabolic control and levels of oral hygiene, are also variable (Sastrowijoto *et al.,* 1989; Rosenthal *et al.,* 1989; Hayden and Buckley, 1989; Nelson *et al.,* 1990; De Pommereau *et al.,* 1992; Miller *et al.,* 1992; Karjalainen *et al.,* 1994). It seems that children and adolescents with diabetes mellitus may have an increased risk of developing gingivitis (Pinson *et al.,* 1995) and adults with diabetes mellitus may have more severe periodontal destruction, despite similar local factors than non-diabetic patients. Recent epidemiological studies suggest an increased odds ratio for diabetes mellitus as a risk factor for periodontitis (Grossi *et al.,* 1993; Haber, 1991). These newer epidemiological studies compensate for the influence of confounding variables and conclude that there is both an increased severity and frequency of periodontitis in diabetes mellitus (Yalda *et al.,* 1994). The possible pathogenic mechanisms of any increased liability to gingival and periodontal disease in diabetes mellitus are indicated in Table 2 (Scully *et al.,* 1991; Yalda *et al.,* 1994, Porter and Scully, 1994).

Connective tissue disease
Gingivitis may arise in systemic lupus erythematosus (SLE) and reduced (Sjostrom *et al.,* 1989), increased (Tolo and Jorkend, 1990) and unchanged (Heasman and Seymour, 1990) levels of periodontal destruction have been reported in different groups of patients with rheumatoid arthritis. An uncontrolled study found that there was no increased liability to peridontal disease in Sjogren's syndrome (Tseng *et al.,* 1990) while a detailed investigation concluded that patients with secondary Sjogren's syndrome and other connective tissue diseases (particularly SLE) had significantly reduced periodontal probing depths compared with healthy control subjects (Mutlu *et al.,* 1991), possibly secondary to the long-term use of non-steroidal anti-inflammatory drugs (see below). Scleroderma does not give rise to any notable gingival or periodontal clinical features although widening of the periodontal ligament may be seen on plain radiographs (White *et al.,* 1977).

Previous studies have suggested that periodontal destruction is not significantly associated with osteoporosis (Kribbs, 1990). However, when the degree of osteoporosis is assessed by accurate techniques such as dual photon-absorptionometry there is some evidence of increased loss of periodontal attachment in osteoporotic persons compared with control subjects (von Wowern *et al.*, 1994). Similary women with high mineral values in the skeleton may retain their teeth with deeper periodontal pockets longer than those with osteoporosis (Klemetti *et al.*, 1994).

Gastrointestinal disease
A recent study suggested that patients with ulcerative colitis or Crohn's disease are at significant risk of periodontal destruction but this investigation did not include a suitable control group (Flemming *et al.*, 1991). Rapidly progressive periodontal disease has been described in a few patients with Crohn's disease possibly secondary to abnormal neutrophil function (*e.g.* reduced chemotaxis possibly due to an inhibitory factor in serum) (Lamster *et al.*, 1978; 1982; Van Dyke *et al.*, 1986) and/or the prescence of a possibly specific periodontal microflora (*e.g.* Campylobacter) (Kalmar, 1994). Increased periodontal disease may occur in hepatic cirrhosis (Movin, 1981) and probably reflects poor oral hygiene, malnourishment and immune dysfunction. Other periodontal aspects of gastrointestinal disease are detailed in other sections of this review

Tobacco
Tobacco smoking seems to predispose to necrotising gingivitis, plaque and calculus formation; and to bone loss and pocket formation (Haber and Kent, 1992; Haber *et al.*, 1993; Stoltenberg *et al.*, 1993). Apart from poorer oral hygiene (Modeer *et al.*, 1980), the mechanisms involved in periodontal disease in smokers are unclear (Rivera-Hidalgo, 1986) but *A. actinomycetemcomitans*, *P. intermedia* and *E. corrodens* may be associated with deep pockets in smokers (Stoltenberg *et al.*, 1993), nicotine may induce gingival vasoconstriction, and smoking impedes neutrophil chemotaxis and phagocytosis (Kraal and Kenney, 1979).

Though some epidemiological evidence suggests little difference in periodontal disease between smokers of cigarettes, cigars or pipes (Ismail *et al.*, 1983b), others have found greater pocket depths in cigarette smokers (Feldman *et al.*, 1983a; Haber and Kent, 1992). Any effect of smoking on plaque accumulation appears less than that of other factors, such as diet (Bergstrom, 1981; MacGregor *et al.*, 1985).

An association between the use of smokeless tobacco and gingival bleeding or destructive periodontal disease has been suggested (Greer and Poulson, 1983; Hoge and Kirkham, 1983) and one controlled study has shown an increase in gingivitis (Modeer *et al.*, 1980). Gingival recession at the site of placement of the smokeless tobacco was a prominent feature in these reports (Weintraub and Burt, 1987). However, smokeless tobacco did not appear to predispose to peridontal disease in an American Indian population (Wolfe and Carolos, 1987).

Apart from mild gingival blanching where the drug was placed, and transient painless vesicles of uncertain pathogenesis in about 15% of users, there appear to be no significant periodontal effects from the use of the tobacco substitute nicotine poloacrilex (Silver *et al.,* 1989).

Other drugs

Antimicrobials such as chlorhexidine, tetracyclines and metronidazole can reduce the development of gingivitis or gingival and/or periodontal destruction (Nuki *et al.,* 1981; Lindhe *et al.,* 1983; Slots and Rosling, 1983) but prolonged use, particularly of systemic agents may be problematic. Iatrogenic immunosuppression can decrease the inflammatory response in the gingiva and periodontium (Oshrain *et al.,* 1979; Tollefsen *et al.,* 1982; Been and Engel, 1982; Sutton and Smales, 1983), although it has recently been reported that methotrexate-induced neutropenia may give rise to alveolar bone destruction in rats (Yoshinari *et al.,* 1994). Non-steroidal anti-inflammatory drugs (NSAIDS) significantly reduce gingival indices, probing depths and alveolar bone loss (Waite *et al.,* 1981; Feldman *et al.,* 1983b), and in most, but not all, animal studies, NSAIDS inhibit periodontitis-associated alveolar bone loss (Nyman *et al.,* 1979; Nuki *et al.,* 1981; Weaks-Dybvig *et al.,* 1982; Williams *et al.,* 1984; Offenbacher *et al.,* 1987) possibly by influencing cyclooxygenase metabolism (Offenbacher *et al.,* 1992).

References

Akula, SK, Creticos, CM, Weldon-Linne, CM. (1989) Gangrenous stomatitis in AIDS. *Lancet*; **I**, 955.

Allen, C.M., Claman, L., Feldman, R. (1984) The acro-osteolysis (Hajdu-Cheney) syndrome, review of the literature and report of a case. *Journal of Periodontology* **55**, 224-229.

Amar, S., Chung, K.M (1994) Influence of hormonal variation on the periodontium in women. *Periodontology 2000* **6**, 79-87.

Ambruso, D.R., McCabe, E.R. Anderson, D. *et al.* (1985) Infectious and bleeding complications in patients with glycogenosis 1b. *American Journal of Diseases in Children.* **139**, 691-697.

Baker, *E.G.,* Crook, H., Swabacher, E. (1967) Personality correlates of periodontal disease. *Journal of Dental Research* **40**, 396-403.

Barr, C, Lopez, MR, Rua-Dobles, A. Periodontal changes by HIV serostatus in a cohort of homosexual and bisexual men. *Journal of Clinical Periodontology* 1992; **19**, 794-801.

Beaudet, A.L., Anderson, D.C. (1987) Reply to Hara et al. Glycogenosis type 1b and periodontitis. *Journal of Pediatrics* **111**, 952.

Beaudet, A.L., Anderson, D.C., Michel, U.V., Arion, W.J., Lange, A.J. (1980) Neutropenia and impaired neutrophil migration in type 1B glycogen storage disease. *Journal of Pediatrics* **97**, 906-910.

Becker, B.C., Karp, C.L., Becker, W., Berg,L. (1988) Personality differences and stressful life events. Differences between treated periodontal patients with and without maintenance. *Journal of Clinical Periodontology* **15**, 49-52.

Been, V., Engel, D. (1982) The effects of immunosuppressive drugs on periodontal inflammation in human renal allograft patients. *Journal of Periodontology* **53**, 245-248.

Bergstrom, J. (1981) Short term investigation on the influence of cigarette smoking upon plaque accumulation. *Scandinavian Journal of Dental Research* **89**, 235-238.

Bimstein, E, Ustman, J, Sela, MN, Ben-Neriah, Z, Soskolne, WA. (1990) Periodontitis associated with Papillon-Lefevre syndrome. *Journal of Periodontology*; **61**, 373-377.

Boraz, R.A. (1984) Familial dysautonomia (Riley-Day syndrome): report of a case. *Journal of Dentistry for Children* **51**, 64-65.

Bullon, P, Pascual, A, Fernandez-Novoa, MC, Borobio, MV, Munianin, MA, Camacho, F. (1993) Late onset Papillon-Lefevre syndrome? A chromosomic, neutrophil function and microbiological study. *Journal of Clinical Periodontology*; **20**, 662-667.

Chapple, I.L.C., Thorpe, G.H.G., Smith, G.M. *et al.* (1992) Hypophosphatasia, a family study involving a case diagnosed from gingival crevicular fluid. *Journal of Oral Pathology and Medicine* **21**, 426-431.

Cohen, DW. Diabetes mellitus and periodontal disease, 2 year longitudinal observations. Part I. *Journal of Periodontology* 1970; **41**, 709-712.

Cohen, M.S., Leong, P.A., Simpson, D.M. (1985) Phagocytic cells in periodontal defence. Periodontal status of patients with chronic granulomatous disease of childhood. *Journal of Periodontology* **56**, 611-617.

D'Angelo, M, Margiotti, V, Ammatuna, P, Sammartano, F. (1992) Treatment of prepubertal periodontitis. A case report and discussion. *Journal of Clinical Periodontology*; **19** 214-219.

Dahlen, G., Bjorklander, J., Gahnberg, L., Slots, J., Hanson, L-A (1993) Periodontal disease and dental caries in relation to primary IgG subclass and other humoral immunodeficiencies. *Journal of Clinical Periodontology* **20**, 7-13.

De Pommereau, V., Dargent-Pare, C., Robert, J.J., Brion, M. (1992) Periodontal status in insulin-dependent diabetic adolescents. *Journal of Clinical Periodontology* **19**, 628-632.

Dreizen, S., Levy, B.M., Bernick, S. (1970) Studies on the biology of the periodontium of marmosets. VIII. The effect of folic acid deficiency on the marmoset oral mucosa. *Journal of Dental Research* **49**, 616-620.

Efeoglu, A., Porter, S.R., Mutlu, S., Gokbuget, A., Scully, C. (1990) Papillon-Lefevre syndrome affecting two siblings. *Journal of Paediatric Dentistry* **6**, 119-124.

Egelberg, J. (1981) Diet and nutrition in prevention of periodontal disease - a review. In: *Prevention of periodontal disease.* Eds, Carranza, F.A. Jr. and Kenney, E.B. Quintessence Publishing Co., Chicago pp 49-63.

Feldman, R.S., Bravacos, J.S., Rose, C.L. (1983a) Association between smoking different tobacco products and periodontal disease indexes. *Journal of Periodontology* **54**, 481-487.

Feldman, R.S., Szet, B., Chauncey, H.H., Goldhaber, P. (1983b) Non-steroid anti-inflammatory drugs in the reduction of human alveolar bone loss. *Journal of Clinical Periodontology* **10**, 317-326.

Fleming, T.F., Shanahan, F., Miyaskai, K.T. (1991) Prevalence and severity of periodontal disease in patients with inflammatory bowel disease. *Journal of Clinical Periodontology* **18**, 690-697.

From, E. et al. (1978) Dyskeratosis benigna intraepithelialis et cutis hereditaria. A report of this disorder in father and son. *Journal of Cutaneous Pathology* **5**, 105-115.

Genco, R.J., Loe, H. (1993) The role of systemic conditions and disorders in periodontal disease. *Periodontology 2000* **2**, 98-116.

Gornitsky, M, Clark, CC, Siboo, *et. al.,* (1991) Clinical documentation and occurrence of putative periodontopathic bacteria in human immunodeficiency virus-associated periodontal disease. *Journal of Periodontology*; **62**, 576-575.

Green, L.W., Tryon, W.W., Marks, B., Huryn, J. (1986) Periodontal disease as a function of life events stress. *Journal of Human Stress* **12**, 32-36.

Greer, R.O. Jr., Poulson, T.C. (1983) Oral tissue alterations associated with the use of smokeless tobacco by teenagers. *Oral Surgery, Oral Medicine and Oral Pathology* **56**, 275-284.

Greer, R.O., Reissner, M.W. (1989) Focal dermal hypoplasia. *Journal of Periodontology* **60**, 330-335.

Grossi, SG, Zambon, JJ, Norderyd, CM *et al.* (1993) Microbiological risk indicators for periodontal disease. *Journal of Dental Research* 72, 206.

Haber, J, Wattes, J, Crowley, R. (1991) Assessment of diabetes as a risk factor for periodontitis. *Journal of Dental Research* **70**, abstract 414.

Haber, J., Kent, R.L. (1992) Cigarette smoking in a periodontal practice. *Journal of Periodontology* **63**, 100-106.

Haber, J., Wattles, J., Crowley, M., Mandell, R., Joshipura, K., Kent, R.L. (1993) Evidence for cigarette smoking as a major risk factor for periodontitis. *Journal of Periodontology* **64**, 16-23.

Hara, T., Mizuno, Y., Okubo, K., Ueda, K. (1987) Glycogenosis type 1b and periodontitis. *Journal of Pediatrics* **111**, 952.

Hartsfield, J.K. Jr., Kousseff, B.G. (1990) Phenotypic overlap of Ehlers-Danlos syndrome types IV and VIII. *American Journal of Medical Genetics* **37**, 465-470.

Hayden, P, Buckley, LA. (1989) Diabetes mellitus and periodontal disease in an Irish population. *Journal of Periodontal Research* ; **24**, 298.

Heasman, P.A., Seymour, R.A. (1990) An association between long-term non-steroidal anti-inflammatory drug therapy and the severity of periodontal disease. *Journal of Clinical Periodontology* 17, 654-658.

Hoge, H.W., Kirkham, D.B. (1983) Clinical management and soft tissue reconstruction of periodontal damage resulting from habitual use of snuff. *Journal of the American Dental Association* **107**, 744-745.

Hugoson, A, Thorstensson, H, Falk, H, Kuylenstierna, J. (1989) Periodontal conditions in insulin-dependent diabetes. *Journal of Clinical Periodontology* **16**, 215-223.

Ismail, A.I., Burt, B.A., Eklund, S.A. (1983a) Relation between ascorbic acid intake and periodontal disease in the United States. *Journal of the American Dental Association* **107**, 927-931.

Ismail, A.I., Burt, B.A., Eklund, S.A. (1983b) Epidemiologic patterns of smoking and periodontal disease in the United States. *Journal of the American Dental Association* **106**, 617-621.

Johnson, B., Addison, I.E., Newman, H.N. (1983) Skin window studies in patients with severe periodontitis, a marked defect in monocyte accumulation and effects of vitamin C. *IRCS Medical Sciences* **11**, 1013.

Karjalainen, K.M., Knuuttila, M.L.E., von Dickoff, K.J. (1994) Association of the severity of periodontal disease with organ complications in type 1 diabetic patients. *Journal of Periodontology* **65**, 1067-1072.

Kraal, J.H., Kenney, E.B. (1979) The response of polymorphonuclear leukocytes to chemotactic stimulation for smokers and non-smokers. *Journal of Periodontal Research* **14**, 383-389.

Kribbs, PJ. (1990) Comparison of mandibular bone in normal and osteoporotic women. *Journal of Prosthetic Dentistry* **63**, 218-222.

Lamster, I., Sonis, S., Hannigan, A., Kolodkin, A. (1978) An association between Crohn's disease, periodontal disease and enhanced neutrophil function. *Journal of Periodontology* **49**, 475-479.

Lamster, I.B., Rodrick, M.L., Sonis, S.T., Falchuk, Z.M. (1982) An analysis of peripheral blood and salivary polymorphonuclear leukocyte function, circulating immune complex levels and oral status in patients with inflammatory bowel disease. *Journal of Periodontology* **53**, 231-238.

Leggott, P.J., Robertson, P.B., Rothman, D.L., Murray, P.A., Jacob, R.A. (1986) The effect of controlled ascorbic acid depletion and supplementation on periodontal health. *Journal of Periodontology* **57**, 480-485.

Lindhe, J., Liljenberg, B., Adielson, B. (1983) Effect of long-term tetracycline therapy on human periodontal disease. *Journal of Clinical Periodontology* **10**, 590-601.

Lucht, E, Teivens, A, Berglund, O, Heimdahl, A, Nord, CE. (1990) Occurrence of micro-organisms in saliva and gingival crevice in HIV-1 infected patients. *Microbiological Ecology in Health and Disease*; **3**, 329-334.

MacFarlane, J.D., Swart, J.G.N. (1989) Dental aspects of hypophosphatasia, a case report, family study and literature. *Oral Surgery, Oral Medicine and Oral Pathology* **67**, 521-526.

MacGregor, I.D., Edgar, W.M., Greenwood, A.R. (1985) Effects of cigarette smoking on the rate of plaque formation. *Journal of Clinical Periodontology* **12**, 35-41.

Mass, E., Sarnat, H., Ram, D., Gadoth, N. (1992) Dental and oral findings in patients with familial dysautonomia. *Oral Surgery, Oral Medicine and Oral Pathology* **74**, 305-311.

Meyle, J. (1994) Leukocyte adhesion deficiency and prepubertal periodontititis. *Periodontology 2000* 26-36.

Michaelides, P.L. (1981) Treatment of periodontal disease in a patient with Turner's syndrome - a case report. *Journal of Periodontology* **52**, 386-389.

Michalowicz, B.S. (1994) Genetic and heritable risk factors in periodontal disease. *Journal of Periodontology* **65**, (suppl) 479-88.

Miller LS, Manwell MA, Newbold D *et al.* (1992) The relationship between reduction in periodontal inflammation and diabetes control, a report of 9 cases. *Journal of Periodontology* **63**, 843-848.

Modeer, T., Lavstedt, S., Ahlund, C. (1980) Relation between tobacco consumption and oral health in Swedish schoolchildren. *Acta Odontologica Scandinavica* **38**, 233-237.

Moghadam, B.K.H., Saedi, S., Gier, R.E. (1991) Adult-onset multifocal histiocytosis X presenting as a periodontal problem. *Journal of Oral and Maxillofacial Surgery* **49**, 417-419.

Moskow, B.S. (1989) Periodontal manifestations of hyperoxaluria and oxalosis. *Journal of Periodontology* **60**, 271-278.

Murray, PA, Grassi, M, Winkler, JR (1989) The microbiology of HIV-associated periodontal lesions. *Journal of Clinical Periodontology*; **16**, 636-642.

Murray, PA, Winkler, JR, Peros, WJ, French, CK, Lipke, JA. (1991) DNA probe detection of periodontal pathogens in HIV-associated periodontal lesions. *Oral Microbiology Immunology*; **6**, 34-40.

Murray, PA, Winkler, JR, Sadkowski, L, *et al.* Microbiology of HIV-associated gingivitis and periodontitis. In: Robertson, PB, Greenspan, JS, eds, *Oral manifestations of AIDS.* PSG Littleton, Massachusetts 1988; 105-118.

Mutlu, S., Scully, C., Richards, A., Maddison, P., Porter, S.R. (1991) Periodontal health in Sjogren's syndrome. In: Gold, S.I., Midda, M. eds. *Recent advances in Periodontology*. Vol II. Amsterdam, Elsevier pp 205-208.

Norhagen-Engstrom, G., Engstrom, P-E., Hammarstrom, L., Edvard Smith, C.I. (1992) Oral conditions in individuals with selective immunoglobulin A deficiency and common variable immunodeficiency. *Journal of Periodontology* **63**, 984-989.

Nuki, K., Soskolne, W.K., Raisz, L.G., Kornman, K.S., Alander, C. (1981) Bone resorbing activity of gingivae from beagle dogs following metronidazole and indomethacin therapy. *Journal of Periodontal Research* **16**, 205-212.

Nyman, S., Schroeder, H.E., Lindhe, J. (1979) Suppression of inflammation and bone resorption by indomethacin during experimental periodontitis in dogs. *Journal of Periodontology* **50**, 450-461.

Offenbacher S, Williams RC, Jeffcoat MK *et al.* (1992) Effects of NSAIDs on beagle crevicular cyclooxygenase metabolites and periodontal bone loss. *Journal of Periodontal Research* **27**, 207-213.

Offenbacher, S., Braswell, L.D., Loos, A.S., *et al.* (1987) Effects of flurbiprofen on the progression of periodontitis in Macaca mulatta. *Journal of Periodontal Research* **22**, 473-481.

Opinya, G.N., Kaimenyi, J.T., Meme, J.S. (1988) Oral findings in Fanconi's anaemia, a case report. *Journal of Periodontology* **59**, 461-463.

Oshrain, H.I., Mender, S., Mandel, I.D. (1979) Periodontal status of patients with reduced immunocapacity. *Journal of Periodontology* **50**, 185-188.

Pack, A.R.C. (1984) Folate mouthwash, effects on established gingivitis in periodontal patients. *Journal of Clinical Periodontology* **11**, 619-628.

Pack, A.R.C., Thomson, M.E. (1980) Effects of topical and systemic folic acid supplementation on gingivitis in pregnancy. *Journal of Clinical Periodontology* **7**, 402-413.

Pinson, M., Hoffman, W.H., Garrick, J.J., Litaker, M.S. (1995) Periodontal disease and type 1 diabetes mellitus in children and adolescents. *Journal of Clinical Periodontology* **22**, 118-123.

Plagmann, H.C., Kocher, T., Kuhrau, N., Caliebe, A. (1994) Periodontal manifestation of hypophosphatasia. A family case report. *Journal of Clinical Periodontology* **21**, 710-716.

Porter, S.R., Scully, C. (1993) Orofacial manifestations in primary immunodeficiencies involving IgA deficiency. *Journal of Oral Pathology and Medicine* **22**, 117-119.

Scully, C., Porter, S.R. (1993) Orofacial manifestations in primary immunodeficiencies, common variable immunodeficiency. *Journal of Oral Pathology and Medicine* **22**, 157-158

Porter, S.R., Scully, C. (1990) Primary immunodeficiencies. In: *Oral manifestations of systemic disease*. Eds, Jones, J.H., Mason, D.K. Balliere Tindall, London pp 112-161.

Porter, S.R., Scully, C. (1994) Orofacial manifestations of primary immunodeficiencies. *Oral Surgery, Oral Medicine and Oral Pathology* **78**, 4 - 13.

Porter, SR, Luker, J, Scully, C, Oakhill, A. Oral features of a family with benign familial neutropenia. *Journal of the American Academy of Dermatology* 1995.

Prichard, J.F., Ferguson, D.M., Windmiller, J., Hurt, W.C. (1984) Prepubertal periodontitis affecting the deciduous and permanent dentition in a patient with cyclic neutropenia. A case report and discussion. *Journal of Periodontology* **55**, 114-122.

Rams, TE, Andriol, M, Feik, D, Abel, SN, McGivern, TM, Slots, J. (1991) Microbiological study of HIV-related periodontitis. *Journal of Periodontology*; **62**, 74-81.

Reichart, PA, Gelderbrom, HR, Becker, J, Kuntz, A.(1987) AIDS and the oral cavity. The HIV infection, virology, etiology, origin, immunology, precautions and clinical observations in 110 patients. *International Journal of Oral and Maxillofacial Surgery*; **16**, 129-153.

Reuland-Bosma, W., Van Dijk, J. (1986) Periodontal diseases in Down's syndrome, a review. *Journal of Clinical Periodontology* **13**, 64-73.

Rivera-Hidalgo, F. (1986) Smoking and periodontal disease. *Journal of Periodontology* **57**, 617-624.

Roberts, M.W., Atkinson, J.C. (1990) Oral manifestations associated with leukocyte adhesion deficiency, a five year case study. *Pediatric Dentistry* **12**, 107-111.

Robertson, P.B., Cooper, M.D. (1974) Oral manifestations of IgA deficiency. In: The immunoglobulin A system. *Advances in Experimental Medicine and Biology.* Eds, Mestecky, J.., Lawton, A.R. Plenum Publishing, New York pp 497-503.

Robinson, P. (1992) Periodontal diseases and HIV infection. Review of the literature. *Journal of Clinical Periodontology*; **19**, 609-614.

Rosensteln: DI, Eigner, TL, LevIn: MP, Chiodo GT. (1989) Rapidly progressive periodontal disease associated with HIV infection, report of a case. *Journal of the American Dental Association* **118**, 313-314.

Rosenthal, I.M., Abrams, H., Kopczyk, R.A. (1989) The relationship of inflammatory periodontal disease to diabetic status in insulin-dependent diabetes mellitus patients. *Journal of Clinical Periodontology* **15**, 425-429.

Rotbart, H.A., LevIn: M.J., Jones, J.F. *et al.* (1986) Noma in children with severe combined immunodeficiency. *Journal of Pediatrics* **109**, 596-600.

Rowland, RW, Escobar, MR, FRiedman, RB, Kaplowitz, LG. (1993) Painful gingivitis may be an early sign of infection with the Human Immunodeficiency Virus. *Clinical Infectious Diseases*; **16**, 233-236.

San Giacomo, TR, Tan, PM, Loggi, DG, ItkIn: AB. (1990) Progressive osseous destruction as a complication of HIV-periodontitis. *Oral Surgery, Oral Medicine and Oral Pathology*; **70**, 476-479.

Sastrowijoto, S.H., Hillemans, P., van Sttenbergen, T.J.M., Abraham-Inpijn, L., de Graaf, J. (1989) Periodontal condition and microbiology of healthy and diseased periodontal pockets in type 1 diabetes mellitus patients. *Journal of Clinical Periodontology* **16**, 316-322.

Scully, C., McFadyen, E.E., Campbell, A. (1985) Orofacial manifestations in cyclic neutropenia. *British Journal of Oral Surgery* **70**, 96-101.

Scully, C., Porter, S.R., Mutlu, S. (1991) Changing, subject-based risk factors for destructive periodontitis. In: Risk markers for oral diseases, Volume 3 - *Periodontal diseases.* Ed, Johnson, N.W. Cambridge University Press pp 139-178.

Seymour, R.A., Heasman, P.A. (1992) *Drugs, disease and the periodontium.* Oxford University Press pp 1-201.

Seymour, R.A., Heasman, P.A. (1988) Drugs and the periodontium. *Journal of Clinical Periodontology* **15**, 1-16.

Slots, J., Rosling, B. (1983) Suppression of the periodontopathic microflora in localised juvenile periodontitis by systemic tetracycline. *Journal of Clinical Periodontology* **10**, 465-486.

Sooriyamoorthy, M., Gower, D.B. (1989) Hormonal influences on gingival tissue, relationship to periodontal diseases. *Journal of Clinical Periodontology* **16**, 201.

Stabholz, A., Soskolne, V., Machtei, E., Or, R., Soskolne, W.A. (1990) Effect of benign familial neutropenia on the periodontium of Yemenite Jews. *Journal of Periodontology* **61**, 51-54.

Stewart, R.E., Hollister, D.W., Rimoln: D.L. (1977) A new variant of Ehlers-Danlos syndrome, an autosomal disorder of fragile skin: abnormal scarring, and generalised periodontitis. *Birth Defects* **13**, 85-93.

Stoltenberg, J.L., Osbourn, J.B., Pihlstrom, B.L., *et. al.* (1993) Association between cigarette smoking, bacterial pathogens, and periodontal status. *Journal of Periodontology* **64**, 1225-1230.

Sutton, R.B.O., Smales, F.C. (1983) Cross-sectional study of the effects of immunosuppressive drugs on chronic periodontal disease in man. *Journal of Clinical Periodontology* **10**, 317-326.

Thomas, R, San Giacomo, DMD, Tan, PM, *et al* (1990). Progressive osseous destruction as a complication of HIV-periodontitis. *Oral Surgery, Oral Medicine and Oral Pathology* **70**, 476-479.

Thomson, M.E., Pack, A.R.C. (1982) Effects of extended systemic and topical folate supplementation on gingivitis of pregnancy. *Journal of Clinical Periodontology* **9**, 275-280.

Tollefsen, T., Koppang, H.S., Messelt, E. (1982) Immunosuppression and periodontal disease in man. Histological and ultrastructural observations. *Journal of Periodontal Research* **17**, 329-344.

Tolo, K., Jorkend, L. (1990) Serum antibodies and loss of periodontal bone in patients with rheumatoid arthritis. *Journal of Periodontal Research* **17**, 288-291.

Tseng, C.C., Wolff, L.F., Rhodus, N., Aeppli, D.M. (1990) The periodontal status of patients with Sjogren's syndrome. *Journal of Clinical Periodontology* **17**, 329-330.

Van Dyke, T.E., Dowell, V.R., Offenbacher, S., Snyder, W., Dersh, T. (1986) Potential role of microorganisms isolated from periodontal lesions in the pathogenesis of inflammatory bowel disease. *Infection and Immunity* **53**, 671-677.

Van Dyke, TE, Mouton, C, Zinney, C, Dowell, VR Jr, Arnold, RR. (1988) The association of the oral microbiota, IgA antibody and neutrophil functional abnormalities with periodontal disease in inflammatory bowel disease patients. In: MacDermott, RP, ed. *Inflammatory bowel disease, current status and future approach.* Amsterdam, Elsevier Science Publishers (Biomedical Division), pp 579-584.

Vrahopoulos, T.P., Barber, P., Liakoni, H., Newman, H.N. (1988) Ultrastructure of the periodontal lesion in a case of Papillon-Lefevre syndrome (PLS). *Journal of Clinical Periodontology* **15**, 17-26.

Waite, I.M., Saxton, C.A., Young, A. *et al.* (1981) The periodontal status of subjects receiving non-steroidal anti-inflammatory drugs. *Journal of Periodontal Research* **16**, 100-108.

Watanabe, H., Umeda, M., Seki, T., Ishikawa, I. (1993) Clinical and laboratory studies of severe periodontal disease in an adolescent associated with hypophosphatasia. A case report. *Journal of Periodontology* **64**, 174-180.

Weaks-Dybvig, M., Sanavi, F., Zander, H., RifkIn: B.R. (1982) The effect of indomethacin on alveolar bone loss in experimental periodontitis. *Journal of Periodontal Research* **17**, 90-100.

Weary, P.E., Bender, A.S. (1967) The Chediak-Higashi syndrome with severe cutaneous involvement. *Archives in Internal Medicine* **110**, 381-386.

Weintraub, J.A., Burt, B.A. (1987) Periodontal effects and dental caries associated with smokeless tobacco use. *Public Health Reports* **102**, 30-35.

White, S.C., Frey, N.W., Blaschke, D.D. *et al.* (1977) Oral radiographic changes in patients with progressive systemic sclerosis (scleroderma). *Journal of the American Dental Association* **94**, 1178-1182.

Williams, CA, Winkler, JR, Grassi, M, Murray, PA. (1990) HIV-associated periodontitis complicated with necrotizing stomatitis. *Oral Surgery, Oral Medicine and Oral Pathology* ; **69**, 351-355.

Williams, R.C., Jeffcoat, M.J., Kaplan, M.L., Goldhaber, P., Johnson, H.G., Wechter, W.J. (1984) Flurbiprofen - a potent inhibitor of alveolar bone resorption in beagles. *Science* **227**, 640-642.

Wilton, J.M.A., Griffiths, G., Curtis, M. *et al.* (1991) Detection of high risk groups and individuals for periodontal diseases. Systemic predisposition and markers of general health. *Journal of Clinical Periodontology* **15**, 339-346.

Winkler, JR, Grassi, M, Murray, PA (1988) Clinical description and etiology of HIV-associated periodontal diseases. In: Robertson, PB, Greenspan, JS, eds, *Oral manifestations of AIDS*. PSG Littleton, Massachusetts 1988; pp 49-70.

Winkler, J.R., Murray, P.A., Hammerle, C. (1989) Gangrenous stomatitis in AIDS. *Lancet* **ii**, 108.

Wolfe, M.D., Carlos, J.P. (1987) Oral health effects of smokeless tobacco use in Navajo Indian adolescents. *Community Dentistry and Oral Epidemiology* **15**, 230-235.

Woolfe, S.N., Kenney, E.B., Hume, W.R. (1980) Ascorbic acid and periodontal disease, a review of the literature. *Journal of the Western Society of Periodontology* **28**, 44.

Wysocki, G.P., Gretzinger, H.A., Laupacis, A., Ulan, R.A., Stiller, C.R. (1983) Fibrous hyperplasia of the gingiva, a side effect of cyclosporin A therapy. *Oral Surgery, Oral Medicine and Oral Pathology* **55**, 274-278.

Yoshida-Minami, I., Kishimoto, K., Suzuki, A. *et al* (1995) Clinical, microbiological and host defense parameters associated with a case of localized prepubertal periodontitis. *Journal of Clinical Periodontology* **22**, 56-62.

Yoshinari, N., Kameyama, Y., Aoyama, Y., Nichiyama, H., Noguchi, T (1994) Effect of long-term methotrexate-induced neutropenia on experimental periodontal lesion in rats. *Journal of Periodontal Research* **29**, 393-400.

Zambon, JJ, Reynolds, HS, Genco, RJ, (1990) Studies of the subgingival microflora in patients with Acquired Immunodeficency Syndrome. *Journal of Periodontology* **61**, 699-704.

Zambon, JJ. Overview of periodontal disease. In: Robertson, PB, Greenspan, JS, eds, *Oral manifestations of AIDS*. PSG Littleton, Massachusetts 1988; 96-104.

4 Gingival manifestations of systemic diseases

Crispian Scully and Stephen R. Porter

Department of Oral Medicine, Eastman Dental Institute for Oral Health Care Sciences, University of London256 Gray's Inn Road, London WC1X 8LD, UK

Introduction

Most gingival disease is dental plaque-related but systemic disorders may cause gingival lesions or modify the gingival response to plaque. This chapter considers gingival lesions due to systemic disease, that can present with various manifestations, particularly swellings, ulceration, bleeding, red lesions or white lesions (Table 1). Physiological changes are not included. Key references only are included: for further details see Porter and Scully (1994a).

Swellings

Gingival swellings due to systemic disease may be congenital, typically hereditary gingival fibromatosis (Table 2) (Takagi *et al.,* 1991). Most affected patients are otherwise healthy, though hirsutism is common. A few patients have gingival fibromatosis as part of a much wider syndrome (Table 3). There appear to be no significant differences in the clinical manifestations of the fibromatosis between the various syndromes and typically it is clinically firm, pink and neither ulcerated, painful or haemorrhagic (Clark, 1987) and typically involving the marginal gingiva rather than solely the interdental areas.

Acquired causes of gingival swellings include drugs, haematological disorders, neoplasms, granulomatous conditions, infections and other disorders (Table 2). The main drugs implicated in gingival hyperplasia are phenytoin, cyclosporin, and calcium channel blockers (Seymour *et al.,* 1985; Seymour, 1992; Seymour and Jacobs, 1992; Miller and Damm, 1992). In addition there have been occasional reports of other drugs (*e.g.* tranexamic acid and sodium valproate) causing gingival enlargement (Diamond *et al.,* 1991; Behari, 1991). The drug-induced gingival enlargement is typically painless, fairly firm and pink and arises initially from the interdental papillae. There can be a superimposed, plaque-related gingivitis (Hancock and Swan, 1992).

Table 1 *Gingival manifestations of systemic disease.*

Manifestation	Main systemic causes		
Swellings	Drugs	-	Phenytoin
			Cyclosporin
			Calcium Channel Blockers
			Other
	Leukaemias	-	Acute myeloid leukaemia
		-	Chronic lymphocytic leukaemia
		-	Other
	Granulomatous disorders	-	Sarcoidosis
		-	Crohn's disease
		-	Wegener's granulomatosis
		-	Orofacial granulomatosis
	Neoplasms	-	Squamous cell carcinoma
		-	Non-Hodgkin's lymphoma
		-	Other
Ulceration	Infections	-	Herpes simplex
		-	Varicella Zoster
		-	Cytomegalovirus
		-	HIV
		-	Acute necrotising ulcerative gingivitis
		-	Other
	Dermatoses	-	Lichen planus
		-	Mucous membrane pemphigoid
		-	Other
	Immune defects	-	Neutropenias
		-	Chronic granulomatous disease
		-	Other
Neoplasms		-	Squamous cell carcinoma
		-	Non-Hodgkin's lymphoma
		-	Other
Bleeding	Platelet disorders	-	Thrombocytopenia
	Telangiectasia	-	Hereditary
		-	Other
	Acute necrotising ulcerative gingivitis		
Red lesions	Infections	-	as above
	Dermatoses	-	as above
	Kaposi's sarcoma		
White lesions	Candidosis		
	Lichen planus		
	Keratoses		
	Neoplasms	-	Squamous cell carcinoma
Hyperpigmentation Drugs		-	Heavy metals (rare)
		-	Antimalarials
		-	Busulphan
		-	Other
	Addison's disease		

Table 2 *Causes of gingival swelling.*

Local causes
Generalised enlargement
    Chronic gingivitis
    Hyperplastic gingivitis due to
    mouth breathing

Localised enlargement
    Abscesses
    Fibrous epulis
    Exostoses
    Cysts
    Pyogenic granuloma (including pregnancy epulis)
    Neoplasms

Systemic causes
Generalised enlargement
    Hereditary gingival fibromatosis
    Mucopolysaccharidoses
    Mucolipidoses

    Drugs: Phenytoin
          Cyclosporin
          Calcium channel
          blockers
          Other

    Pregnancy
    Sarcoidosis
    Crohn's disease
    Leukaemia
    Wegener's granulomatosis
    Scurvy
    Amyloidosis

Localised enlargement
    Pregnancy
    Sarcoidosis
    Crohn's disease
    Orofacial granulomatosis
    Wegener's granulomatosis
    Midline lethal granuloma
    Amyloidosis
    Neoplasms

Table 3 *Gingival fibromatosis syndromes.*

Name	Associated features
Gingival fibromatosis	± Hypertrichosis ± Epilepsy ± Mental retardation
Jones' syndrome	Progressive sensineural deafness
Murray-Puretic-Drescher syndrome	Multiple hyaline fibromas White skin Flexion contracts Osteolytic bone lesions Recurrent infection
Mucolipidosis II (I-cell disease)	Short stature Loose facies Psychomotor retardation
Rutherfurd syndrome	Corneal opacities Multiple root resorption
Zimmerman-Laband syndrome	Hypoplasia of terminal phalanges of toes and fingers Ear and nose abnormalities Hepatomegaly and splenomegaly
Cross syndrome	Microphthalmia Mental retardation Athetosis Hypopigmentation
Ramon syndrome	Hypertrichosis Cherubism Mental retardation Growth retardation Epilepsy
Gingival fibromatosis with growth hormone deficiency	Growth hormone deficiency
Byars-Jurkiewicz syndrome	Giant fibroadenomas of breast and secondary kypothosis Hypertrichosis

The leukaemias are the most common group of haematological disorders that can cause gingival swelling and there may be associated gingival or oral purpura and haemorrhage, ulceration and/or infection. Gingival enlargement is most common in acute myeloid leukaemia (Declerck and Vinkier, 1988), although there have been occasional reports of acute and chronic lymphocytic leukaemia giving rise to gingival enlargement (Porter *et al.,* 1994). Gingival swellings may also be seen in other haematological disorders, for example, aplastic anaemia (Luker *et al.,* 1991), the preleukaemic disorders (Deasy *et al.,* 1976) and acute myeloid leukaemia secondary to myelodysplasia (Porter *et al.,* 1994b). Lymphomas are uncommon in the mouth, though gingival and faucial non-Hodgkin's lymphomas are now increasingly being seen in HIV-infected persons (Porter and Scully, 1994c).

The most common gingival malignant neoplasm is squamous cell carcinoma which may present as a swelling or ulcer (or occasionally a white or red lesion) and cause localised bone destruction (Sankaranayanan *et al.,* 1989). Kaposi's sarcoma was extremely rare in the mouth before the HIV epidemic but is now seen mainly in those who have contracted HIV infection sexually. Though the main oral site is the palate, lesions can involve the gingivae and elsewhere. Starting as a dusky macule, Kaposi's sarcoma progresses to a purplish, bluish, reddish or brown papule or nodule (Porter and Scully, 1994c), causing destruction of adjacent periodontal tissues and resultant tooth mobility. Other neoplasms are rare on the gingiva, but any lump persisting for more than three weeks should be biopsied for a definitive diagnosis.

Gingival swellings may be a feature of oral Crohn's disease, orofacial granulomatosis, sarcoidosis or Wegener's granulomatosis. Oral Crohn's disease and orofacial granulomatosis can present with diffuse gingival swelling or discrete firm, salmon-pink lumps or tags (Scully and Eveson, 1991). Sarcoidosis can present with gingival nodules, as well as pulmonary and other lesions (Cohen and Reinhardt, 1982). Wegener's granulomatosis is caused by a vasculitis and presents with gingival swelling that has an appearance like a strawberry, or ulcer (Parsons *et al.,* 1992; Eufinger *et al.,* 1992); pulmonary and renal problems may be associated. Localised gingival swellings may be secondary to pregnancy (pregnancy epulides).

Infections typically may produce gingival ulceration but swelling may sometimes be a feature. For example, herpetic stomatitis typically presents with diffuse, purplish gingival swelling, with scattered oral ulcers, cervical lymphadenopathy and fever (Scully, 1985). Human papillomaviruses on the other hand, produce painless, pink or whitish warty lesions such as papillomas, verrucae, or condyloma acuminatum and the patient or sexual partner may have similar lesions (Scully and Samaranayake, 1992). The systemic mycoses such as histoplasmosis and paracoccidiodomycosis can give rise to gingival enlargement and ulceration (Almeida *et al.,* 1991).

Ulceration

Gingival ulceration is mainly a result of infectious, dermatological, gastrointestinal or haematological causes (Table 4). Ulceration of the gingival tissues is typically associated with acute necrotising ulcerative gingivitis (ANUG) (Sabiston, 1986) and

C. Scully & S. R. Porter

Table 4 *Causes of gingival ulceration.*

Trauma (physical, chemical, radiation, thermal)

Aphthae and associated syndromes
Recurrent aphthous stomatitis
Behcet's syndrome

Infections
Primary or recurrent herpes simplex virus infection
Varicella zoster virus
Epstein Barr virus
Human herpes virus 8 (Karposi's sarcoma herpes virus)
Cytomegalovirus
Coxsackie virus
ECHO virus

Acute necrotising ulcerative gingivitis (ANUG)
Treponema pallidum
Neisseria gonorrhoeae
Mycobacterium tuberculosis
Atypical mycobacteria
Lepromatous leprosy
Tularaemia
Leishmaniasis
Aspergillosis
Histoplasmosis
Cryptococcosis
Coccidioidomycosis
Blastomycosis
Paracoccidioidomycosis
Candidosis

Dermatoses
Lichen planus
Mucous membrane pemphigoid
Pemphigus vulgaris
Dermatitis herpetiformis
Linear IgA disease
Erythema multiforme
Lupus erythematosus

Haematological disorders
Neutropenia(s)
Leukaemia(s)
Myelodysplasia
Multiple myeloma
Haematinic deficiencies
Gastrointestinal disorders
Crohn's disease and related disorders
Ulcerative colitis

Drugs
Cytotoxics and others

Malignancy
Carcinoma and others

Vasculitides
Wegener's granulomatosis
Polyarteritis nodosa

Other - lipoid proteinosis
Amyloid-like disease

Table 5 *Systemic causes of gingival bleeding.*

Any condition causing exacerbation of gingivitis (*e.g.* pregnancy)
Leukaemia
HIV infection
Scurvy
Other causes of purpura
Clotting defects
Drugs (*e.g.* anticoagulants)
Acute necrotising ulcerative gingivitis

viral infections, particularly primary herpes simplex (herpetic gingivostomatitis). Less commonly varicella zoster virus (VZV) causes unilateral gingival ulceration; in immunocompromised patients VZV can cause gingival ulceration that progresses to locally destructive periodontal breakdown (Wright *et al.,* 1989). Rare viral causes of gingival ulceration include Epstein-Barr virus (EBV), cytomegalovirus (CMV),Human herpes virus 8 (Porter *et. al.,* 1997a), Coxsackie and ECHO viruses (Scully and Samaranayake, 1992). Primary or secondary syphilis can rarely cause gingival ulceration (MacFarlane and Samaranayake, 1990).

Other bacterial infections which occasionally give rise to gingival ulcerative lesions include *Mycobacterium tuberculosis* (MacFarlane and Samaranayake, 1990). Very rarely systemic mycoses can cause large, often exophytic areas of gingival ulceration particularly in immunosuppressed individuals (Almeida *et al.,* 1991).

Ulceration and miliary abscess formation of the gingivae can arise in pyostomatitis vegetans in ulcerative colitis (Chan *et al.,* 1991). Other acquired causes of gingival ulceration include dermatological diseases (see below), leukaemias, neutropenias and neoplasms.

Bleeding

Bleeding from the gingival margins is common and is usually a consequence of gingivitis which may be more obvious in patients taking oral contraceptives and in pregnant women, especially during the second and third trimesters. Gingival haemorrhage, may however also be an early sign of platelet disorders or vascular disorders, and is common in patients with leukaemia or HIV infection (Table 5).

Red lesions

Red gingival lesions are usually caused by inflammation, vascular lesions, purpura, or mucosal desquamation or atrophy (Table 6). Congenital lesions include angiomas - usually isolated but sometimes as part of the Sturge-Weber syndrome of encephalo-trigeminal angiomatosis - then with epilepsy, mental impairment, glaucoma and hemiplegia (Porter and Scully, 1994a). Telangiectasia may represent

Table 6 *Systemic causes of red lesions of the gingiva.*

Congenital
Mucoepithelial dysplasia syndrome
Hereditary Haemorrhagic telangiectasia

Acquired
Trauma (physical, chemical, radiation, thermal)
Drugs *e.g.*   Chlorhexidine
        Cinnamonaldehyde

Candidosis
Other infections

Desquamative gingivitis
        Lichen planus
        Mucous membrane pemphigoid
        Pemphigoid
        Pemphigus vulgaris
        Dermatitis herpetiformis
        Linear IgA disease
        Lupus erythematosus

Psoriasis
Wegener's granulomatosis
Sarcoidosis
Plasma cell gingivastomatitis
Dermatomyositis
Primary biliary cirrhosis
Leukaemia(s)

Premalignancy (*e.g.* erythroplakia)
Malignancy - Kaposi's sarcoma

hereditary haemorrhagic telangiectasia (Osler-Rendu-Weber syndrome) in which telangiectasia may be found in the aerodigestive and gastrointestinal tracts; chronic haemorrhage and anaemia can result (Flint *et al.*, 1988). The most common acquired red lesion, apart from plaque-related gingivitis, is desquamative gingivitis. Typically causing chronic soreness and seen in females over middle-age, this is usually a consequence of lichen planus or mucous membrane pemphigoid. Several other dermatoses can present as desquamative gingivitis (Table 6). Histopathological examination and immunostaining of perilesional tissue are therefore indicated since the differential diagnosis may include potentially life-threatening conditions such as pemphigus (Porter and Scully, 1994a). Inflammatory lesions also include allergic

Table 7 *Systemic causes of white lesions of the gingiva.*

Congenital
    Pachyonychia congenita
    Hyperkeratosis palmoplantaris
    White sponge naevus
    Acrodermatitis enteropathica

Acquired
    Trauma
    Tobacco
    Candidosis
    Lichen planus
    Discoid lupus erythematosus
    Psoriasis
    Reiter's syndrome
    Pyostomatitis vegetans
    Xanthomatosis

Premalignancy - leukoplakia
Malignancy - *e.g.* squamous cell carcinoma

disorders such as plasma cell gingivostomatitis (Porter *et al.,* 1997b), and infections such as herpes simplex stomatitis, candidosis (*e.g.* erythematous and pseudomembranous) and HIV-gingivitis (see chapter 3). Some malignant, premalignant and granulomatous conditions can also produce reddish lesions. Erythroplasia (arerythroplakia) - a velvety red patch - is typically premalignant (Craig *et al.,* 1989), and some carcinomas are red. Kaposi's sarcoma (i.e. Human herpes virus 8 infection), Wegener's granulomatosis and sometimes Crohn's disease or sarcoidosis can also give rise to red gingival lesions.

White lesions

White lesions of the gingiva can be caused by surface deposits or by keratosis (Table 7). Hyperkeratotic areas can occur on the gingiva in congenital disorders such as pachyonychia congenita (Jadassohn-Lewandowsky syndrome; Jackson-Lawler dyskeratosis congenita, syndrome) (Young and Lenox, 1978), hyperkeratosis palmoplantaris (Gorlin, 1976) and white sponge naevus (Pindborg, 1990).

Acquired causes of gingival white lesions include traumatic keratosis, smoker's keratosis pseudomembranous candidosis, lichen planus and idiopathic leukoplakia. Rare acquired causes include discoid lupus erythematosus (Porter and Scully, 1997), psoriasis (Pindborg, 1990) and Reiter's syndrome (Pindborg, 1990).

C. Scully & S. R. Porter

Summary

It is evident that many systemic disorders can give rise to gingival manifestations. Drug-induced gingival enlargement is probably the most well-known of the systemically-associated gingival disorders. Nevertheless, in view of the range of diseases that can affect the gingival tissues, it is important always to review the medical and social history of patients who present with unusual gingival signs or symptoms and look for extra-oral as well as intra-oral lesions.

References

Almeida, OPD, Jorge, J, Scully, C, Bozzo, L. (1991) Oral manifestations of paracoccidioidomycosis (South American blastomycosis). *Oral Surgery, Oral Medicine, and Oral Pathology* **72**, 430-435.

Behari, M. (1991) Gingival hyperplasia due to sodium valproate (letter). *Journal of Neurology, Neurosurgery and Psychiatry* **54**, 279-280.

Chan, SWY, Scully, C, Prime, SS, Eveson, J.W. (1991) Pyostomatitis vegetans, oral manifestation of ulcerative colitis. *Oral Surgery, Oral Medicine, and Oral Pathology* **72**, 689-692.

Clark, D. (1987) Gingival fibromatosis and related syndromes. *Journal of the Canadian Dental Association* **6**, 137-140.

Cohen, DM, Reinhardt, RA (1982) Systemic sarcoidosis presenting with Horner's syndrome and mandibular paresthesia. *Oral Surgery, Oral Medicine, and Oral Pathology* **53**, 577-581.

Craig, RM Jr., Vickers, VA, Correll, RW (1989) Erythroplastic lesion on the mandibular marginal gingiva. *Journal of the American Dental Association* **119**, 543-544.

Deasey, M, Vogel, R, Annes, I, Simon, B. (1976) Periodontal disease associated with preleukaemic syndrome. *Journal of Periodontology* **47**, 41-45.

Declerck, D, Vinckier, F. (1988) Oral complications of leukemia. *Quintessence International* **8**, 575-583.

Diamond, JP, Chandna, A, Williams, C, Easty, DL, Scully, C, Eveson, J, Richards, A (1991) Tranexamic acid-associated ligneous conjunctivitis with gingival and peritoneal lesions. *British Journal of Ophthalmology* **75**, 753-754.

Eufinger, H, Machtens, E, Akuamoa-Boateng, E (1992) Oral manifestations of Wegener's granulomatosis, review of the literature and report of a case. *International Journal of Oral and Maxillofacial Surgery* **12**, 50-53.

Flint, SR, Keith, O, Scully, C, (1988) Hereditary haemorrhagic telangiectasia, family study and review. *Oral Surgery, Oral Medicine, and Oral Pathology* **66**, 440-444.

Gorlin, R.J. (1976) Focal palmoplantar and marginal gingival hyperkeratosis syndrome. *Birth Defects* **12**, 239-242.

Hancock, R.H, Swan, RH (1992) Nifedipine-induced gingival overgrowth. *Journal of Clinical Periodontology* **19**, 12-14.

Luker, J, Scully, C, Oakhill, A (1991) Gingival swelling as a manifestation of aplastic anaemia. *Oral Surgery, Oral Medicine, and Oral Pathology* **71**, 55-56.

MacFarlane, T.W, Samaranayake, L. (1990) Systemic infections. In: *Oral manifestations of systemic disease*. Eds, Jones JH, Mason DK. Balliere Tindall, London pp 339-386.

Miller, CS, Damm, DD (1992) Incidence of verapamil-induced gingival hyperplasia in a dental population. *Journal of Periodontology* **63**, 453-456.

Parsons, E, Seymour, RA, Macleod, RK, Nand, N, Ward, MK (1992) Wegener's granulomatosis, a distinct gingival lesion. *Journal of Clinical Periodontology* **19**, 64-66.

Pindborg, JJ (1990) Diseases of the skin. In: *Oral manifestations of systemic disease.* 2nd Edition Eds, Jones, JH, Mason, DK. Balliere Tindall, London pp 537-592.

Porter, SR, Scully, C (1994a) Periodontal aspects of systemic disease. A system of classification. In: *European Workshop of Periodontology.* Ed, Lang, N. Karring, T Quintessence, pp 415-438.

Porter, SR, Scully, C (1994b) Gingival and oral mucosal ulceration as the initial features of myelodysplasia. *Oral Oncology* (European Journal of Cancer Part B) **30B**,346-360.

Porter, SR, Scully, C (1994c) HIV disease, the surgeon's perspective 2. Diagnosis and management of non-malignant oral manifestations. *British Journal of Oral and Maxillofacial Surgery* **32**, 231-240.

Porter, SR, DiAlberti, L, Kumar, N (1997a) Human herpes virus 8. Oral Oncology. *European Journal of Cancer Part B* (in press).

Porter, S.R, Scully, C, Evesan, J, Langdon, J, Fan, K, Hopper, C (1997b) Management of plasma cell gingivastomatitis with photodynamic therapy. *Journal of the American Academy of Dermatology* (in press).

Porter, S.R., Scully, C, Matthews, RW (1994) Gingival enlargement in chronic lymphocytic leukaemia. *Journal of Periodontology* **21**, 559-561.

Sabiston, CB Jr. (1986) A review and proposal for the etiology of acute necrotizing gingivitis. *Journal of Clinical Periodontology* **13**, 727-734.

Sankaranarayanan, R, Duffy, SW, Padmakumary, G, Day, NE, Padmanabhan, TK (1989) Tobacco chewing, alcohol and nasal snuff in cancer of the gingiva in Kerala, India. *British Journal of Cancer* **60**, 638-643.

Scully, C, Eveson, JW (1991) Orofacial granulomatosis (Leading article). *Lancet* **i**, 20-21

Scully, C, Porter, SR (1997) Desquamative gingivitis - a review. *Seminars in Clinical Dermatology* (in press).

Scully, C, Samaranayake, LP (1992) *Clinical virology in dentistry and oral medicine.* Cambridge University Press pp 1-489.

Scully, C (1985) Ulcerative stomatitis, gingivitis and rash, a diagnostic dilemma. *Oral Surgery, Oral Medicine, and Oral Pathology* **59**, 261.

Seymour, RA, Heasman, PA (1992) *Drugs, disease and the periodontium.* Oxford University Press pp 1-201.

Seymour, RA, Jacobs, DJ (1992) Cyclosporin and the gingival tissues. *Journal of Clinical Periodontology* **19**, 1-11.

Seymour, RA, Smith, DG, Turnbull, DN (1985) The effects of phenytoin and sodium valporate on the periodontal health of adult epileptic patients. *Journal of Clinical Periodontology* **12**, 413-419.

Takagi, M, Yamamoto, H, Mega, H, Hsieh, KJ, Shioda, S, Enomoto, S (1991) Heterogeneity in the gingival fibromatoses. *Cancer* **68**, 2202-2212.

Wright, WE, Davis, DL, Geffen, DB, MartIn: SE, Nelson, MJ, Straus, SE (1983) Alveolar bone necrosis and tooth loss, a rare complication associated with herpes zoster infection of the fifth cranial nerve. *Oral Surgery Oral Medicine and Oral Pathology* **56**, 39-46.

Young, LW, Lenox, JA (1973) Pachyonychia congenita, a long-term evaluation of associated oral and dermal lesions. *Oral Surgery, Oral Medicine, and Oral Pathology* **36**, 663-666.

5   The role of neutrophils in periodontal inflammation

J. Meyle

Abteilung Parodontologie, Zentrum für Zahn-, Mund- u. Kieferheilkunde, Justus-Liebig-Universität Giessen, Schlangenzahl 14, D- 35392 Giessen, Germany

Introduction

Periodontal diseases mostly are chronic bacterial infections. Bacteria of the plaque and their products induce a host response. The visible inflammatory reaction is a consequence of the immunologic reactions to the antigenic proteins present in the pockets.

Many different cells, and effector molecules act synergistically or antagonistically to inactivate and kill the infectious agents and their products.

Among leukocytes the polymorphs (neutrophils) are the most important phagocytic cells. At the local inflammatory site they represent the major percentage of white blood cells (40-60 %) and form the first line of defense. Neutrophils are produced in great numbers in bone marrow at a turnover of 1.5×10^9 /kg body weight/day[1]. Their half life is rather short. After maturation in the bone marrow they only rest for some hours in the blood and then enter the tissues were they finish their life with in 1-4 days.

The structural features of the mature neutrophil illustrate the unique relationship to the function of the cell. The cytoplasm contains numerous vesicles that are specalized lysosomes that have been classified as primary, secondary and tertiary granules. The peroxidase positive azurophilic or primary granules are formed during the promyelocytic stage of neutrophil development and contain acid hydrolases, neutral proteases, cationic proteins, myeloperoxidase and lysozyme [2-8].

The specific or secondary granules are formed during the myelocytic stage and contain lysozyme, lactoferrin, collagenase and vitamin B 12-binding protein.[9,10,11]

Tertiary or secretory granules contain cytochrome b, alkaline phosphatase and are more readily secreted upon stimulation of the cells. There contents probably modify the cell surface and affect adhesion. After stimulation with chemotaxins the contents of specific granules are selectively released, which facilitates diapedesis and penetration of the tissues [15,16]. Secretory and specific granules are also discussed as storage areas of new receptors, which are released and integrated in the outer membrane at the leading front of the cell, thereby playing an important role in cell sensing and orientation. Based on their unique properties and structure these cells are able to react to infectious agents with a number of different highly specialized functions listed in Table 1.

Table 1 *Neutrophil functions.*

1. Adherence
2. Chemotaxis
3. Degranulation and enzyme secretion
4. Phagocytosis
5. Microbicidal activity and killing

Adherence

Leukocyte adherence to endothelial cells and tissues is regulated by several different types of receptors among them integrins of the beta-2 familiy are of considerable importance for strong adhesion to the surface[17,18]. These receptors recognize in their active center a sequence of 3 amino acids (Arg-Gly-Asp) which are present on many different substrata. Genetic inborn disorders of these receptors result in a greatly enhanced susceptibility to bacterial infections. These persons also suffer from severe and early onset periodontitis, which results in premature loss of (all) deciduous teeth [19,20].

Chemotaxis

After diapedesis the cells are guided by chemotactic factors to the site of inflammation [21]. Different proteins which stem from the bacteria have chemotactic properties as well as different cytokines (*e.g.* Il-1, TNF-a). In a number of studies the chemotactic behaviour of PMNs has been investigated showing that the cells are able to detect a gradient of 1-2 % from the leading front to the end of their body. They are rapidly crawling (not swimming!) towards the source of the chemotactic stimuli [22-26].

Guanine nucleotides have been shown to play an important role in the regulation of the hormone-receptor interaction in several receptor systems. Regulation of receptor-ligand interactions by guanine nucleotides has been linked to their ability to cause interconversion between high and low affinity states [27]. For beta adrenergic receptors it has been shown, that the signal transduction is mediated by a nucleotide regulatory protein (G-Protein). Receptor occupancy by f-Met-LEU-[^{3}H] - Phe facilitates the substitution of GDP by GTP during activation and subsequent reactions. When coupled to the G-unit carrying GDP or GTP the receptor is expressed in it's low affinity state. If the receptor is bound to G in the absence of any nucleotide, then the high affinity state is expressed. Neutrophils contain receptors for chemoattractants and opsonins on their cell surface. Ligand binding initiates coordinated cellular responses in a dose dependent manor. Some of the first reactions

Table 2 *Publications describing chemotactic alterations in patients with periodontitis.*

Author	Year	Evaluation	CTN	Patients	CT	CT-H	
Clark	1977	Cr-rad	CDCF	9	JP	7/9/0	37.7%
				5	AP	0/5/0	4.4%
				4	RPP	-/-/-	-
Cianciola	1977	BC	BF CDCF LDCF	9	JP	-/-/-	-
Lavine	1979	LI	BF	14	LJP	12/2/0	24-56%
				19	AP	9/10/0	18-48%
Van Dyke	1980	BC	BF	32	LJP	26/4/2	8-49%
			FMLP	10	PLJP	7/3/0	-
			LDCF	8	GJP	5/1/2	-
				23	AP	2/11/10	-
Van Dyke	1981	BC	FMLP	7	LJP	-	50%
Man.-Pour	1981	BC	EAS	8	SPD	inhibited	40-45%
			FMLP	7	SP	0	0
Larjava	1984	LF	CAS	8	JP	0	0
Suzuki	1984	BC	FMLP	29	LJP	6/0/0	-
				24	GJP	10/0/0	-
Page	1984	Cr-rad	FMLP	5	JP	26/1/0	-
				27	RPP	26/1/0	-
Ellegaard	1984	Cr-rad	CAS	12	JP	-	-
				10	AP	-	-
Katsuragi	1988	BC	FMLP	13	RPP	-	-
				16	AP	-	-
Van Dyke	1987	BC	EAS	16	LJP	12/4/0	59%
			FMLP	5	GJP	5/0/0	50%
Van Dyke	1990	BC	FMLP				
17	LJP	12/5/0	-				
				4	AP	-	-

AP: adult periodontitis; BC:bottom counts; BF: bacterial factor; Cas:casein; CDCF: complement-dep. chemotact. factors; Cr-rad: radioact. Chrom; CT-H: inhibition of chemotaxis (%); CT: 0/0/0 = chemotaxis reduced/normal/enhanced; CTN:chemotaxin; EAS: Endotoxin-activated serum; GJP:generalised JP; LF: leading front technique; PLJP:post LJP; SPD: severe periodontitis with diabetes mellitus; – .no data

are shape change, cytoskeletal rearrangement and receptor capping at the uropod [28]. Together with the chemotactic reactions these are stimulated already by very low chemotaxin concentrations. Microbicidal and cytotoxic functions require 10 to 50-fold higher concentrations of these agents [29,30].

Neutrophil activation by chemotactic factors results primarily from the release of calcium and activation of protein kinase C. Involved in this process are Phosphatidyl-inositol 4,5-biphosphate (PIP2), Inositoltriphosphate (IP3) and Diacylglycerol (DAG). Increases in DAG and calcium activate the respiratory burst suggesting that this is also mediated by protein kinase C and calcium-dependent processes [31,32].During the migration from the blood vessel to the inflammatory site a steady rearrangement of receptors occurs, *i.e.* receptor-ligand-complexes are moved to the rear of the cell and either shed in small membrane droplets or internalized and recycled to be used again at the leading front of the cell [33]. New or recycled receptor complexes are integrated into the membrane which happens together with the release of specific granule contents. Therefore exposure of human neutrophils to degranulating agents enhances the number of chemotactic factor receptors on the cells[34]. The contents of the specific granules (lysozyme, beta glucuronidase *etc.*) facilitate the penetration of the tissue by local enzymatic digestion.

Degranulation, phagocytosis and intracellular killing

After contact with foreign material through Fc-and C3b-receptors primary granules are released intra- and extracellularly. Their contents (collagenase, elastase *etc.*) are involved in the killing and digestion of the phagocytosed material [35,36]. The killing potential of the neutrophil can be divided into oxygen-dependent and independent mechanisms. Under certain circumstances (high number of bacteria simultaneously contacting the cell, i. e. a high number of bacteria: low number of neutrophils) granule contents are also released in considerable amounts extracellularly, which is called "frustrated phagocytosis" [37]. Together with the uptake of foreign material the oxygen consumption of the cell increases 100-fold [38]. Within this respiratory burst reactive oxygen compounds are produced and released (O_2, H_2O_2, OH^-, $HOCl$) which are all toxic for the ingested microorganisms [39,40]. If the cell has ingested numerous bacteria, the membrane of one of the phagolysosomes will rupture and destroy the PMN through the action of the enzymatic activities. The destructive process is limited by enzymes of the cytoplasm, which, like superoxide dismutase, transform oxygen radicals and together with catalase result in the release of H_2O and oxygen [41,42]. Also ceruloplasmin has been demonstrated to be an effective superoxide anion scavenger [43].

Disorders of neutrophil functions in periodontitis

A number of reports has been published describing neutrophil functional abnormalities as primary or secondary to a variety of diseases. In juvenile periodontitis (JP) and rapidly progressive periodontitis (RPP) in 1977 Cianciola *et al.* and Clark *et al.* reported about chemotactic abnormalities [44,45]. Since then many studies appeared showing that chemotactic disorders may be present in a great number of these cases[45-53] (Table 2).

Hence the method for testing chemotaxis is crucial for the results obtained because a negative or abnormal test result has to be differentiated from a false negative test, which is often more difficult then to differentiate a positive from a false positive.

If chemotaxis is tested in Boyden chamber assays or modified Boyden chambers, the test should be performed at least in triplicate and the triple assays should be checked for homogeneity before comparing the results of the healthy volunteers with the patients.

Table 3 *Defective chemotaxis (p < 0.001) in patients with severe periodontitis. Comparison of regression coefficients and leukotactic indices.*

a) f-Met-Leu-Phe-Chemotaxis

	Number	Severity of inhibition(%)
LP	2	57.6
JP	2	61.8
RPP	1	63.8
AP	1	46.2
Total	6 =12.2% of all patients (*n*=49)	

b) Poolserum-Chemotaxis

	Number	Severity of inhibition(%)
LP	1	70.9
JP	1	57
RPP	1	72.6
AP	1	76.2
Total	4 = 10.8% of all patients (n=37)	

LP:less severe periodontitis 3 teeth with p.d. > 5 mm
JP:juvenile periodontitis <19 years, at least 2 teeth p.d. > 5mm
RPP:rapidly progressive periodontitis >8 teeth p.d. >5 mm >18 and< 30years

In most of these studies (Table 2) evaluation was performed by counting the number of cells on the lower filter surface ("bottom counts"), which can be erroneous. After migration through the filter the PMNs will fall of the surface thus very fast migrating cells would appear as a defective response. According to the data published by Van Dyke *et al.* (1980) in localized juvenile periodontitis (LJP) approximately 75 % of the cases show defective chemotactic responses to bacterial peptides (f-Met-Leu-Phe). Later these data have been criticized, because it has been observed, that the chemotactic behavior of PMNs differs between Caucasians and Blacks [54]. Therefore if in earlier studies neutrophils from black patients were compared with the cells from Caucasian volunteers the "defects" may be due to racial differences.

In our own investigation in 49 patients (all Caucasians) we detected a rather low percentage of chemotactic abnormalities (Table 3). According to Van Dyke *et. al.* (1985) there may be a genetic base for the defects, since they observed an enhanced percentage of disorders in families were siblings were suffering from LJP [55]. Further studies suggested that there was an intrinsic defect of the f-Met-Leu-Phe-receptor and the number, but not the affinity, of the receptors in these patients was reduced as compared with healthy controls [56,57].Recently published data suggest that the reduced cell function may be caused by an abnormality in the signal transduction process of the PMN, which results in elevated diacylglycerol levels and there may also be a defect in a surface glycoprotein of a molecular weight of 110 kDa (GP 110) which is involved in the signal transduction from the chemotactic receptor to intracellular molecules [57,58].

Since chemotactic disorders are also seen in other types of the disease elevated serum cytokine levels could also influence this cell function as published by Agarwal *et al.* (1991), who reported about the effect of elevated TNF-alpha concentrations on PMN chemotaxis. In our own study where we observed slightly elevated TNF-alpha levels we did not detect a correlation between the serum concentrations of this cytokine and the functional state of the granulocytes [60].

Several other functions of the neutrophils seem to be altered in periodontitis patients. Microbicidal activity and O_2- -production was elevated, which could be due to a priming effect of bacterial LPS. Also phagocytosis and killing appear to be abnormal. Kalmar *et al.* (1987) found that bactericidal activity of LJP neutrophils was depressed, in fact they observed a specific killing defect of LJP-neutrophils [61]. This finding was consistent over time similar to the chemotaxis defect.

Summary and conclusions

Congenital disorders of the phagocytic system often result in severe breakdown of all/periodontal tissues [62]. Receptor defects disturbing the adherence of the cell to the capillary endothelium result in leukocyte adhesion deficiency disease (LAD). This syndrome is accompanied by an early onset periodontitis already affecting the primary dentition [63].

Severe chemotactic defects as seen in the Chediak-Higashi-Syndrome, which also are accompanied by early onset periodontitis underline the importance of this cellular function for the healthy periodontium [64]. According to our current knowledge at least in certain cases there may be an intrinsic cellular defect of neutrophil function which facilitates the early onset of periodontal infection (LJP/JP). On the other hand it is known that bacterial infections themselves are able to alter and influence neutrophil function.

Some of the pathogens present in deep pockets, like *Actinobacillus actinomycetemcomitans* possess a number of virulence factors, which, like the leukotoxin are able to kill neutrophils and therefore possibly influence cell function[65].

Although the explosion of knowledge in biology and immunology has had a strong impact on our understanding of periodontal infection, still many questions are open and remain to be answered. Improvements in basic periodontal research unveiling some of the key features leading to early periodontal destruction will change therapeutic approaches completely and therefore an international concerted action would be a desirable goal.

References

1.Davis JM, Gallin JI. The Neutrophil. In: Oppenheim JJ, Rosenstreich DL, Potter M, ed. *Cellular functions in immunity and inflammation*. New York, Amsterdam: Elsevier, 1981: 77.
2. Bainton, D. F. 1972. The origin, content, and fate of polymorphonuclear leukocyte granules, In: *Phagocytic Mechanisms in Health and Disease*, Williams, R. C. and Fudenberg, H. H. Eds, New York, Intercontinental Medical Books, 123.
3. Wright DG. *Advances in Host Defense Mechanisms* Vol. 1. Raven Press: New York, 1982: 75-110.
4. Lehrer, R. I., Ladra, K. M., and Hake, R. B., 1975. Nonoxidative fungicidal mechanisms of mammalian granulocytes: demonstration of components with candidacidal activity in human, rabbit, and guinea pig leukocytes, *Infect Immun*, **11**, 1226.
5. DeChatelet, L. R., Cooper, M.R., and McCall, C.E., 1971. Studies of leukocyte phosphatases. III. Inhibition of leukocyte acid phosphatase by zinc, *Clin Chem*, **17**, 1176.
6. DeChatelet, L. R., McCall, C. E., Cooper, M. R., and Shirley, P. S., 1972. Inhibition of leukocyte acid phosphatase by heparin, *Clin Chem*, **18**, 1532.
7. Avila, J. L. and Convit, J., 1973. Heterogeneity of acid phosphatase activity in human polymorphonuclear leukocytes, *Clin Chim Acta*, **44**, 21.
8. Yeh, A. K., Tulsiani, D. R., and Carubelli, R., 1971. Neuraminidase activity in human leukocytes, *J Lab Clin Med*, **78**, 771.
9. Davies, P., Rita, G. A., Krakaur, K., and Weissmann, G.,1971. Characterization of neutral protease from lysosomes of rabbit polymorphonuclear leukocytes, *Biochem J*, **123**, 559.
10. Dewald, B., Rindler-Ludwig, R., Bretz, U., and Bagiolini, M., 1975. Subcellular localization and heterogeneity of neutral proteases in neutrophilic polymorphonuclear leukocytes, *J Exp Med*, **141**, 709.
11. Lazarus, G. S., Brown, R. S., Daniels, J. R., and Fullmer, H. M., 1968. Human granulocyte collagenase, *Science*, **159**, 1483.
12. Clark, J. M., Vaughan, D. W., Aiken, B. M., and Kagan, H. M., 1980. Elastase-like enzymes in human neutrophils localized by ultrastructural cytochemistry, *J Cell Biol*, **84**, 102
13. Spitznagel, J. K., Dalldorf, F. G., Leffell, M. S., Folds., J. D. Welsh, I. R. H., Cooney, M. H., and Martin, L. E., 1974. Character of azurophil and specific granules purified from human poly-morphonuclear leukocytes, *Lab Invest*, **30**, 774
14. Baggiolini, M., Hirsch, K. G., and DeDuve, C., 1969. Resolution of granules from rabbit heterophil leukocytes into distinct propulations by zonal centrifugation, *J Cell Biol*, **40**, 529.
15. Brentwood, B. J. and Henson, P. M., 1989, The sequential release of granule constituents from human neutrophils, *J Immunol*, **124**, 855.
16. Gallin JI. 1985:Neutrophil specific granules: a fuse that ignites the inflammatory response. *Clin Res* 320-328.
17. Gallin JI.1985, Leukocyte adherence-related glycoproteins LFA-1 Mo1 and p150,95: a new group of monoclonal antibodies, a new disease, and a possible opportunity to understand the molecular basis of leukocyte adherence. *J Infect Dis*: **152,** 661-664.
18. Springer, T. A., Dustin, M. L., Kishimoto, T. K., and Marlin, S. D, 1987. The lymphocyte function-accociated CFA-1, CD2. and LFA-3 molecules: cell adhesion receptors of the immune system, *Annu Rev immunol*, **5**, 223.
19. Baab, D.A., Page, R.C. and Morton, T., 1985. Studies of a family manifesting premature exfoliation of deciduous teeth. *J Periodontol* **56**, 403.

20. Baab DA, Page RC, Ebersole JL, Williams BL, Scott CR. 1986. Laboratory studies of a family manifesting premature exfoliation of deciduous teeth. *J Clin Periodontol* **13**: 677-683.

21. Zigmond, S. H., 1977. The ability of polymorphonuclear leukozytes to orient in gradients of chemotactic factor, *J Cell Biol,* **137**, 387

22. Zigmond, S. H. and Hirsch, J. G., 1973. Leukocyte locomotion and chemotaxis. New methods for evaluation and demonstration of cell-derived chemotactic factor, *J Exp Med*, **137**, 387.

23. Stecher, V. J., Sorkin, E., and Ryan, G. B., 1971. Relation between blood coagulation and chemotaxis of leukocytes, *Nature (London)*, **233**, 95.

24. Ward, P. A., Lepow, I. H., and Mewman, L. J., 1968. Bacterial factors chemotactic for polymorphonuclear leukocytes, *Am J Patho*, **52**, 725.

25. Snyderman, R. and Goetzl, E. J., 1981. Molecular and cellular mechanisms of leukocyte chemotaxis, *Science*, **213**, 830.

26. Schiffmann, E., Corcoran, B. A., and Wahl, S. M., 1975. N-Formylmethionyl peptides as chemoattracts for leukocytes, *Proc Natl Acad Sci U.S.A*, **72**, 1059.

27. Snyderman, R., Pike, M.C., Edge, S. and Lane, B.C 1984. A chemoattractant receptor on macrophages exist in two affinity states regulated by guanine nucleotides, *J Cell Biol*, **98**, 444.

28. Omann, G. M., Allen, R. A., Bokoch, G. M. *et al.*, 1987. Signal transduction and cytoskeletal activation in the neutrophil, *Physiol Rev*, **67**, 285.

29. Goldstein, I., Hoffstein, S., Gallin, j. and Weissman, G. 1973. Mechanism of lysosomal enzyme release form human leukocytes: microtubule assembley and membrane fusion induced by a component of comlement, *Proc Natl Acad Sci USA*, **70**, 2916.

30. Klebanoff, S.J. and Clark, R.A. 1978. *The neutrophil: function and clinical disorders*, North Holland, New York, 172.

31. Berridge, M.J. and Irvine, R.F. 1984. Inositol triphosphate: a novel second messenger in cellular signal transduction, *Nature*, **312**, 315.

32. Cockroft , S. 1986. The dependence on Ca^{2+} of the guanine-nucleotide activated polyphosphoinositide phosphodiesterase in eutrophil plasma menbranes, *Biochem J* **240**, 503

33. Fletcher MP and Gallin JI. 1983. Human neutrophils contain an intracellular pool of putative receptors for the chemoattractant n-formyl-methionyl-leucyl- phenylalanine. *Blood* **62**: 792-799.

34. Fletcher , M.P., Seligmann, B.E. and Gallin, J.I. 1982. Correlation of neutrophil secretion, chemoattractant receptor mobilization, and enhanced functional leukocytes. *J. Exp Med*, **128** , 941.

35. Janoff, A. and Scherer, J., 1968. Mediators of inflammation in leukocyte lysosomes. IX. Elastinolytic activity in granules of human poly-morphonuclear leukocytes, *J Exp Med*, **128**, 1137.

36. Lazarus, G. S., Daniels, J. R., Brown, R. S., Bladen, H. A., and Fullmer, H: M., 1968. Degradation of collagen by human granulocyte collagenolytic system, *J Clin Invest*, **47**, 2622.

37. Goldstein , I.M., 1976. Polymorphonuclear leukocyte lysosomes and immune tissue injury, *Prog. Allergy*, **20**, 301

38. Cheson , B.D., Curnutte, J.T. and Babior, B.M. 1977. The Oxidative killing mechanism of the neutrophil. *Clin Immunol*, **3**,1.

39. Tauber, A. I., Borregaard, N., Simons, E. *et al.*, 1983. Chronic granulomatous disease: a syndrome of phagocyte oxidase deficiencies, *Medicine*, **62**, 286.

40. Spielberg, S. P. Boxer, L. A., Oliver, J. M. *et al.*, 1979. Oxidative damage to neutrophils in glutathione synthetase deficiency. *Br J Haematol*, **42**, 215.

41. Rohrer, G. F., Von Wartburg, J. P., and Aebi, H., 1966. Myeloperoxidase aus menschlichen Leukocyten. I. Isolierung und Charakterisierung des Enzyms, *Biochem Zeitschr*, **344**(5), 478.

42. Schultz, J. and Kaminker, K., 1962. Myeloperoxidase of the leukocyte from normal human blood. I. Content and localization, *Arch Biochem*, **96**, 465.

43. Golstein, I.M., Kaplan, H.B., Edelson, H.S. and Weissman, G., 1979. Ceruloplasmin a scavenger of superoxide anion radicals, *J Biol Chem*, **254**, 4040.

44. Cianciola LJ, Genco RJ, Patters MR, McKenna J, Van Oss CJ. 1977. Defective polymorphonuclear leukocyte function in a human periodontal disease. *Nature,* **265**, 445-447.

45. Clark RA, Page RC, Wilde G. 1977. Defective neutrophil chemotaxis in juvenile periodontitis. *Infect Immun* **18**, 694-700.

46. Van Dyke, T. E., Horoszewicz, H. U., and Genco, R. J., 1982b. The polymorphonuclear leukozyte (PMNL) locomotor defect in juvenile periodontitis. Study of random migration, chemokinesis and chemotaxis, *J Periodontol*, **53**, 682.

47. Ellegaard B, Borregaard N, Ellegaard J. 1984. Neutrophil chemotaxis and phagocytosis in juvenile periodontitis. *J Periodont Res,* **19**, 261-268.

48. Larjava H, Saxén L, Kosunen T, Gahmberg CG. 1984. Chemotaxis and surface glycoproteins of neutrophil granulocytes from patients with juvenile periodontitis. *Archs Oral Biol,* **29**, 935-939.

49. Lavine WS, Maderazo EG, Stolman J, Ward PA, Cogen RB, Greenblatt I, Robertson PB. 1979. Impaired neutrophil chemotaxis in patients with juvenile and rapidly progressing periodontitis. *J Periodont Res* **14**, 10-18.

50. Suzuki JB, Collison BC, Falker WA, Naumann JR, Naumann RK. 1984. Immunologic profile of juvenile periodontitis. *J Periodontol* **55**, 461-467.

51. Suzuki JB, Sarah K, Falkler P, Falkler WA. 1984. Immunologic profile of juvenile periodontitis. *J Periodontol* **55**, 453-460.

52. Page RC, Sims TJ, Geissler F, Altman LC, Baab DA.1984. Abnormal leukocyte motility in patients with early - onset periodontitis. *J Periodont Res* **19**,591-594.

53. Van Dyke TE, Horoszewicz HU, Cianciola LJ, Genco RJ. 1980. Neutrophil chemotaxis dysfunction in human periodontitis. *Infect Immun* **27**,124-132.

54. Best AM, Schenkein HA, Gunsolley JC. 1991. Race differences in neutrophil chemotactic responses of periodontally healthy subjects. *J Dent Res* **70**, 442

55. Van Dyke TE, Schweinebraten M, Cianciola LJ, Offenbacher S, Genco RJ. 1985. Neutrophil chemotaxis in families with localized juvenile periodontitis. *J Periodont Res* **20**, 503-541.

56. Van Dyke TE, Warbington M, Gardner M, Offenbacher S. 1990. Neutrophil surface protein markers as indicators of defective chemotaxis in LJP. *J Periodontol*, **61**, 180-184.

57. Van Dyke TE, Wilson-Burrows C, Offenbacher A, Henson P. 1987. Association of an abnormality of neutrophil chemotaxis in human periodontal disease with a cell surface protein. *Infect Immun*, **55**, 2262-2267.

58. Tyagi, S., Lambeth, J. D., and Van Dyke, T. E.. 1992. Altered signal transduction pathways in neutrophils from individuals with localized juvenile periodontitis. *Infect Immun*, **60**, 2481.

59. Agarwal, S. and Suzuki, J.B. 1991 Altered neutrophil function in localized juvenile periodontitis, intrinsic cellular defect or effect of immune mediators? *J Periodont Res*, **26**, 276.

60. Meyle, J. 1993. Neutrophil chemotaxis and serum concentration of tumor necrosis-factor-alpha (TNFA), *J Periodontal Res* **28**, 491.
61. Kalmar, J.R., Arnold, R.R. and Van Dyke, T.E., 1987. Direct ionteraction of Actinobacillus actinomycetemcomitans with normal and defective (LJP) neutrophils, *J Periodont Res*, **22**, 179.,
62. Hill, H.R., Sauls, H.S., Dettloff, J.L. and Quie, P.G. 1974b. Impaired leukotactic responsiveness in patients with juvenile diabetes mellitus. *Clin Immunol Immunopathol*, **2**, 395.
63. Page, R.C. Beatty, P. and Waldrop, T.C. 1987. Molecular basis for the functional abnormality in neutrophils from patients with generalised pre-pubertal periodontitis. *J Periodontal Res*, **22**, 182.
64. Tempel, T.T., Kimball, H.R., Kakehasi, H.R. and Amen, C.R., 1972. Host factors in periodontal manifestation of Chediak-Higashi syndrome, *J Periodont Res*, **7**, 26.
65. Tsai, C.C., McArthur, W.P., Baehni, P.C., Hammond, B.F. and Taichman, N.S., 1979. Extraction and partial characterization of a leukotoxin from a plaque-derived Gram-negative microorganism, *Infect Immun*, **25**, 427.

6 Local and systemic immunologic markers and their diagnostic potential

N.W. Johnson

Royal College of Surgeons of England Department of Dental Sciences/Department of Oral Medicine and Pathology, Kings College School of Medicine and Dentistry, Caldecot Road, London SE5 9RW, UK

Introduction

One of the most active and successful fields of periodontal research over the past decade has been the area of diagnostic procedures. It has been increasingly realised that only a minority of the population is at risk of developing destructive periodontitis and that not all susceptible individuals will have active disease at any particular observation point. Accurate diagnosis therefore depends on separating disease potential from disease activity. More fundamentally, it depends on a satisfactory classification of the different types of disease which affect the periodontium, and of thresholds of severity and extent of damage to the periodontal tissues which are regarded as constituting significant disease.

This paper therefore begins with a summary of current knowledge of the different types of periodontal disease and their global distribution, considers the natural history of disease progression and lists the various scientific approaches to the determination of disease susceptibility and activity. It then concentrates on local and systemic immunological markers and their diagnostic potential.

The opinions expressed are largely personal. No attempt is made comprehensively to review the literature because a number of exhaustive versions have been published in recent years. Rather, some examples drawn from the work of the author's laboratory and from other relevant, recently published, studies will be used to emphasise the value of using host response variables in the diagnosis and management of periodontal diseases. Direct examination of microbial markers is considered by others in this volume.

The paradigm against which the discussion is set holds that an ecological shift in the bacterial flora colonising the gingival margin results in a local and systemic immune inflammatory response which, in susceptible individuals, causes local (bystander) tissue injury [1]. There may also be injuries in other tissues.

Classification of periodontal diseases

For the purposes of this discussion we are considering only plaque-related inflammatory conditions and excluding neoplasms, metabolic diseases of bone, acute mucogingival infections such as herpes simplex-induced gingivo-stomatitis and dermatoses which can affect the gingivae such as lichen planus and mucous membrane pemphigoid[2]. Even so, no satisfactory classification exists. Our knowledge is still so incomplete that no logical spine for an ideal classification can be applied - be it based on a list of causative organisms, clinical features or host factors. Textbooks contain variably complex classifications. Many work with that of the American Academy of Periodontology[3]. After thorough debate, the 1st European Workshop on Periodontology[4] proposed a simple classification distinguishing between: (1) early onset periodontitis; (2) adult periodontitis and (3) necrotising periodontitis.

However the Workshop recommended that as many as possible secondary descriptors should be added. These would include distribution within the dentition (severity and extent), rate of progression, response to treatment, nature of the associated microflora, ethnic group, familial or genetic predisposition, drug therapy, smoking status, intercurrent disease able to influence the host response (*e.g.* diabetes, immune-suppression, stress, immune defect, structural tissue defect). Several comprehensive reviews of the latter are available [5-8].

In an ideal world, periodontists everywhere would record all this detail, to common criteria and repeatedly on every patient over many years. We would then be able retrospectively to apply cluster and discriminant analyses to identify how many genuinely different kinds of periodontitis there are! Such a scenario is improbable, though large organisations such as the American, and even the European, Academies of Periodontology probably have the authority and mechanisms to implement such a programme. However, unless and until such studies are performed, clinicians will no doubt go on using terms such as rapidly progressive periodontitis, refractory periodontitis, and localised juvenile periodontitis. In doing so it is important to realise how poorly defined are these supposed entities: *e.g.* disease can progress rapidly at any age in a minority of cases, independent of when disease began; the response to treatment depends on the nature and appropriateness of the therapy delivered and on the skill of the operator; juvenile (onset) periodontitis may have a "classical" localised distribution, but in my experience a continuous spectrum of involvement within the dentition exists [9]. Finally it remains fundamentally important to distinquish between disease limited to the gingivae and that which involves the deeper tissues, the periodontium: here we are really only concerned with destructive periodontitis.

The existence of high risk cohorts

The fact that severe early onset destructive periodontitis is uncommon (*e.g.* typical "juvenile periodontitis" has a prevalence of the order of 0.8 % in blacks [10], 0.2 % in Asians and 0.1 % in European Caucasians: prepubertal periodontitis associated with leucocyte adhesion deficiency [11] and Papillon - Lefevre syndrome are even rarer) tells us that the risk groups are small. This is independent of arguments as to whether the risk relates to risk of becoming infected by certain organisms or to host-based susceptibility - though we know that most of the basis of this risk is genetic [12].

Truly rapidly progressive periodontitis is rare: no genuine population-based prevalence or incidence data exist and there are no widely agreed diagnostic criteria; nevertheless such cases form quite a small proportion of patients even in specialist referral clinics. [13]The proportion of the adult population which develops significant periodontal destruction is variously reported as between 10 and 30 per cent depending, inter alia, on sample size, method of examination, diagnostic threshold, the index used for reportage, and age - the signs of destructive disease being cumulative over the life time of the individual. [10; 14-17]. Most of the data which might allow international comparisons use CPITN methodology and are held in the World Health Organisation's (WHO) Global Oral Data Bank [18]. This index has severe limitations and needs to be appropriately adjusted to its purpose [19]. Nevertheless it is clear that most of the significant disease resides in a minority of individuals in any community [10;16;17;20;21].

Approaches to periodontal diagnosis

Setting aside the presence or absence of gingivitis - a manifestation of local tissue response to bacterial plaque and of poor predictive value for periodontal breakdown - clinical observation remains the mainstay of diagnosis. "Severe disease for age" [22], as recorded by pocketing, loss of attachment and/or of bone or teeth by physical probing and/or radiography remains the best diagnostic and prognostic method. Much recent work has refined this concept to show site-specific markers of risk of further breakdown, *e.g.* current pocket depth, tooth type and site [23;24]. Plaque levels and bleeding on probing have limited predictive value [25].

Clinical examination of first degree relatives, sometimes more widely, helps to identify those with an inherited susceptibility and should be mandatory in all early onset forms of destructive periodontitis.Diagnosis by identification of micro-organisms present is dealt with elsewhere in this volume. This is rational in that we can identify a list of 6-10 likely contributory pathogens. However, the mere presence of an organism in these polymicrobial, multifactorial inflammatory diseases has no predictive value [26]. Tests which quantify the numbers of putative pathogens present and, most importantly, the nature and concentration of the virulence factors produced, may prove of value in the future.The second European Workshop on Periodontology agreed that measures of the host response show some promise as diagnostic tools: furthermore they shed light on aetiology and pathogenesis [27].

Diagnostic theory

An appreciation of diagnostic theory is fundamental to approaching the usefulness of local and systemic markers of the immune response. Such theories are described in

71

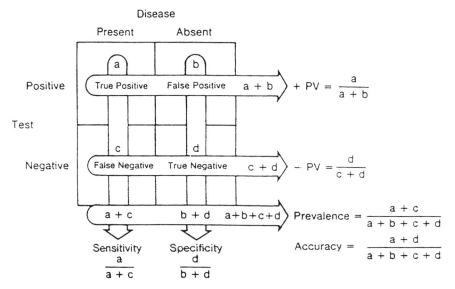

Figure 1 *Characteristics of diagnostic tests and formulae for the main outcome measures.(Design courtesy of the Department of Clinical Epidemiology and Biostatistics, Macmaster Health Sciences Centre, Canada.)*

many textbooks of medicine, epidemiology and of biostatistics. It is well summarised, in the context of periodontal diseases, by Lang [25]. The strengths and limitations of clinical and laboratory diagnostic tests for periodontal diseases have been critically evaluated by both the First and Second European Workshops on Periodontology. It is worth summarising some of the key principles here.

(1) Evaluating a diagnostic test requires a "gold standard": viz, a truly accurate knowledge of the presence or absence of disease in all circumstances in which a new test is being applied. Such a gold standard does not exist for the periodontal diseases. The best we can do is to record attachment loss over time, and this is beset by serious measurement error [28].

(2) Tests must be evaluated in terms of their sensitivity, specificity and predictive values (Figure l). It is impossible to achieve 100% sensitivity (viz. no false negatives) and 100% specificity (viz. no false positives). There is always a trade off, which should be evaluated by formal study of receiver-operator characteristics.

(3) A test is only useful if it adds to more readily available information about the patient or the site. This means that the test result must have good predictive values: These are, however, strongly influenced by the prevalence of disease in the population under study. This is a problem in the diagnosis of periodontal disease activity, which at any particular examination point will be present in a small proportion of individuals and, probably, at few sites.

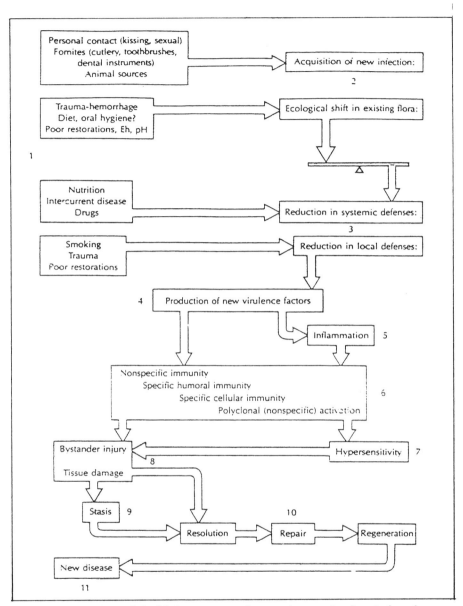

Figure 2 *Flow chart of the likely sequence of events in a cycle of periodontal disease activity. The numbers indicate conceptual domains, provocations in the case of domain 1; shifts in the nature and activity of aetiological agents in 2; shifts in the threshold of host defence in 3, and the nature of the tissue changes in various phases of an episodic disease process in 4-10. Each of these domains provides many ideas for possible markers of periodontal disease activity in GCF. (From ref 29).*

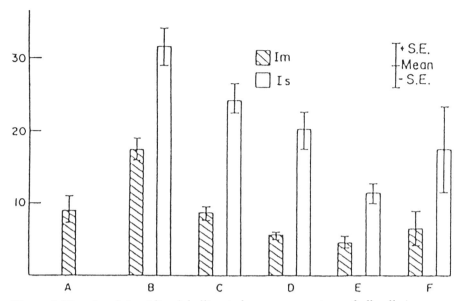

Figure 3 *The triated thymidine labelling index as a percentage of all cells in various compartments of gingival epithelium. Junctional epithelium has a high labelling index and consequently a high replacement rate. (From ref 31). A is junctional epithelium. B is oral sulcular epithelium. C, D, E are successive 1 mm segments of the oral aspects of free and attached gingiva. F includes the micro-gingival junction.*

(4) Most of the available tests are better at identifying low risk patients/sites. As this represents the majority of the population this is very useful information.

(5) It is helpful to consider an heirarchy of tests, *e.g.* 'discovery', 'exclusionary' and 'confirmatory' tests which quite properly vary in their sensitivity, specificity and predictive values.

(6) Available tests show greater potential for monitoring the effect of therapy than in diagnosis of current disease activity or predicting future disease.

Potential diagnostic markers

We shall now look at the defence mechanisms of the periodontium and at some aspects of the diagnostic potential of each component of the immune response, both locally (as measured in gingival crevicular fluid - GCF) and systemically (as measured in peripheral blood). These are intimately interrelated: GCF and its constituents derive principally from the blood stream with local additions and modifications (Figure 2)[29]. Equally, the body responds to periodontal infections in many of its tissues and organs - principally those of the immune system - and these responses are reflected in peripheral blood.Thus we approach our selective survey under headings describing the various (interactive) structural and functional components of host defence.

Tissue integrity.

Epithelium

The stratified squamous epithelia of the body's integument - epidermis and the epithelial components of all mucous membranes - is, together with the chemicals secreted onto its surfaces, the first line of defence against potentially damaging microbes. Though controversial, it does not seem reasonable to regard the epithelial attachment to the tooth as an inherently weak link. Junctional epithelium (JE) is a remarkable tissue, firmly bound to both tooth surface and gingival lamina propria by a sophisticated system of adhesion molecules[30] and with a remarkably high rate of cell renewal and repair capacity Figure 3 [31]. Molecular markers of increased catabolism or anabolism of these tissue components might usefully be investigated for their diagnostic potential.In periodontitis, as well as responding to cytokines produced by the underlying inflammatory infiltrate, keratinocytes of JE and of oral sulcular epithelium themselves produce cytokines (notably interleukins and, indeed, gelatinase (Type IV collagenase) which can damage the basement membrane and contribute to tissue destruction and epithelial downgrowth. [32].

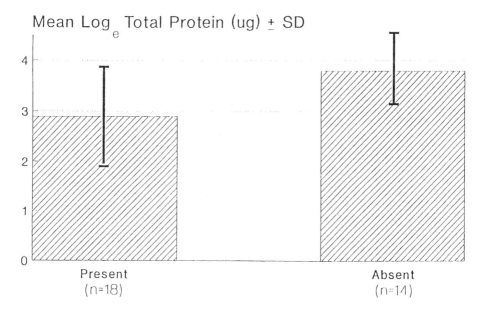

Figure 4 *The presence or absence of detectable pyrodinoline in GCF samples from periodontal pockets in relation to the total protein concentration sampled at the site over a standard 30 second period.* f = 8.21; 1, 30 d.f. *p = 0.0072 (sig. at 1%)*

The stratified squamous epithelia of the body's integument - epidermis and the epithelial components of all mucous membranes - is, together with the chemicals secreted onto its surfaces, the first line of defence against potentially damaging microbes. Though controversial, it does not seem reasonable to regard the epithelial attachment to the tooth as an inherently weak link. Junctional epithelium (JE) is a remarkable tissue, firmly bound to both tooth surface and gingival lamina propria by a sophisticated system of adhesion molecules [30] and with a remarkably high rate of cell renewal and repair capacity Figure 3 [31]. Molecular markers of increased catabolism or anabolism of these tissue components might usefully be investigated for their diagnostic potential.In periodontitis, as well as responding to cytokines produced by the underlying inflammatory infiltrate, keratinocytes of JE and of oral sulcular epithelium themselves produce cytokines (notably interleukins and, indeed, gelatinase (Type IV collagenase) which can damage the basement membrane and contribute to tissue destruction and epithelial downgrowth. [32].

Homeostasis of connective tissues
It has been established for many years that collagen of the gingival tissues turns over faster in health than almost any other site in the body [33]. Not only does this indicate an important defence, but suggests that various catabolic and anabolic moieties in GCF might mark disease activity [34]. Early work concentrated on measurements of hyaluronidase levels in GCF. More recently we, and now several research groups , have measured the collagen cross-linking molecules pyrodinoline and deoxypyrodinoline which, cross-sectionally at least, show a correlation with disease severity [35]. When the assay methods improve, it may be possible to distinguish bone-derived, and soft connective tissue derived, collagen breakdown products. Indeed Giannobile *et al.*[36] have shown that it is possible to detect sites of rapid bone turnover in beagle dogs using pyridinoline cross links and osteocalcin assays.Breakdown products of connective tissue ground substance have also been extensively investigated, notably sulphated glycoseaminoglycans [37], and we have demonstrated their relationship to sustained chronic inflammation at periodontal sites [38]. This whole exciting field, has just been reviewed exhaustively and critically by Bartold [39].

Non-specific immunity

Acute-phase proteins
There are few recent studies. We [40] recently compared the levels of acute-phase proteins in the peripheral blood of cases of adult periodontitis with matched controls and found statistically significantly lower levels of transferrin in cases. This might be important because many of the putative periodontal pathogenic bacteria, notably Porphyromonas gingivalis, require iron containing proteins for growth (notably haem). It is possible that foci of periodontal infection have sequestered iron and that this is reflected in peripheral blood. We do not know, however, whether this is cause or effect, nor how it may relate to disease activity, as this was a cross sectional study. Other acute phase reactants were not significantly different (Table 1).

Table 1 *Acute phase proteins in adult periodontitis.case vs control, paired t-tests on differences.*

Analyte	No of pairs	Mean difference	p
Mannan binding protein	20	705	0.22
Transferrin	20	-0.45	0.02
Pre-albumin	19	-1.58	0.86
α1- antichymotrypsin	20	-0.03	0.50
C- reactive protein	19	0.05	0.92

Curtis MA, Slaney JM, Johnson NW *et al.* 1995; MRC Dental Research Unit, unpublished.

Do levels of acute phase proteins in GCF indicate site specific disease activity? We have shown that the proportion of complexed α2-macroglobulin (α2-M) (or spent, inactivated enzyme inhibitor) in GCF, irrespective of pocket depth, is consistently of the order of 70% - higher than in any other inflammatory site described in the literature (Figure 5). In deep sites, the total α2-M concentration , viz. Free plus Complexed, is positively correlated with the proteolytic activity in the same GCF sample. Likewise α1-antitrypsin (α1-AT), the main physiological inhibitor of neutrophil elastase, is predominantly in complexed form [41]. These findings perhaps demonstrate the importance and efficacy of these non-specific, largely plasma-derived, enzyme inhibitors in containing the destructive elements of periodontal inflammation. They imply, however, that measurements of α2-M and α1-AT in GCF may not prove a very sensitive marker of disease activity. This is borne out by the observations of Adonogianaki *et al.* [42], in which levels of α2-M, α1-AT, transferrin and lactoferrin failed to differentiate between active and stable periodontitis sites at the baseline of a 3 month longitudinal study.

Polymorphonuclear leukocyte (PMN): numbers and function

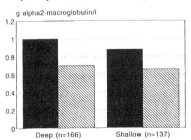

Figure 5 *The concentrations of total and of complexed alpha 2 macrogobulin in standardised GCF samples from deep and shallow periodontal pockets. Black box, total. Hatched box, complexed In both cases approximately 70% of the total (α2-M is in the complexed form. (From ref. 40).*

Polymorphonuclear leukocyte (PMN): numbers and function

It has long been accepted that PMN (predominantly neutrophilic -PMN) leucocytes constitute a key defence system of the periodontium, though their degranulation *in situ* produces products which exacerbate inflammation and which cause bystander tissue injury. They sweep in vast numbers quickly from capillaries and aggregate in the periodontal crevice or pocket, where they actively phagocytose and kill bacteria, and also kill bacteria by close range extracellular mechanisms. All of these roles have been comprehensively reviewed many times, very recently in ref.43.

Constitutional defects in PMN function - migration, response to chemotaxis, phagocytosis and/or killing have been described in patients with early onset periodontal diseases, particularly in the USA [44], though this has not been shown in some European studies [45]. A relatively well understood genetic deficiency in PMN surface receptors underlies susceptibility to so-called prepubertal periodontitis [11].

Two pieces of recent evidence point to the possibility that constitutional defects in PMN are associated with adult periodontitis, though it is not yet possible to tell whether the changes in peripheral blood leukocytes (pbl) represent a contributory cause or an effect of periodontal disease. Firstly our group has shown [46] that the susceptibility of pbl to the damaging effects of culture supernatant, and to purified trypsin-like protease of Porphyromonas gingivalis, is greater in cases of adult periodontitis than in matched controls - as measured by the important function of phagocytic ability. Secondly, Gustafsson and Asman [47] have shown that patients with adult periodontitis demonstrate a more than 2 fold higher release of oxygen free radicals from Fcγ -receptor stimulated pbl compared to healthy controls. This is also true of cases of early onset periodontitis. There is also a tendency for greater release of neutrophil elastase: thus by both mechanisms there is increased potential for by-stander tissue destruction. Measures of pbl (pmn) function may be an approach to detecting individuals at risk.

Substances released from pmn in individual periodontal sites have been explored as markers of disease activity for many years [29;48]. Lactoferrin and β-glucuronidase appear to be fairly non-specific markers of pmn numbers. Neutrophil elastase, however, is potentially destructive and much work has gone into study of its diagnostic and prognostic potential, with very encouraging results [49].

Other host derived proteinases

Members of the family of matrix metalloproteinases (MMP's: including collagenases) act synergistically at neutral pH to digest structural components of connective tissues - both in normal tissue turnover and in disease. They act in balance with tissue inhibitors of metalloproteinases (TIMP's), and disturbances of this balance, mediated by cytokines such as IL-1 and TGF β produced by, particularly , monocyte/macrophage cells in an inflammatory focus, can lead to net connective tissue loss. This important area has been reviewed concisely and well by Reynolds[50]. Furthermore, there is considerable evidence that phospholipases from periodontal pathogenic bacteria can trigger host cells to release MMP's: the released proteases are then triggered to an active form by the proteases of plaque bacteria [51]. This knowledge might form the basis for the use of specific protease inhibitors in the

Table 2 *Polymorphonuclear leukocyte phagocytosis (mean per cent)by cases and controls of* P.gingivalis. *Effects of culture supernatant and purified TLPase activated with dithiothreitol.*

Treatment	Case	Control	p
None	49.6 ± 6.5	52.3 ± 8.4	0.55
Supernatant	9.3 ± 5.3	12.4 ± 5.1	0.02
TLPase	16.0 ± 6.5	17.2 ± 8.4	0.06

Data from Ref 46.

prevention or treatment of periodontal tissue destruction [1]. Collagenase levels in GCF and in saliva are useful screening tools for patients with active periodontitis [52].

On the other hand, using synthetic peptide substrates and suitable assay conditions, Eley and Cox have demonstrated, in an impressive series of papers, that they can distinguish host-derived and bacteria-derived dipeptidyl peptidases (DDP) in GCF. In a study in which 48 adult periodontitis patients were followed at 3 month intervals over 2 years, GCF DDPII and IV levels (at critical values of 5mU per 30 second samples, or 25mU per ml of GCF) showed remarkable sensitivity and specificity (99-100%) and positive predictive values from 55-71% in the prediction of sites of attachment loss [53]. DPP II appears to arise from tissue macrophages and fibroblasts and from cells in GCF; DPP IV has been localised to monocytes, macrophages, fibroblasts and CD4 and CD8 lymphocytes.

Prostaglandins
Other potential diagnostic markers derived from host cells, particularly monocytes and macrophages, are eicosanoid products of the arachadonic acid cascade. Work in the 1980's and early 1990's suggested that whole mouth, and to a lesser extent site-specific, GCF levels of PGE2 could differentiate attachment loss sites [54]. A number of groups, including our own [5], have tended to use PGE2 as a standard against which experimental analytes were compared. It is somewhat surprising that more recent longitudinal data have not been published.

Cytosolic enzymes
The release of the non cell-specific cytosolic enzyme aspartate amino-transferase (AST) into the circulation has long been exploited as a marker of tissue damage, *e.g.*in cardiac infarction or liver disease. AST levels in GCF form the basis of a commercially available diagnostic kit, as research in both animals and man a few years ago showed the method to have diagnostic and prognostic value. A recent multicentre trial [55] is described and a careful account is given of study design and of appropriate methods for statistical analysis. So far only the results of response to treatment have been presented and these, not surprisingly, show significant falls in

Table 3a *Levels of IL1β in GCF at visit one for sites whose composite index improved, deteriorated, or remained unchanged at visit two (see text)*

	Concentration (log pg/ml GCF)	Amount (log pg/ml eluate)
Improved	2.27	2.65
No change	0.99	1.40
Deteriorated	3.09	3.34
	$p = 0.022$	$p = 0.054$

Table 3b *The change in GCF IL1-β levels from first to second visit (V2 - V1).*

	Concentration (Δ pg/ml GCF)	Amount (Δpg/ml eluate)
Improved	1.14	0.43
No change	1.81	2.17
Deteriorated	-0.42	-0.31
	$p=0.026$	$p=0.024$

(From Johnson NW, Powell JR, Harrap G J *et al.*, unpublished)

AST at sites which have been effectively treated. Data on the utility of this kit for predicting future disease and for detecting active sites are awaited.

Cytokines
Cytokines are short range chemical messengers produced by many different host cells and with actions on many types of target cell - by autocrine or paracrine binding to specific cell surface receptors. Their concentrations increase both locally and systemically in inflammation, and their activity is modulated by receptor-antagonists and by soluble forms of the receptors. Howells [56] has recently proposed that disregulation of these inhibitors of IL-1β and TNF α , rather than overproduction per se, may play a central role in destructive periodontal diseases.

Several years ago we showed increased levels of the proinflammatory cytokines IL-1β, IL-6 and TNFα, detected by immuno assay (and thus not necessarily all in bioactive form) at diseased periodontal sites, though there was no correlation with static clinical markers of disease severity [57-59]. Subsequent work has shown however that the total amount of IL-1β at a site is positively correlated with GCF volume, plaque score, bleeding index and probeable crevice depth.

Table 4 *Principles of antibody responses in disease.*

Antibody titres reflect antigenic load and history
Rising titres indicate infection
High titres might indicate immunity or convalescence
Low titres might indicate susceptibility

Table 5 *Mean levels of IgG1, IgG2, IgG3 and IgG4 in the serum of cases and controls.*

	IgG1	IgG2	IgG3	IgG4
Cases	4.429 ± 1.750[a]	3.756 ± 1.684	0.407 ± 0.233	0.615 ± 0.404
Controls	4.268 ± 1.785	2.882 ± 1.559	0.396 ± 0.277	0.685 ± 0.511

[a] g/l ± standard deviation $n = 35$ pairs

Given the pleiotropic effects of these cytokines, particularly IL-1, it is unlikely that changes in their concentration will reflect any specific component or phase of a cycle of disease activity, through to resolution and healing. Although IL-1β is an important activator of osteoclasts, levels in GCF are more likely to reflect the intensity of gingivitis. Nevertheless, in a longitudinal study sampling 10 sites in 33 patients with adult periodontitis, at two visits, 3 months apart, we found that high levels of IL- 1β in GCF at the first visit predicted change - in either direction - viz. a deterioration or improvement - in a composite index of the status of a site compiled from plaque and bleeding scores, pocket depths and attachment levels; the corollary is clear: the lowest levels indicate stable sites (Table 3a). Furthermore a rising concentration from visit 1 to visit 2 indicates sites likely to be stable or improving and a falling level indicates deterioration of a site. (Table 3b).Turkish colleagues have made a useful contribution to the measurement of IL-1β and TNF-α in GCF [60].

Specific immune responses

If we regard destructive periodontitis as a bacterial disease, then there are well established principles of the local and systemic immune response which can guide our approach to diagnosis, prognosis and assessment of the outcome of intervention (Table 4). Prevention by immunization is also a rational aim; further discussion of immunization is outwith the scope of the present chapter but we have addressed the principles elsewhere[1].There is an extensive literature on measurements of the systemic humoral response to presumed periodontal pathogens, which we reviewed in 1991[61]. That review concluded that serology had little place in diagnosis and prognosis and made recommendations for future studies to focus on responses to

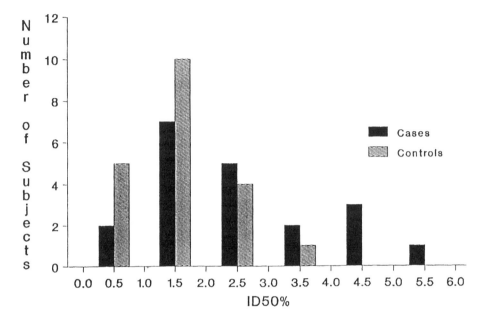

Figure 6 *The avidity of IgG antibodies to the 47 kDa antigen of* Porphyromonas gingivalis *in the serum of cases with adult periodontitis and matched controls. Whilst there is a shift to the right in the case population, note that a substantial proportion of cases have low avidity antibodies comparable to those of healthy controls. The technique is ammonium thiocyanate disassociation of binding measured in an ELISA (From ref. 68).*

known or putative virulence factors of periodontal pathogens, and to more functional assays of serum antibodies. There has been considerable progress since then, reviewed more recently by Ebersole and Taubman [62].

In case:control studies (Table 5), total serum IgG2 is raised in cases, perhaps reflecting polyclonal B cell responses to a mixture of carbohydrate-containing antigens, and this response may prove ineffective because IgG2 antibodies are non-opsonic [63]. IgGl and IgG4 (the latter characteristically reflecting chronic antigenic stimulation) antibodies to whole cells of *Porphyromonas gingivalis* (Pg) are significantly higher in cases as a group but, potentially importantly, some patients still have low levels; this may indicate that Pg is not an important pathogen in these patient's disease or that they are constitutionally unable to mount an effective response – hence constituting a susceptible group [64].

We know that there are a number of species–specific antigens of Pg which are discriminatory in adult periodontitis [65;66], including a protein of approximately 47 kDa which contains much of the trypsin-like protease activity of this organism - an important virulence factor because it not only has the potential to damage host tissue but also to interfere with the host's defences by disarming the natural protease inhibitors present in plasma [1;67]. We have recently measured circulating antibody titres and avidities to this antigen, as well as to Pg whole cells, in cases and controls with periodontitis[68]. It is important to add avidity - a measure of the strength of binding between antibody and antigen and an indication of its functional ability. These studies again show an overall case:control difference, but again with overlap (Figure 6), tempting the speculation that those individuals with respectable antibody titres but low avidities may be constitutionally susceptible. Similar arguments have been advanced by the Page group as described elsewhere in the present volume.

It has now become common for studies of humoral immunity to periodontal diseases to include avidity assays and to look at Ig isotype and subclass responses. Amongst others, important new data are emerging from the laboratories of Kinane *et al.* , whose work shows lower aviditties of IgG, and particularly IgM, antibodies to Pg and Aa in patients with rapidly progressive periodontitis compared to adult periodontitis [70] and, in a longtitudinal study, that antibody avidities to Pg were higher in patients who did not go on to suffer further attachment loss than in those who did [71]. Furthermore the initial antibody titre to Pg influenced development of antibody avidity and the success of treatment [72]. Ebersole *et al.* [73] have shown that, in early onset and adult periodontitis patients harbouring Aa, 70% of patients with progressive disease showed an increase in IgG antibody level 2-4 months prior to the clinical detection of disease activity. This was associated with a rise in numbers of Aa infected sites and implies that the antibody response is ineffective: furthermore the spectrum of Aa antigens recognized differed in those with active disease as mentioned above. Holbrook *et al.* [74] have shown, in a small group of patients refractory to treatment, that they were unable to produce antibody titres to Pg and Aa significantly higher than matched control subjects and that, although antibody avidities to these pathogens were higher in the patients, no change in avidity was noted during the course of treatment.

Control of the systemic immune response is mediated by a complex set of interactions between antigen presenting cells (predominantly cells of the monocyte/macrophage/Langerhan's cell lineage) and T and B lymphocytes. Major histocompatability (MHC) antigens are central to the specificity and efficacy of antigen recognition, and MHC differences clearly underly some of the inherited differences in suspectibility referred to earlier [7;9]. New knowledge on the priming, early in life or on first contact of the host's immune system with an antigen, shows that important decisions are made as to whether a Thy 0 naive T cell differentiates into a Thy 1 or Thy 2 cell (Figure 7). The former preferentially produce the cykokines IL-2, IL-10, IL-12 and IFN γ, resulting in a predominantly T cell lesion which, in periodontitis, seems to represent an effective innate immune response and to contain disease. The presence of IL-4 and low IFN γ leads to differentiation of Thy 2 cells which secrete IL-4, IL-5 and IL-6 resulting in B cell recruitment and further IL-4 production, in which case disease is likely to be more severe, partly through IL-1 production (see earlier), even if antigen-specific B cells do produce some protective antibody. This area has been researched in an outstanding series of papers from the Seymour group in Brisbane [75]. Pg antigens have a tendency to trigger unfavourable pathways in Pg-infected subjects who develop periodontitis compared with Pg-infected subjects whose disease remains restricted to gingivitis, possibly explaining and indicating susceptible individuals [76].

In GCF, immune responses can of course also be measured. We[58] have shown in collaboration with Unilever Dental Research (as have others), elevated IgG2 and IgG4 in diseased sites, indicating sustained chronic inflammation of the site and continual B cell recruitment and both specific and non specific (polyclonal) plasma cell activity. Clearly much of this activity is ineffective in eliminating subgingival colonisation/infection and is thus likely to mark sites at risk of disease progression.Attempts are being made to combine studies of all the foregoing immunological and inflammatory events into a coherent diagnostic strategy [77].

Conclusions

From this selective review it is evident that the science of periodontology is progressing rapidly, exploiting new knowledge of basic immunology and cell biology, and indeed contributing to it. We have several likely explanations of the genetic basis for susceptibility to some early-onset forms of destructive periodontitis, and working hypotheses for some instances of adult-onset disease. GCF-based

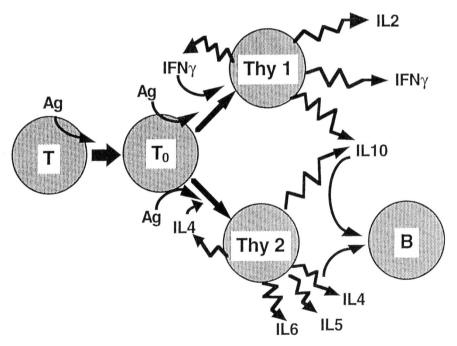

Figure 7 *Diagramatic representation of the differentiation of Thy1 and Thy2 lymphocytes and their cytokine profiles.*

analyses for detecting site-specific disease activity and the likelihood of progression are a reality. These latter have, unfortunately, been brought prematurely to the market place, but the more promising of them are now having their clinical utility properly assessed in multicentre trials designed to strict protocols, international guidelines for which are being promulgated to a high standard by bodies such as the American Academy of Periodontology [78] and the European Academy of Periodontology[79]. This level of co-operation between scientists in many countries and between clinicians, academics and industry augers well for continuing progress.

References

1. Johnson NW, Curtis MA. Preventive therapy for periodontal diseases. *Adv. Dent. Res.* 1994; **8**, 337-348.

2. Holmstrup P, Johnson NW. Use of chemicals in the diagnosis of the most common skin and mucous membrane disorders with gingival affection. In: *Proceedings of the 2nd European Workshop on Periodontology.* Lang NP, Karring T. Eds, Quintessance, 1996. 366 - 379.

3. *Proceedings of the World Workshop in Clinical Periodontics.* American Academy of Periodontology 1989 pp. 1-23, 2

4. *Proceedings of the First European Workshop on Periodontology.* Lang NP, Karring T eds. Quintessance 1994, 120.

5. Johnson NW. Risk factors and diagnostic tests for destructive periodontitis. In: Lang NP, Karring T eds. *Proceedings of the 1st European Workshop on Periodontology.* Quintessence 1994, 90-119.

6. Johnson NW. Facturs de risque et marquers de la parodontitie severe. *J. de Paradontol* 1994, **13**, 139-167.

7. Genco RJ, and Loe H. The role of systemic conditions and disorders in periodontal disease. *Periodontology 2000* 1993; **2**, 98-116.

8. Porter SR, Scully C. Periodontal aspects of systemic disease, classification. In: Lang NP, Karring T eds. *Proceedings of the 1st European Workshops on Periodontology.* Quintessence 1994, 375-414.

9. Moses JH, Tsichti P, Donaldson O, Smith PB, Johnson NW, Bodmer JG. HLA and susceptibility to periodontitis in Afro-caribbeans. *Tiss Antigens* 1994; **43**, 316-319.

10. Brown LJ, Loe H. Prevalence, extent, severity and progression of periodontal disease. *Periodontology 2000* 1994; **2**, 57-71.

11. Katsuragi K, Takashiba S. Kurihara H, Murayama Y. Molecular basis of leukocyte adhesion molecules in early onset periodontitis. Patients with decreased CD11/CD18 expression on leucocytes. *J. Periodontol* 1994; **65**, 949-957.

12. Michalowicz BS. Genetic and heritable risk factors in periodontal disease. *J. Periodontol* 1994; **65**, 479-488.

13. Page RC. Severe forms of periodontitis in children, juveniles and adults, worldwide prevalence. In: Johnson NW ed, Risk Markers for Oral Diseases Vol 3, *Periodontal Diseases, Markers of Disease Susceptibility and Activity.* Cambridge Univ. Press 1991, 76-105.

14. Burt BA. The distribution of periodontal destruction in the populations of industrialised countries. In: Johnson NW ed, *Risk Markers for Oral Diseases* Vol 3, Periodontal Diseases; Markers of Disease Susceptibility and Activity. Cambridge University Press 1991, 76-105.

15. Baelum V, Manji F. Fejerskov O. The distribution of periodontal destruction in the populations of non-industrialised countries, evidence for the existence of high risk groups and individuals. In Johnson NW ed, *Risk Markers for Oral Diseases* Vol 3, Periodontal Diseases; Markers of Disease Susceptibility and Activity. Cambridge University Press 1991, 76-105.

16. Johnson NW, Huws A, Maiden MFJ, Griffiths GS. Inflammatory Periodontal Diseases. In: *Oral Diseases in the Tropics.* Prabhu R, Daftary DK, Wilson DF, Johnson NW, eds, Oxford Univ. Press 1992; 598-633.

17. Baelum V, Chen X, Manji F, Luan WM, Fejerskov O. Profiles of destructive periodontal disease in different populations. *J. Perio Res* 1996; **31**, 17-26.

18. Miyazaki H, Pilot T, Leclecq MH. *Periodontal profiles; an overview of CPITN data in the WHO Global Oral Data bank for the age groups 15-19 years, 35-44 years and 65-74 years.* Geneva 1994 World Health Organization.

19. Page RC, Morrison EC. Summary of outcomes and recommendations of the Workshop on CPITN. *Int. dent. J.* 1994; **44**, 589-594.

20. Pilot T. The implications of the high risk strategy and of improved diagnostic methods for health screening and public health planning in periodontal diseases. In: Johnson NW Ed. *Risk Markers for Oral Diseases* Vol 3, Periodontal Diseases, Markers of Disease Susceptibility and Activity. Cambridge Univ. Press 1991, 76-105.

21. Papapanou PN. Epidemiology and natural history of periodontal disease. In: *Proceedings of the 1st European Workshop and Periodontal Disease.* Lang NP, Karring T. eds, Quinntessence 1994; 23-41.

22. *World Health Organisation/Federation Dentaire Internationale. Guidelines for community periodontal care.* FDI World Dental Press, 1992; London.

23. Grossi SG, Zambon JJ, Ho AW *et al..* Assessment of risk for periodontal diseases. 1. Risk indicators for attachment loss, *J. Periodontol* 1994; **65**, 260-267.

24. Lamster IB, Smith QT, Celenti RS, Singer RE, Grbic JT. Development of a risk profile for periodontal disease, Microbial and host response factors. *J. Periodontol* 1994; **65**, 511-520.

25. Lang NP. Clinical markers of active periodontal disease. In: Johnson NW ed. *Risk Markers for Oral Diseases* Vol 3, Periodontal Diseases; Markers of Disease Susceptibility and Activity. Cambridge University Press 1991, 76-105.

26. Cattabriga M, Pedrazolli V. Microbial-based chemical agents in diagnostics. In Lang NP, Karring T eds, *Proceedings of 2nd European Workshop on Periodontal diseases* 1996; Quintessance. In press.

27. Kinane DF. Host response-based chemical agents in diagnosis. In: *Proceedings of the 2nd European Workshop on Periodontal diseases.* Lang NP, Karring T. eds, 1996. Quintessance. In Press.

28. Claffey NP. Gold standard, Clinical and radiological assessment of disease activity. In: *Proceedings of the 1st European Workshop on Periodontology.* Lang NP, Karring T. eds. Quintessance 1994; 42-53.

29. Johnson NW. Crevicular fluid - based diagnostic tests. *Current Opin. Dent.* 1991; **1**, 52-65.

30. Larjava H, Haapasalmi K, Salo T, Wiebe C, Uitto. Keratinocyte integrins in wound healing and chronic inflammation of the human periodontium. *Oral Diseases* 1996; **2**, 77-86.

31. Johnson NW, Hopps RM. Epithelial cell proliferation in gingiva of macaque monkeys studied by local injections of [^{3}H] thymidine. *Archs oral Biol* 1974; **19**, 265-268.

32. Bampton JL, Shirlaw PJ, Topley S, Weller P, Wilton JM. Human junctional epithelium, demonstration of a new marker, its growth in vitro and characterisation by lectin reactivity and keratin expression. *J. invest. Dermatol.* 1991; **96**, 708-717.

33. Narayanan AS, Page RC. Connective tissues of the periodontium. A summary of current work. *Coll Rel Res* 1983; **3**, 33-64.

34. Embery G, Waddington R. Gingival crevicular fluid, biomarkers of periodontal tissue activity. *Adv. Dent Res.* l994; **8**, 329-336.

35. Meng HX, James IT, Skingle L, Thompson O, Johnson NW. Collagen cross links in human gingival crevicular fluid. *J. Dent Res* 1991; **70**, 714 (Abs.)

36. Giannobile WV, Lynch SE, Denmark RG, Paquette DW, Fiorellini JP, Williams RC. Crevicular fluid osteocalcin and pyrodinoline cross-linked carboxy terminal telopeptide of type I Collagen (ICTP) as markers of rapid bone turnover in periodontitis. A pilot study in beagle dogs. *J. Clin Perio* 1995; **22**, 903-910.

37. Shibutani T, Nishino W, Shiraki M *et al.*. ELISA detection of glycosaminoglycans in gingival crevicular fluid. *J. Periodont Res* 1993; **28**, 17-20.

38. Powell J. Mediators of inflammation and tissue destructive metabolism in gingival crevicular fluid. *J dent. Res.* 1992; **71**,747 (Abs.)

39. Bartold PM. Turnover in periodontal connective tissues, dynamic homeostasis of cells, collagen and ground substances. *Oral Dis.* 1995 ; **1**, 238-252.

40. Rosin M, Benjamin P, Rogers P *et al.*. Elevated conversion of α2- macroglobulin to the complexed form in gingival crevicular fluid from adult periodontitis patients. *J. Perio Res* 1995; **30**, 436-444.

41. Petropoulou P, Winyard PG, Zhang Z, Hughes FJ, Curtis MA, Johnson NW. Molecular mechanisms of α-1-antitrypsin inactivation in chronic adult periodontitis. *J. Dent Res.* 1996; **75** , 1154 (Abs.)

42. Adonogianaki E, Mooney J, Kinane DF. Detection of stable and active periodontitis sites by clinical assessment and gingival crevicular acute phase protein levels. *J. Periodont Res.* 1996; **31**, 135-143.

43. Hart TC, Shapira L, Van Dyke TE. Neutophil defects as risk factors for periodontal diseases. *J Periodontol* 1994; **65**, 521-529.

44. Van Dyke TE, Vaikuntam J. Neutrophil function and dysfunction in periodontal disease. *Curr. Opin. Periodontol.* 1994; 19-27.

45. Kinane DF, Cullen CF, Johnston FA, Evans CW. Neutrophil chemotactic behaviour in patients with early onset forms of periodontitis, Assessment using the under agarose technique. *J. Clin Periodontol* 1989; **16**, 247-251.

46. Wilton JMA, Hurst TJ, Scott EE. Inhibition of polymorphonuclear phagocytosis by Porphyromonas gingivalis culture products in patients with adult periodontitis. *Archs Oral Biol* 1993; **38**, 285-289.

47. Gustafsson A, Asman B. Increased oxygen free radicals from peripheral neutrophils in adult periodontitis after Fc γ–receptor stimulation. *J. Clin Periodontol* 1996; **23**, 38-44.

48. Lamster IB, Grbic JT. Diagnosis of periodontal disease based on analysis of the host response. *Periodontology 2000* 1995; **7**, 83-89.

49. Armitage GC, Jeffcoat MK, Chadwick DE, *et al.*. Longitudinal evaluation of elastase as a marker of the progression of periodontitis. *J. Periodontol* 1994; **68**, 120-128.

50. Reynolds JJ. Collagenases and tissue inhibitors of metalloproteinases, a functional balance in tissue degradation. *Oral Dis.* 1996; **2**, 70-76.

51. Ding Y, Uitto VJ, Firth J *et al.*. Modulation of host matrix metalloproteinases by bacterial virulence factors relevant in human periodontal diseases. *Oral Dis*1995 ; **1**, 279-286.

52. McCulloch CAG. Host enzymes in GCF as diagnostic indicators of periodontitis. *J*. *Clin. Periodontol.* 1994; **21**, 497-506.

53. Eley BM, Cox SW. Correlation between gingival crevicular fluid dipeptidyl peptidase II and IV activity and periodontal attachment loss. A 2-year longitudinal study in chronic periodontitis patients. *Oral Diseases* 1995; **1**, 201-213.

54. Offenbacher S, Heasman PA, Collins JG. Production of host PGE2 secretion as a determinant of periodontal disease expression. *J. Periodontol.* 1993; **64**, 432-444.

55. Persson GR, Alves MEA, Chambers DA, *et al.*. A multicentre clinical trial of Perio Gard TM in distinguishing between diseased and healthy periodontal sites. (1) Study design, methodology and therapeutic outcome. *J. Clin Periodontol.* 1995; **22**, 794-803.

56. Howells GL. Cytokine networks in destructive periodontal disease; *Oral Dis.* 1995; **1**, 266-270.

57. Wilton JMA, Bampton JVM, Griffiths GS, Curtis MA, Life JS, Johnson NW. Interleukin-1 beta levels in gingival crevicular fluid from adults with previous evidence of destructive periodontitis, A cross sectional study. *J. Clin. Periodontol.* 1992; **19**, 53-57.

58. Wilton JM, Bampton JLM, Hurst TJ, Caves J, Powell JR. Interleukin - 1β and IgG subclass concentration in gingival crevicular fluid from patients with adult periodontitis. *Arch. Oral Biol* 1993; **38**, 55-60.

59. Wilton JMA, Austin AK, Rogers P, Johnson NW, Powell JR. Interleukin 6 in crevicular fluid from adult periodontitis subjects. *J. Dent Res* 1992; 71 Spec Issue, 698 (Abst).

60. Yavuzyilmaz E, Yamalik N, Bulut S, Ozen S, Ersoy F, Saatci U. The gingival crevicular fluid Interleukin-1β and tumour necrosis factor-α levels in patients with rapidly progressive periodontitis. *Aust. Dent. J.* 1995; **40**, 46-49.

61. Wilton JMA, Johnson NW, Curtis MA *et al.*. Specific antibody responses to subgingival plaque bacteria as aids to the diagnosis and prognosis of destructive periodontitis. *J. Clin. Periodontol* 1991; **18**, 1-15.

62. Ebersole JL, Taubman MA. The protective nature of host responses in periodontal diseases. *Periodont 2000* 1994; **5**, 112-141.

63. Wilton JMA, Hurst TJ, Sterne JAC, Caves J, Tilley C, Powell JR. Elevated levels of the IgGg2 subclass in serum from patients with a history of destructive periodontal disease, a case: control study. *J. Clin Periodontol* 1992; **19**, 318-321.

64. Wilton JMA, Hurst TJ, Austin AK. IgG subclass antibodies to Porphyromonas gingivalis in patients with destructive periodontal disease. *J. Clin. Periodontol.* 1992; **19**, 646-651.

65. Duncan AJ, Carman RJ, Harper FH, Griffiths GS, Curtis MA. Porphyromonas gingivalis: Presence of a species-specific antigen which is discriminatory in chronic inflammatory adult periodontal disease. *Micro Ecol Health Dis.* 1992; **5**, 15-20.

66. Gemmell E, Polak B, Reinhardt RA, Eccleston J, Seymour GJ. Antibody responses of Porphyromonas gingivalis-infected gingivitis and periodontitis subjects. *Oral Dis.* 1995; **1**, 63-69.

67. Curtis MA, Slaney JM, Carman RJ, Pemberton PA. Interaction of a trypsin-like enzyme of Porphyromonas gingivalis W83 with antithrombin III. *FEMS Microbiol. Lett.* 1993; **108**, 169-174.

68. Benjamin PA, Rogers P, U S, Johnson NW, Cole MF, Curtis MA. Increased titre and avidity of IgG antibodies to Porphyromonas gingivalis whole cells and a cell surface protein in subjects with adult periodontitis. *J. Perio Res.* 1997, **32,** 31-39.
69. Whitney C, Ant J, Moncla B, Johnson B, Page RC and Engel D. Serum immunogloblin G to Porphyromonas gingivalis in rapidly progressive periodontitis. Titer, avidity and subclass distribution. *Infect. Immun.* 1992; **60**, 2194-2200.
70. Mooney J, Kinane DF. Humoral immune responses to Porphyromonas gingivalis and Actinobacillus actinomycetemcomitans in adult periodontitis and rapidly progressive periodontitis. *Oral Microbiol Immunol* 1994; **9**, 321-326.
71. Mooney J, Adonogianaki E, Kinane DF. Relative avidity of serum antibodies to putative periodontal pathogens in periodontal diseases. *J. Periodont Res.* 1993; **28**, 444-450.
72. Mooney J, Adonogianaki E, Riggio MP *et al.*. Initial serum antibody titre to Porphyromonas gingivalis influences development of antibody avidity and success of therapy for chronic periodontitis. *Infect and Immun.* 1995; **63**, 3411-3416.
73. Ebersole JL, Capalli D, Steffen MJ. Longitudinal dynamics of infection and serum antibody in A. actinomycetemcomitans periodontitis. *Oral Dis.* 1995; **1**, 129-138.
74. Holbrook WP, Mooney J, Sigurdsson T, Kitsiou N, Kinane DF. Putative periodontal pathogens, antibody titres and avidities to them, in a longitudinal study of patients with resistant periodontitis. *Oral Dis.* 1996; **2**, 217-223.
75. Seymour GJ, Gemmell E, Kjeldsen M, Yamazaki K, Nakajima T, Hara K. Cellular immunity and hypersensitivity as components of periodontal destruction. *Oral Dis.* 1996; **2**, 96-101.
76. Gemmell E, Kjeldsen M, Yamasaki K, Nakajima T, Aldred MJ, Seymour GJ. Cytokine profiles of Porphyromas gingivalis infected subjects. *Oral Dis.* 1995; **1**, 139-146.
77. Okada H, Murakami S, Kitamura M *et al.*. Diagnostic strategies of periodontitis based on the molecular mechanisms of periodontal tissue destruction. *Oral Dis.* 1996; **2**, 87-95.
78. Proceedings of the 1996 World Workshop in Periodontics. American Academy of Periodontology.
79. Proceedings of the Second European Workshop on Periodontology. Lang NP and Karring T. Eds. Quintessance 1996.

7 Multifactorial approach to periodontal diagnosis

I. B. Lamster

Division of Periodontics, Columbia University School of Dental and Oral Surgery, 630 W. 168th Street, New York, NY 10032, USA

Today the evaluation of periodontal disease continues to rely upon clinical findings (probing depth, attachment level, measures of tissue inflammation) and standard intraoral radiography. While these procedures determine disease severity, and allow assignment of a diagnosis (i.e. acute inflammatory gingivitis, chronic adult periodontitis), they are subject to technical errors, and are poor predictors of sites at-risk for progressing disease. Newer concepts concerning the diagnosis of periodontal disease focus on identification of disease activity, which differs from disease severity. Disease activity is defined as probing attachment loss or radiographic evidence of alveolar bone loss occurring over a defined interval of time. A multifactorial approach to periodontal diagnosis is now being developed, and combines use of patient-derived clinical data and knowledge of the risk for active disease associated with the systemic status of the individual (i.e. presence of systemic disease such as diabetes mellitus, or smoking). If the patient is felt to be at risk for active disease due to the presence of clinical or systemic risk factors, consideration should be given to the use of pathogenesis-based evaluation of the periodontal lesion. This involves analysis of the microbial challenge and host response (based primarily on assessment of subgingival plaque for periodontal pathogens and analysis of gingival crevicular fluid for the local inflammatory response). These components are now being integrated into a risk profile for patients with periodontal disease. The application of this profile will likely result in improved clinical management of patients.

Introduction

Evaluation of the patient with periodontal disease today relies upon three components: the medical/dental history, clinical findings and radiographic findings. These three parts of the diagnostic process are intended to provide the clinician with information about systemic factors that could influence the development and treatment of periodontal disease, and the status of the periodontium in terms of the extent of existing disease.

The medical history has traditionally been part of the periodontal examination to determine if patients were able to tolerate dental treatment. Patients with recent, acute disease (*i.e.* history of myocardial infarction within the past 6 months) or patients with debilitating chronic diseases (*i.e.* malignancy, Alzheimer's disease) could be recognized as poor candidates for extensive periodontal and prosthodontic care. In addition, the medical history could be used to identify patients for which therapy had to be modified (*i.e.* a history of a seizure disorder being treated with phenantoin with resulting gingival hyperplasia, or pregnancy).

The clinical evaluation of periodontal disease relies primarily upon the evaluation of the depth of the probable crevice ("pocket" or probing depth), as well as qualitative or semiquantitative assessment of the degree of tissue inflammation as evaluated by bleeding following probing and tissue erythema. The amount of supragingival dental plaque is usually recorded, as are other measures of disease such as tooth mobility and gingival recession.

Radiographic findings provide a two-dimensional view of mineralized and other radioopaque structures of the teeth and jaws. Properly exposed and aligned periapical and bitewing radiographs can provide one measure of the remaining support for the dentition, as well as identify other findings that can influence the status of the periodontium, such as untreated periapical pathology and improperly contoured restorations.

The standard or traditional periodontal examination provides the clinician with information that can help to arrive at a diagnosis. The information gathered will allow differentiation of acute inflammatory gingivitis from chronic adult periodontitis, or chronic adult periodontitis from localized juvenile periodontitis. Furthermore, a traditional periodontal evaluation can help in the development of a treatment plan. Mobility, existing probing depth and total alveolar bone support can be used to evaluate teeth for periodontal therapy. The need for periodontal surgery to reduce deep probing depths, and the use of certain teeth in various restorative schemes are based on clinical and radiographic findings. The clinician's experience can often be a critical factor in these decisions.

Nevertheless, there are important inherent problems in the clinical and radiographic approach to diagnosis of periodontal disease as described above. We recognize that there are some inherent inaccuracies in the currently employed diagnostic protocol. First, some of the measurements are subject to inherent errors. For example, the measured probing depth can be influenced by many factors. The probe will pass into the tissue (through the junctional epithelium and into the lamina propria) when an inflammatory cell infiltrate is present in the connective tissue[1]. Greater force applied to the probe will cause deeper penetration, and without a stent being used clinicians cannot be sure if they are measuring probing depth at the same point on the tooth at each evaluation, or if the angle of probe entry into the crevice is constant from examination to examination. In addition, comparison between radiographs taken at different times is an inexact process unless a patient-specific positioning device is employed. These considerations lead to caution when

Natural History of Periodontal Disease: Continuous Progression

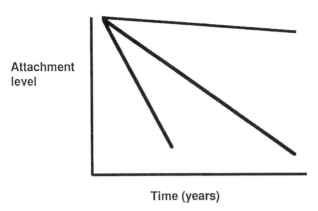

Time (years)

Figure 1 *Periodontal disease had been thought to progress at a near constant rate over time. The top line represents a patient who experienced minimal attachment loss, the middle line represents a patient who experienced moderate attachment loss and the bottom line represents a patient who experienced rapid and severe attachment loss.*

comparing data from different examinations. Furthermore, clinical variables at individual sites have been proven to be unreliable indicators of the risk for active disease[2]. In fact, the evaluation of the accuracy of clinical findings as predictors of probing attachment loss (PAL = demonstrated loss of support along the root surface over a defined interval of time) were associated with a false positive rate of 95% to 97%. These studies have determined that relatively few sites undergo disease progression over a few months to a year[3]. Consequently, many sites with deeper probing depths and evidence of tissue inflammation will not experience PAL over the defined time interval.

New approaches for the evaluation of the periodontal patient

During the past decade, there have been a number of important conceptual advances relating to the evaluation of the patient with periodontal disease. Application of research findings will allow this process to be more quantitative.

Disease severity versus disease activity

We can now begin to discuss periodontal disease in the context of both cross-sectional and longitudinal evaluations. Disease severity can be defined as the evaluation of existing periodontal disease. Parameters such as probing depth, attachment level, bleeding on probing, plaque accumulation, presence of suppuration and tooth mobility are collected, as well as alveolar bone support and other pathological findings on traditional bitewing and periapical intraoral radiographs. This type of assessment allows assignment of a diagnosis (*i.e.* acute inflammatory gingivitis, chronic adult periodontitis, localized juvenile periodontitis), as well as help with the development of a treatment plan (a needs assessment, to determine the type of periodontal therapy, prosthodontic therapy, endodontic therapy, *etc.*). Nevertheless, this is different than assessment of disease activity, which is the progression of periodontal disease as determined by PAL or radiographic evidence of alveolar bone support. PAL is the loss of support along the root surface as evidenced by increased measurement from a fixed point (the cementoenamel junction or other fixed point such as provided by a prepared stent). Quantitative evidence of radiographic bone loss can be provided by subtraction radiography[4]. The importance of identification of active disease relates to our improved understanding of the natural history of periodontal disease. Disease progression was thought to be slow, with loss of support occurring at a mean constant rate over time. Periodontal disease is now recognized to follow a pattern typical of chronic disorders with periods of exacerbation and remission (Figures 1 and 2). Longer periods of stable disease are punctuated by shorter periods of active progression[3]. This finding has obvious clinical implications. Identification of an active phase (or the increased risk for

Natural History of Periodontal Disease: Discontinuous Progression

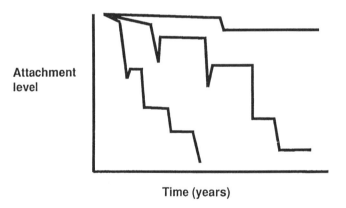

Attachment level

Time (years)

Figure 2 *Periodontal disease is now considered to be episodic, with periods of exacerbation (activity) and remission (inactivity). The top line represents a patient who experienced minimal attachment loss, with long periods of inactivity (horizontal component) and only one episode of active disease (vertical component). The middle line represents a patient who experienced moderate attachment loss, and the disease is characterized by periods of inactivity,as well as active disease (downward vertical component) followed by repair (upward vertical component). The bottom line represents a patient who experienced rapid and severe attachment loss, and the disease is characterized by periods of inactivity and activity. Little repair is observed.*

entering an active phase) should necessitate a different approach to treatment when compared to therapy required for a patient with quiescent disease.

New approaches for evaluating the periodontal tissues

The examination of the periodontal tissues has relied upon the manual periodontal probe for many decades. As noted earlier, there are problems associated with the use of this device. In addition to variables such as force applied to the probe and the angle of insertion, the inherently complex anatomy associated with deeper probing depths on molar teeth leads to concern about significance of the findings.

New devices for assessing the periodontal tissues have recently been introduced to provide a more quantitative evaluation of periodontal pathology, and in some cases offer a different measure of disease. Examples can be provided.

To respond to some of the limitations of manual probing, automated computer-linked probing devices have been introduced. These devices (*i.e.* the Florida Probe) have in common the use of a fixed force and automatic data recording for ease of data collection and retrieval[5]. Principles of construction may differ, but the intent is to reduce operator variability. These devices have been shown to reduce the standard deviation of repeat measurement, and as a result reduce the threshold for identifying active disease. While proving to be useful research tools, these instruments have not found widespread acceptance in clinical dental practice.

Tooth mobility is generally assessed by placing dental instruments on the buccal and lingual/palatal aspects of teeth, and then alternately tapping on the tooth surfaces to determine if the teeth are firm or mobile. Mobility is assessed on an semiquantitative scale (*i.e.* 0 to 3, with the score based on the number of millimeters of movement, or on relative movement ranging between no mobility and severe mobility characterized by depressibility of the tooth in its socket). An electronic mobilometer has been introduced to quantitate movement of the tooth in its socket[6]. This device utilizes an impeller to deliver a standard laterally-directed force. The tooth moves in response to the force, and the time required to rebound to the original position is quantitated on a scale ranging from 0 to +50. Negative numbers will be displayed if the tooth is ankylosed and does not have physiologic movement. The diagnostic significance of tooth mobility is not well defined. While the presence of tooth mobility has been shown to be associated with an increased risk for probing attachment loss, this clinical finding does not occur alone, and is often associated with other indicators of past disease such as furcation involvement[7]. Furthermore, occlusal forces and endodontic involvement can also influence tooth mobility. Evaluation of the stability of dental implants may offer a valid clinical application for this device.

The gingival crevice is the contact surface between the subgingival microflora and the host. The evaluation of the host response in the crevicular environment is currently determined by semiquantitative or qualitative means such as bleeding following probing. In an attempt to more specifically define events in the crevicular environment that occur with development of periodontal disease, quantitative devices to evaluate other aspects of the lesion have been introduced. An intracrevicular temperature probe has been developed to determine the temperature within the crevice[8]. An increase in temperature is one of the hallmarks of an acute inflammatory response, and represents increased blood flow to an inflamed site. The handpiece is shaped as a periodontal probe, and the disposable tips contain a thermacouple device that allows assessment of temperature in increments of $0.1°C$. The temperature is referenced to the core temperature taken sublingually. Differences in temperature have been observed between crevices from periodontally-diseased teeth versus healthy teeth, with the most pronounced differences noted in the anterior region. In longitudinal studies, elevated intracrevicular temperature has been associated with an increased risk of PAL for teeth with probing depths of less than 4mm[9].

There is interest in the development of other intracrevicular test systems. This type of device would offers the clinician the opportunity to test for some disease-associated change at the site of the lesion. As an example, an intracrevicular sulfide-detection probe has recently been introduced for evaluation of periodontal disease. This probe will detect volatile sulfur compounds (VSC), which can be by-products of metabolism by Gram-negative microorganisms. This device provides a digital readout to quantitate the amount of intracrevicular VSC.

There recently has been considerable interest in the diagnostic potential of assessing the microbial challenge and host response in periodontal disease. The focus of this approach has been the specific identification of putative periodontal pathogens associated with periodontitis, as well as identification of specific inflammatory mediators associated with the host response to the subgingival microflora. This pathogenesis-based evaluation of the periodontal patient has been a major focus of the effort to develop diagnostic tests for periodontal disease. Specifically, the association of a number of subgingival microorganisms with the most severe forms of periodontal disease (*i.e. Porphyromonas gingivalis, Actinobacillus actinomycetemcomitans* and *Bacteroides forsythus*) has been recognized[10]. In addition, while many host-derived immune and inflammatory mediators have been identified in gingival crevicular fluid (GCF), a limited number of these have been shown to identify a patient's risk for active periodontal disease (PAL or alveolar bone loss). Specifically, prostaglandin E_2 (PGE$_2$;[11]), the lysosomal glycohydrolase β-glucuronidase (βG;[12]), the serine protease neutrophil elastase (NE;[13]), as well as the cytoplasmic enzyme aspartate aminotransferase (AST;[14]) in GCF have all been shown to hold promise as diagnostic tests, and serve as surrogate markers for active disease.

The goal of identifying the risk for active periodontal disease represents a new approach to both categorizing patients and choosing the appropriate type of therapy for each individual. In an era of cost containment in health care, however, these tests must be used under appropriate situations.

In summary, it is apparent that our diagnostic paradigm for periodontal disease is shifting from determining disease severity to identification of the risk for disease activity. Recognizing that assessment of the risk for disease activity by relatively expensive diagnostic tests must be used judiciously, new schemes should be developed for patient evaluation. In the next section a new approach to the diagnostic process will be proposed.

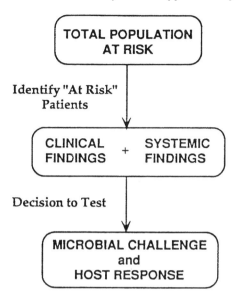

Figure 3 *Flow chart for multifactorial approach to periodontal diagnosis. After collection of clinical data, and establishing a diagnosis, consideration is given to the risk for active disease associated with patient-derived clinical variables such as age and mean attachment level, as well as the risk for periodontitis associated with systemic diseases/modifiers such as diabetes mellitus and cigarette smoking. If the risk for active disease is high, the clinician may decide to proceed with pathogenesis-based testing, including evaluation of the subgingival microbial challenge and host response in gingival crevicular fluid.*

Multifactorial approach to periodontal diagnosis

The proposed new paradigm for evaluation of the patient with periodontal disease is a three-tiered process that utilizes data from recent longitudinal studies that have improved our understanding of the pathogenesis of periodontal disease, as well as helped to identify specific risk factors for occurrence of active disease (Figure 3). The first tier is the collection of traditional periodontal examination data, including the evaluation of probing depth, existing probing attachment loss, and bleeding on probing. Together with an appropriate radiographic series, these data can, as noted earlier, help the clinician in classifying the type of disease, as well as identifying specific problems that need to be corrected. The next tier is comprised of two parts. The first part represents a relatively new use for the clinical data: the calculation of patient (mean) values to be used for identifying the risk for active disease. The second part employs recent studies evaluating the risk for periodontitis associated with modification of the patient's systemic status.

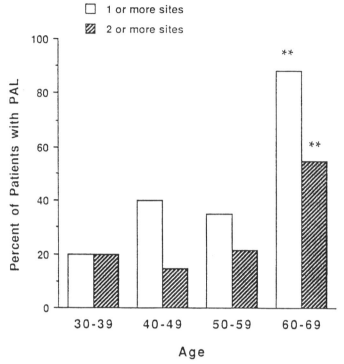

Figure 4 *The relationship of probing attachment loss (PAL) and age. Adults with chronic periodontitis were monitored for 6 months, and PAL was characterized for the patient as 1 or more sites, or 2 or more sites demonstrating at least 2.5mm of PAL. Age was stratified by decade (30-39 years N=10, 40-49 years N=30, 50-59 years N=25, 60-69 years N=9). A statistically significant difference was observed between the 60-69 year old age group and the other groups (**p< .005).*

Clinical data used to identify the risk for active periodontal disease

A study was conducted to identify clinical parameters that could be used to identify the patient at risk for active periodontal disease as defined by PAL[15]. A total of 75 adults with chronic periodontitis were evaluated. The clinical and epidemiological parameters collected at the initiation of monitoring were evaluated in reference to PAL during the following 6 months. The mean values (calculated for each patient as an average of all sites) for probing depth (mm), recession (mm), attachment level (mm), bleeding (%) and number of teeth, as well as the epidemiologic variables of age, health status, gender, marital status, level of education and occupation were related to active disease.

The results were tabulated relative to the detection of PAL of 2.5 mm at one or more sites, or two or more sites. Thirty-one of 75 patients (41%) demonstrated at least one PAL site, while 16 patients (21%) demonstrated at least two sites with PAL.

The parameters of health status, gender, marital status, level of education and occupation failed to demonstrate a statistically significant relationship to occurrence of PAL, though we did observe a trend relating PAL to marital status (increased risk when married) and being male. There was, however, a significant relationship of PAL and increasing age. 89% of individuals over 60 displayed at least one site with PAL, while 56% displayed at least two sites (Figure 4). Compared to PAL occurring in the youngest age group of 30 to 39 years, the relative risk of PAL in this older age group was 4.5 for at least 1 site and 2.8 for at least 2 sites.

Evaluation of baseline mean clinical parameters to the risk for PAL revealed that existing periodontal disease as defined by mean attachment loss (MAL) was a significant risk factor for active disease. 85% of patients with MAL of 5.0mm demonstrated at least one site experiencing PAL, while 62% of these individuals demonstrated at least 2 active sites (Figure 5). Similar patterns were observed for mean probing depth and mean recession. Bleeding on probing was divided into

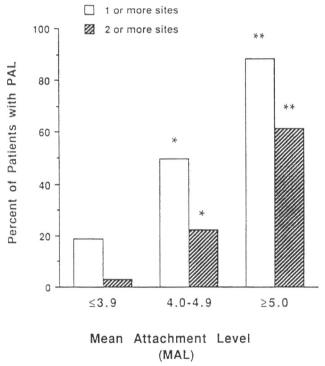

Figure 5 *The relationship of probing attachment loss (PAL) and mean attachment level. Adults with chronic periodontitis were monitored for 6 months, and PAL was characterized for the patient as 1 or more sites, or 2 or more sites demonstrating at least 2.5mm of PAL. Mean attachment level was stratified as less than or equal to 3.9mm, 4.0-4.9mm and equal to a greater than 5.0mm. Statistically significant differences were observed between the ≤3.9mm group and the 4.0-4.9mm group (*p < .01) and the 4.0-4.9mm group and the <.005 mm group (**p < .005).*

categories of 0-20%, 21-40%, 41-60% and greater than 60% of sites. An increased incidence of % BOP was associated with increased risk for PAL. For those individuals that displayed the most bleeding at baseline, 63% had at least one site and 40% had at least 2 sites of PAL.

Using both correlation analysis and logistic modelling, it was determined that age and MAL were independent risk factors for PAL. As noted, other clinical parameters were associated with the risk for PAL, but these measures were correlated to MAL, and MAL demonstrated the strongest association of any of the clinical parameters and PAL.

This study demonstrated that patient-derived variables could be used to identify individuals at risk for occurrence of active disease. It is important to remember, however, that the patients studied in this trial were specifically selected for certain criteria, including the presence of a minimum of 18 natural teeth. Some controversy exists concerning the susceptibility of older individuals to periodontal disease. For example, there is data suggesting that development of gingivitis is slower in older individuals[16]. Nevertheless, the overwhelming concensus is that aging is a risk factor for periodontitis.

Calculation of mean clinical parameters can be performed quite easily as an extension of a routine evaluation of patients in the clinical setting. In addition, recent reports concerning systemic risk factors for periodontal disease can provide additional information about the status of patients who present for treatment.

Systemic risk factors

A number of systemic risk factors for periodontal disease have been identified in the literature. Among the most thoroughly studied are cigarette smoking[17], diabetes mellitus[18], HIV infection[19] and genetic/familial factors[20]. Recent data has suggested that the increased risk for periodontal disease associated with a number of systemic disorders/modifiers is identifiable, and hence can be used as part of a risk profile for periodontal disease.

Cigarette Smoking

The health hazards associated with cigarette smoking are well recognized, and include increased risk for malignancy and cardiovascular disease. Recent evidence has implicated cigarette smoking as a major risk factor for periodontal disease[17].

Studies have suggested that gingival inflammation is reduced in patients who smoke[21,22]. In contrast, recent studies have suggested that periodontitis as measured by existing attachment loss and alveolar bone loss is more severe in smokers versus nonsmokers. Haber and Kent[23] conducted a case-control study and evaluated both clinical and radiographic measures of periodontal disease. Comparing patients with moderate to advanced periodontitis to dental patients without periodontal disease, the age and gender adjusted odds ratio of having periodontitis if an individual is a current smoker was 3.3, and 2.1 if the patient had been a smoker.

Similarly, Grossi et al.[24] used mean existing attachment loss as the outcome variable, and examined 1426 adults in Erie County in New York. The relative risk for attachment loss was 2.05 for light smokers (5.3-15.0 packyears) and 4.75 for heavy smokers (30.1-150.0 packyears).

The effect of smoking on periodontal disease may be relatively more pronounced in younger individuals. Studying adults 20-33 years of age, Linden and Mullally determined the odds ratio of smokers versus nonsmokers presenting with established periodontitis was 14.1[25]. Severe attachment loss (6mm) was observed in 19% of smokers and 3% of nonsmokers.

Alveolar bone loss has also been shown to be greater in smokers versus nonsmokers. Examining a population of adults with good oral hygiene, Bergstrom and Eliasson [26] evaluated alveolar bone height as a percent of root length, and determined alveolar support for smokers versus nonsmokers. Smokers displayed slightly less support (78% versus 83%), but the difference was significant. In a larger study, Grossi *et al.*[27] examined risk factors for alveolar bone loss in 1361 adults. A close association of smoking to alveolar bone loss was observed. The odds ratio of severe bone loss occurring in light smokers (0-5.2 packyears) compared to nonsmokers was 1.48. Heavy smokers (30 packyears) demonstrated an odds ratio of 7.28.

A review of this field by Bergstrom and Preber[17] emphasized that patients who smoke are at increased risk for development of periodontal disease. Depending on the outcome variable chosen, the relative risk is 2.5 to 6.0.

Diabetes mellitus
An association of periodontal pathology and diabetes has been recognized for many years. Diabetes is generally divided into type 1, or insulin-dependent diabetes mellitus (IDDM) and type 2, or noninsulin-dependent diabetes mellitus (NIDDM). The population distribution is 1:8 for type 1:type 2. Many reports have examined the relationship of diabetes mellitus to periodontal disease [18], and the importance of this risk factor has been emphasized by studies of the Pima Indians in Arizona. Having access to a large population, and comparing diabetics and nondiabetics, NIDDM was associated with a relative risk of 2.8 for the presence of attachment loss and a relative risk of 3.4 for the presence of radiographic bone loss [28]. When age was considered, the greatest differences were observed for younger individuals. For example, the relative risk of having at least one site with 5mm of probing attachment loss was 4.8 for diabetics between 15 and 24, but only 1.1 for diabetics older than 55 years of age. Similarly, Grossi *et al.* [24] found that diabetes was associated with an odds ratio of 2.3 for the presence of probing attachment loss.

The data concerning IDDM and periodontal disease is not as extensive as that relating NIDDM and periodontal disease. Nevertheless, the available information suggests an increased risk for periodontal disease in individuals with type I diabetes [29]. Additional evidence indicating that IDDM is also a true risk factor for periodontal disease is provided by data demonstrating increased periodontal disease in patients with long-term diabetes or diabetic complications. Hugoson *et al.* [30] demonstrated a greater number of sites with at least 6 mm of probing depth and more alveolar bone loss in certain long-term diabetics compared to short-term diabetics or nondiabetics. In addition, diabetics with retinopathy have been shown to have five times the risk for periodontal disease as compared to those individuals who did not have retinopathy [31].

In summary, diabetes appears to be a systemic disorder that can be considered an important risk factor for periodontal disease. The risk has been demonstrated in a number of large scale studies, and while apparently not as great as what is observed for cigarette smoking, the relative risk is 2.0 to 3.0.

Pathogenesis-based evaluation of the patient with periodontal disease

There has been enormous interest in the use of laboratory measures of periodontal disease to evaluate the patient's risk for active disease (PAL, loss of crestal alveolar bone as assessed by radiography). This interest developed as a result of improved understanding of the nature of periodontal disease, with understanding of the role of both the microbial challenge and host response in development of disease. This topic has been the subject of a number of major reviews [32, 33], and will be discussed briefly. This pathogenesis-based evaluation of periodontal disease represents the third tier in the proposed multifactorial approach to patient evaluation. Pathogenesis-based evaluation of the periodontal patient currently relies upon analysis of samples of subgingival plaque, gingival fluid and serum for both the nature of the microbial challenge and the host response to that challenge.

The attempt to identify specific bacteria associated with periodontitis has been the subject of intensive research over the past 25 years. The most recent findings suggest that a group of microorganisms appear to be associated with the development of periodontal disease in the susceptible host. Specifically, organisms such as *Porphyromonas gingivalis, Bacteroides forsythus* and *Actinobacillus actinomycetem-comitans* have been shown to be present in the subgingival environment in patients with periodontal disease [34, 35].

The diagnostic significance of infection with specific microbial pathogens for progression of periodontal disease has been examined. Haffajee and co-workers [36] determined that individuals with probing attachment loss occurring at many sites had *lower* levels of microorganisms than patients demonstrating a limited number of sites with attachment loss. That study also emphasized the importance of other factors for the active event, such as increased levels of certain protective bacterial species as decreasing the risk for probing attachment loss, and elevated temperature as a requirement for the presence of specific pathogens. They stated that active periodontal disease was a multifactorial process involving, among other factors, the subgingival plaque microorganisms and the host response.

A study by Wolff *et al.* [37] examined the relationship of *P. gingivalis* and *A. actinomycetemcomitans* to progressive attachment loss in a group of individuals selected for the presence or absence of these microorganisms in subgingival plaque at the baseline examination. No clear trends were observed that could indicate that a threshold level of 10^3 organisms was a risk factor for progressive disease. However, just the presence of *P. gingivalis* at baseline was associated with an increased risk for probing attachment loss. The finding of the variable relationship of the presence of certain indicator bacteria to progressive disease has been observed by other investigators. The importance of the bacterial challenge to progression of disease has been examined by Wennstrom *et al.*[38]. They determined that the absence of specific pathogens (*P. gingivalis, A. actinomycetemcomitans* and *Prevotella intermedia*) was a better predictor of the absence of disease progression than the presence of the organism was an indicator of risk for progression. These data emphasized the importance of the host response to the microbial challenge.

The microbiological findings suggest that progressive probing attachment loss is not solely dependent upon the presence of putative periodontal pathogens. In evaluating this conclusion, the role of the host response must be considered as the important alternate variable. Consequently, the analysis of the acute inflammatory, cellular immune and humoral response in periodontal disease may offer important diagnostic information, and analysis of these responses has been proposed as part of the diagnostic evaluation of patients with periodontitis.

Evaluation of the host response as part of a diagnostic evaluation of patients with periodontal disease relies upon identification of specific host mediators in GCF, blood and saliva [39]. During the past few years the application of GCF analysis has received the most attention. While numerous mediators representing the acute inflammatory, humoral immune and cellular immune responses have been identified in GCF, a very limited number have been shown to have a relationship to the risk for disease progression as measured by PAL or radiographic bone loss. Four mediators associated with the acute inflammatory response have been most intensely studied, including the arachidonic acid metabolite prostaglandin E_2 [11] the neutrophil lysosomal enzymes β-glucuronidase [12] and elastase [13] and the cytoplasmic enzyme aspartate aminotransferase [14].

The sampling of GCF has generally been accomplished using precut methylcellulose filter paper strips [11, 12, 14], or a specially prepared sampling device of similar size with assay reagents contained on the sample collector [13]. These sampling devices are easy to use and very minimally invasive. This allows repeated sampling of sites/teeth over time.

The analysis of the PGE_2 concentration in GCF from patients with periodontitis was shown by Offenbacher *et al.* to identify the risk for active disease as defined by PAL of 3mm [11]. A GCF sample was collected from each tooth, and a patient mean concentration was determined. Using a threshold level of 66.2 mg/ml, which was 2 standard deviations above the concentration of PGE_2 in GCF from healthy subjects, they determined that elevated PGE_2 in GCF was associated with evidence of PAL 3 months later. The investigators calculated that PGE_2 had a sensitivity of 76% and specificity of 96% as a diagnostic test for active periodontitis.

Lamster *et al.* [12] evaluated the relationship of the neutrophil marker β-glucuronidase in GCF to PAL in a multicenter study of 140 patients. One GCF sample was collected from all teeth excluding third molars, and algorithms were created to determine the relationship of elevated levels of the enzyme (upper 10% of total enzyme activity) in 2 or 3 GCF samples to the occurrence of PAL of 2.0 or 2.5 mm at 2 or 3 sites in the mouth. The algorithms related the levels of enzyme at baseline, and two weeks and 3 months after conservative therapy, to PAL detected at 6 months. Given these criteria, elevated βG activity was associated with a relative risk of PAL of 6 to 14, and the total predictive value of βG as a diagnostic test was 81% to 90%. A similar relationship of neutrophil elastase in GCF to active disease [13] supports the concept that disease progression can be associated with an exuberant neutrophil response [40].

Lastly, an association between elevated levels of the cytoplasmic enzyme aspartate aminotransferase and PAL has been described. A study by Chambers *et al.* [14] followed 31 patients who were on maintenance recall. Individuals were seen every 3 months for 2 years, with 2 sites being followed in each individual. The odds ratio of PAL being associated with elevated levels of AST was 9 to 16, which was greater than the odds ratio relating AST and gingivitis (5 to 9), or AST and inactive periodontitis (3 to 12).

While elevated levels of inflammatory mediators have been shown to be associated with an increased risk of active disease, it is recognized that the periodontal lesion represents a complex interplay of the microbial challenge and the multifaceted host response. Other aspects of the host response that may ultimately be included in a diagnostic profile include analysis of the serum antibody titer to putative pathogens [41]. Furthermore, a complete diagnostic evaluation of the periodontal patient may involve the concurrent evaluation of the microbial challenge and host response. This may help to accurately identify at-risk patients [42].

Conclusions

The following general conclusions can be drawn from the preceeding review.
(1) Periodontal diagnosis should be viewed as a stepwise process. Depending upon history and individual patient considerations, different patients will require different diagnostic evaluations.
(2) Pathogenesis-based evaluation for the periodontal patient is an important, new component in the diagnostic process. Application of these tests to the clinical setting will ultimately be available in a variety of configurations, but tests that can be performed in the dental office will be most widely utilized.
(3) The ultimate result of this comprehensive approach to periodontal diagnosis will be improved patient management. This should result in improved clinical care as treatment can be directed to the specific needs of each patient.

References

1. Fowler C, Garrett S, Crigger M, Egelberg J. Histologic probe position in treated and untreated human periodontal tissues. *J Clin Periodontol* 1982;**9**, 373-385.
2. Haffajee AD, Socransky SS, Goodson JM. Clinical parameters as predictors of destructive periodontal disease activity. *J Clin Periodontol* 1983;**10**, 257-265.
3. Socransky SS, Haffajee AD, Goodson JM, Lindhe J. New concepts of destructive periodontal disease. *J Clin Periodontol* 1984;**11**, 21-32.
4. Jeffcoat MK, Wang I-C, Reddy MS. Radiographic diagnosis in periodontics. *Periodontol 2000* 1995, **7**, 54-68.

5. Gibbs CH, Hirschfeld JW, Lee JG, *et al.* Description and clinical evaluation of a new computerized periodontal probe, the Florida probe. *J Clin Peirodontol* 1988;**15**, 137-144.

6. Schulte W. The new Periotest® method. *Compend Contin Educ Dent* 1988;Suppl no. **12**, S410-S417.

7. Wang H-L, Burgett FG, Shyr Y, Ramfjord S. The influence of molar furcation involvement and mobility on future clinical periodontol attachment loss. *J Periodontol* 1994;**65**, 25-29.

8. Kung RTV, Ochs B, Goodson JM. Temperature as a periodontal diagnostic. *J Clin Periodontol* 1990;**17**, 557-563.

9. Haffajee AD, Socransky SS, Goodson JM. Subgingival temperature (II). Relation to future periodontal attachment loss. *J Clin Periodontol* 1992;**19**, 409-416.

10. Socransky SS, Haffajee AD. The bacterial etiology of destructive periodontal disease, current concepts. *J Periodontol* 1992;**63**, 322-331.

11. Offenbacher S, Odle BM, Van Dyke TE. The use of crevicular fluid prostaglandin E$_2$ levels as a predictor of periodontal attachment loss. *J Periodont Res* 1986;**21**, 101-112.

12. Lamster IB, Holmes LG, Williams Gross KB *et al.* The relationship of β-glucuronidase activity in crevicular fluid to probing attachment loss in patients with adult periodontititis. Findings from a multicenter study. *J Clin Periodontol* 1995;**22**, 36-44.

13. Palcanis KG, Larjava IK, Wells BR, *et al.* Elastase is an indicator of periodontal disease progression. *J Periodontol* 1992;**63**, 237-242.

14. Chambers DA, Imrey PB, Cohen RL, Crawford JM, Alves MEAF, McSwiggin TA. A longitudinal study of aspartate aminotransferase in human gingival crevicular fluid. *J Periodont Res* 1991;**26**, 65-74.

15. Grbic JT, Lamster IB, Celenti RS, Fine JB. Risk indicators for future clinical attachment loss in adult periodontitis. Patient variables. *J Periodontol* 1991;**62**, 322-329.

16. van der Velden U. Effect of age on the periodontium. J *Clin Periodontol* 1984;**11**, 281-294.

17. Bergström J, Preber H. Tobacco as a risk factor. *J Periodontol* 1994;**65**, 545-550.

18. Oliver RC, Tervonen T. Diabetes - a risk factor for periodontitis in adults? *J Periodontol* 1994;**65,** 530-538.

19. Lamster I, Grbic J, Fine J, *et al.* A critical review of periodontal disease as a manifestations of HIV infection. In: Greenspan JS, Greenspan D, eds. *Oral manifestations of HIV infection.* Chicago, Quintessence Books, 1995, 247-256.

20. Michalowicz B. Genetic and heritable risk factors in periodontal disease. *J Periodontol* 1994;**65**, 479-488.

21. Bergström J, Floderus-Myrhed B. Co-twin control study of the relationship between smoking and some periodontal disease factors. *Community Dent Oral Epidemiol* 1983;**11**, 113-116.

22. Bergström J, Preber H. The influence of cigarette smoking on the development of experimental gingivitis. *J Periodont Res* 1986;**21**, 668-676.

23. Haber J, Kent RL. Cigarette smoking in a periodontal practice. *J Periodontol* 1992;**63**, 100-106.

24. Grossi SG, Zambon JJ, Ho AW, *et al.* Assessment of risk for periodontal disease. I. Risk indicators for attachment loss. *J Periodontol* 1994;**65**, 260-267.

25. Linden GJ, Mullally BH. Cigarette smoking and periodontal destruction in young adults. J Periodontol 1994;65, 718-723.

26. Bergström J, Eliasson S. Cigarette smoking and alveolar bone height in subjects with a high standard of oral hygiene. *J Clin Periodontol* 1987;**14**, 466-469.
27. Grossi SG, Genco RJ, Machtei EE, *et al.* Assessment of risk for periodontal disease. II. Risk indicators for alveolar bone loss. *J Periodontol* 1995;**66**, 23-29.
28. Emrich LJ, Shlossman M, Genco RJ. Periodontol disease in non-insulin dependent diabetes mellitus. *J Periodontol* 1991;**62**, 123-131.
29. Glavind L, Lund B, Löe H. The relationship between periodontal state and diabetes duration, insulin dosage and retinal changes. *J Periodontol* 1968;**39**, 341-347.
30. Hugoson A, Thorstensson H, Falk H, Kuylenstierna J. Periodontal conditions in insulin-dependent diabetics. *J Clin Periodontol* 1989;**16**, 215-223.
31. Löe H. Periodontal disease. The sixth complication of diabetes mellitus. *Diabetes Care* 1993;**16** (Suppl 1), 329-334.
32. Listgarten MA. Microbiological testing in the diagnosis of periodontal disease. *J Periodontol* 1992;**63**, 332-337.
33. Page RC. Host response tests for diagnosing periodontal diseases. *J Periodontol* 1992;**63**, 356-366.
34. Slots J, Bragd L, Wikström M, Dahlen G. The occurrence of Actinobacillus actinomycetemcomitans, Bacteroides gingivalis and Bacteroides intermedius in destructive periodontal disease in adults. *J Clin Periodontol* 1986;**13**, 570-577.
35. Savitt ED, Strzempko MN, Vaccaro KK, Peros WJ, French CK. Comparison of cultural methods and DNA probe analyses for the detection of Actinobacillus actinomycetemcomitans, Bacteroides gingivalis and Bacteroides intermedius in subgingival plaque samples. *J Periodontol* 1988;**59**, 431-438.
36. Haffajee AD, Socransky SS. Microbial risk indicators for periodontal attachment loss. *J Periodontol Res* 1991;**26**, 293-296.
37. Wolff L, Dahlen G, Aeppli D. Bacteria as risk markers for periodontitis. *J Periodontol* 1994;**64**, 498-510.
38. Wennström JL, Dahlen G, Svensson J, Nyman S. Actinobacillus actinomycetemcomitans, Bacteroides gingivalis and Bacteroides intermedius. Predictors of attachment loss? *Oral Microbiol Immunol* 1987;**2**, 158-163.
39. Lamster IB, Grbic JT. Diagnosis of periodontal disease based on analysis of the host response. *Periodontal 2000* 1995;**7**, 83-99.
40. Weiss JJ. Tissue destruction by neutrophils. *N Engl J Med* 1989;**320**, 365-376.
41. Ebersole JL. Systemic humoral immune responses in periodontal disease. *Crit Rev Oral Biol Med* 1990;**1**, 283-331.
42. Lamster IB, Smith QT, Celenti RS, Singer RE, Grbic JT. Development of a risk profile for periodontal disease. Microbial and host response factors. *J Periodontol* 1994;**65**, 511-520.

8 Host-parasite interactions in periodontal diseases

Mariano Sanz

Facultad de Odontologia, Universidad Complutense Madrid, Spain

Gingivitis and periodontitis are caused by bacteria that colonise the gingival crevice and attach to tooth surfaces. The pathogenic potential of bacteria within the plaque varies from individual to individual and from site to site. Small amounts of plaque in a healthy person can be tolerated without causing gingival or periodontal disease, probably because the control exerted by host defence mechanisms. When specific bacteria within the plaque increase to significant numbers and produce virulent factors beyond the individual patient's control threshold, the balance shifts from health to disease. Disease may also occur as a result of a reduction in the host defence capacity. Therefore, host defences play an important role in the pathogenesis of many types of periodontal diseases by directly contributing to the disease process or by modulating the effects of the bacteria. The immune system plays a key role in limiting the bacterial infections to the gingival crevice or the tissues within the vicinity. The immune system also orchestrates the alterations of the connective tissues in a complex remodelling process involving cycles of destruction and reconstruction.

The response against bacteria is normally mediated by leukocytes, as most periodontal pathogens are known to be resistant to the antimicrobial mechanisms of serum[1]. This response takes place first as an acute inflammatory response mediated by neutrophils, and if this bacterial infection is not resolved then a chronic inflammation process begins. This chronic inflammatory response is mediated mainly by macrophages and lymphocytes. This chronic immune cells elaborate cytokines and other effector molecules which induce the differentiation and activation of local immune cells and potentially signal the destruction or repair of the surrounding connective tissues[2-4].

Innate immune responses:neutrophil - bacteria interaction

Polymorphonuclear leukocytes or neutrophils (PMNs) are the cellular hallmark of an acute inflammatory response. These cells are the most numerous (90%) of the leukocytes found in the peripheral blood, and they constitute the body's first line of defence against microbial attack.

On initiation of the microbial challenge, the neutrophil responds to stimulus by a series of well co-ordinated mechanisms that can be categorised as follows:

(1) *Adherence*. This process involves margination and attachment of the PMNs to vascular endothelium via specific molecules present on the surface of the PMN and the endothelial cell[5]. There are two phases in this process, a selectin-dependent phase and an integrin dependent-phase. In the first phase inflammation causes endothelium to express P-selectin and to synthesise E-selectin. This molecules increase the binding between the leukocyte and the endothelial cell. Inflammation also induces endothelium to produce interleukin-8 (IL-8) which induces the leukocyte to express b2-integrins. This integrins interact with endothelial intercellular adhesion molecules (ICAMs) and mediate the trans-endothelial migration of the PMNs. The neutrophil eventually works its way to the serosal side of the endothelium and enters the connective tissues.

(2) *Chemotaxis*. This process is the directed movement of a cell along a chemical gradient. The neutrophil is attracted by chemical signals from multiple sources what requires that this cell possesses specific chemotaxin receptors for all this molecules. Among these include complement fragment C5a, FLMP (a synthetic bacterial peptide), and the arachidonic metabolite LTB4. The chemotactic response is initiated following binding of a ligand to its specific receptor on the surface of the PMN what creates a stimulus that triggers a response through a defined activation pathway.

(3) *Recognition and phagocytosis*. The invading organisms are coated with molecules called opsonins. Opsonization refers to the process of coating a particle with recognisable molecules to enable phagocytic ingestion. There are two types of opsonins to be considered: the complement metabolite, iC3b and immunoglobulin G (IgG). Both the alternative and classic pathways of complement activation produced C3b bound covalently to the target surface. The PMNs possess a specific receptor CR1 that binds to C3b to form iC3b which facilitates the endocytosis. Phagocytic adhesion is also mediated by antibody using the surface receptors denominated Fc receptors. Once the attachment between the neutrophil and the bacteria occurs, the process of phagocytosis begins. This involves the engulfment of the bacteria (endocytosis) and then their subsequent killing.

(4) *Antimicrobial systems*. Neutrophils have oxidative and non-oxidative mechanisms for exerting antimicrobial effects. Oxidative mechanisms are based on reduction of oxygen with resultant formation of toxic oxygen metabolites. Non-oxidative mechanisms in general appear to be based on membrane-disruptive antibiotic-like activities of peptides within larger proteins. Specific granules contain lactoferrin, lysozyme and B12-binding protein. Azurophil granules contain myeloperoxidase. Oxidative antibacterial effects are mediated mainly by the NADPH oxidase system and myeloperoxidase

Neutrophil function in periodontal disease
Primary neutrophil defects are often associated with severe forms of periodontal disease and pyogenic infections of the host[6]. Localized juvenile periodontitis (LJP)

has been used as a model to study neutrophil function and has helped to elucidate the mechanisms of PMN dysfunction as they relate to periodontal disease[7]. This dysfunction has been described at different levels. Neutrophils from individuals with LJP are characterised by a decrease in chemotactic responses to a variety of chemotactic factors, including C5a, FMLP and LB4[8]. This dysfunction is associated with a functional decrease in chemotaxin receptors on the PMN surface. Van Dyke *et. al.*[9] have described about a 40% deficiency in a 110-kDa membrane glycoprotein denominated GP110 which intervenes in the signal transduction of all chemotactic receptors[10]. The inheritance model of this defect is still unclear, although some data suggest an autosomal dominant mode of inheritance. Neutrophils with individuals with LJP also may exhibit increased levels of O_2 production and a selective decrease in ability to kill *A. actinomycetemcomitans*, despite normal phagocytosis. This defect probably lies in the decreased ability of LJP neutrophils to undergo phagosome-lysosome fusion[11]. The reason that LJP is limited to certain sites is unknown. It has been proposed that the site limitation is the result of a time-dependent "window of opportunity". Antibody plus complement are required for the opsonization of *A. actinomycetemcomitans*. This indicates that antibody responses must be initiated before neutrophils can kill the bacteria. The time required to produce antibodies of proper isotype, specificity, and affinity may be prolonged by the immunosuppresive factors elaborated by this specific bacteria, period which the organism may be able to induce considerable local tissue destruction.

The presence of PMNs in the crevicular epithelium serves to protect the periodontal tissues against microbial invasion and microbial attack by phagocytosing and ultimately killing the bacteria and by releasing lysosomal enzymes into the crevicular environment. Therefore, neutrophils at the gingival crevice are the first line of defence against periodontopathic bacteria. However, these bacteria are equipped with their own arsenal of potent toxins that counteract the effect of leukocytes.

Among the most important mechanisms to circunvent the neutrophil function the following have been reported[12]:

A. actinomycetemcomitans secretes a potent leukotoxin, collagenase, endotoxin, epitheliotoxin, and a fibroblast inhibiting factor. The leukotoxin acts on the PMN plasma membrane resulting in osmotic lysis.

Bacterial LPS from gram-negative bacteria has a priming effect on the neutrophil that confuses the cell, leading to alteration of its normal activity. There appears to be a difference in the virulence of LPS among different organisms. LPS from *P. gingivalis* has a more profound effect than LPS from other periodontopathic bacteria.

P. gingivalis also has ability to circumvent phagocytosis by decreasing adherence and has demonstrated resistance to neutrophil granule compounds[13].

PMNs secrete cytoplasmic granules. Fusion of the granules and the phagosome leads to discharge of its content into the phagosome. Many of the neutrophil granule constituents (myeloperoxidase, lysosome, b-glucoronidase, elastase, collagenase, lactoferrin and cathepsin-D) have been found at sites of periodontal destruction, and some of these constituents have been used as predictors of periodontal disease activity[14]. Although primary granules are released intracellularly, the secretory and secondary granules are released extracellularly and thus have the potential to cause localised tissue destruction.

Activated PMNs have been shown to be damaging to periodontal ligament fibroblasts and to cause detachment of gingival epithelial cells.

The formation of hydrogen peroxide and superoxide anion are by-products resulting from neutrophil activation. The release of hydrogen peroxide is not damaging in itself, but when it combines with myeloperoxidase from the PMN and halide ions from the plasma membrane result in the formation of hypochlorous acid, which is a potent oxidant and potential damage to host cells. The production of superoxide has the same oxidative and thus damaging effect on the host cells.

Modulation of neutrophil function

In recent years, a regulatory role for PMNs in adult periodontal disease has been postulated[15]. This idea is based on the observation that these cells are necessarily end cells but are also able of secreting a range of regulatory cytokines, including interleukin-1 and interleukin-1 antagonist. Other mediators with PMN origin have been identified such as: interleukin-6, interleukin-8, tumour necrosis factor-α, and granulocyte-macrophage-colony-stimulating factor. The ability of the innate immune system to regulate or to direct the adaptive immune response is beginning to be recognised and may have an important role in the differences of periodontal disease susceptibility shown among different individuals. According to this hypothesis, a strong innate immune response would result in a stable form of disease and a week response would result in the progressive forms of the disease.

Adaptive immune responses

The term adaptive immune response is mediated by the chronic inflammatory cell system. This is a network of cells including, monocytes, other antigen-presenting cells, and lymphocytes. This system performs three main tasks with respect to the periodontium: (a) protect the deep periodontal tissues from infection; (b) mediates connective tissue destruction to prevent bone and systemic infection and (c) orchestrates connective tissue repair and healing.

Monocytes and macrophages

Unlike neutrophils, monocytes exist in the bone marrow in a functionally immature condition. As a result, they arrive from blood to the tissues as multipotential cells capable of differentiating in a variety of different ways in order to kill pathogens, regulate clearance of tissue debris, regulate tissue remodelling and process exogenous antigens. The monocytes once into the tissues are termed macrophages which differentiate in response to environmental factors. For example, T-cells release IFN-α which induces the differentiation of macrophages into antigen-processing and -presenting cells.

Antigen processing is the partial degradation of proteins that result in antigen presentation. Antigen presentation refers to the expression of peptides on the cell surface in association with molecules encoded within an important gene complex known as major histocompatibility complex (MHC). Periodontal bacterial infections are extracellular, therefore the macrophage must ingest the antigen by phagocytosis, binding the target particle using the CR3 or the IgG binding F receptors, and digest it within the phagolysosome. MHC classII molecules are sequestered within the membrane of lysosomes and become available when the phagosome fuses the lysosome. Peptides associate with the MHC class II molecules in the phagolysosome, and this complex is expressed on the phagocyte surface by exocytosis, where it is adequately recognised by the specific immune system.

Lymphocytes T cells are involved in nearly all immunoregulatory interactions both *in vivo* and *in vitro*. When the immune system encounters an antigen, it mounts a specific reaction that ultimately eradicates the infection. Antigen is first taken up by antigen presenting cells (APC), processed, and reexpressed on the cell membrane in association with class I or class II MHC molecules, which can then be recognised by the CD8+ or CD4+ T cells, respectively. This interaction leads to the production of growth and differentiation factors by both the APC and the T cell, which in turn are responsible for the rapid expansion and differentiation of the initially small numbers of antigen specific lymphocytes present in a previously unchallenged host. The result is a clone of effectors in sufficient numbers to mediate an immune response.

Part of the pathogenesis of periodontal diseases including gingivitis and periodontitis involves a net increase in the number of gingival lymphocytes and monocytes within the periodontal connective tissues. In gingivitis in children the dominant cell type in this infiltrate are T lymphocytes. In adult periodontitis the lymphocitic infiltrate is primary cells of the B-lineage (both activated B-blasts and plasma cells), although the density of T-cells is similar to gingivitis lesions. Therefore, the persistence of the T-cell populations in periodontitis and the net increase of B-cell activity led to the postulation that the T-cell to B-cell ratio decrease is due not to a decrease in T-cells, but to an increase in B-cells and therefore advance the concept that periodontitis was a B-cell lesion[16]. Also the persistence of the T-cell populations led to the postulation that the T-cell regulation of B-cells was altered in periodontal disease. In studies where the lymphoid cell populations have been characterised have indicated that T-cells are always present in all stages of inflammation and probably play a key regulatory role. To study this function, the T-helper to T-suppressor ratios (T4:T8) have received considerable attention. Local T4:T8 ratios in health or gingivitis are generally considered to be similar to the peripheral blood ones. Conversely a significant decrease in T4:T8 ratios has been observed in periodontitis sites, which has been attributed to a significant decrease in the T-helper/inducer phenotype.

The increased B-cell activation seems paradoxical in the presence of increased proportions of suppressor CD8+ T cells. This fact has been termed as the "B cell paradox". The activation of B cells in the presence of "inverted" CD-4-to-CD-8 ratios may be explained in terms of subpopulations of CD4+ T cells[17,18]. These cells have also been characterised in terms of their expression of CD45RO, CD45RA and Cdw29 differentiation markers which is linked to the functional status of T-cells, being naive and memory cells[19]. Naive CD4+ cells suppress polyclonal Ig production and have been functionally associated with suppressor-inducer activity, while memory cells respond with intense proliferation to the previously primed antigen and seem to be important in helper activity. The majority of the periodontal lymphocytes express a memory phenotype. T-cell "disregulation" may result in the apparent activation of IgG-, IgA-, or IgE-bearing B cells in a polyclonal manner. Although it is clear that antibody within the periodontal tissues can be antigen specific and react with such pathogens as *A. actinomycetemcomitans* or *P. gingivalis*, the vast majority of the immunoglobulins found in the periodontal tissues do not appear to be reactive to specific antigens. Importantly, the polyclonal nature of the antibody response in periodontitis has been suggested to preclude the formation of insoluble immune complexes what makes type III immunopathologic reactions unlikely. Polyclonal B-cell activation may lead to the production of IL-1, which activates osteoclasts and impedes immunologic clearance of the pathogen.

A functional characterisation of the immunohistochemical isotype profiles of gingival antibody producing cells has also been carried out in gingival and periodontal lesions[20]. B-cell responses in the periodontium are generally of IgG mostly IgG1 and IgG3 and some IgA. Serologic studies have also shown a good correlation between microbiologic culture of subgingival plaque in different periodontal diseases and serum antibody[21]. Generally, individuals with adult advanced periodontitis demonstrate antibodies against *P. gingivalis* and individuals with LJP possess antibodies to A. actinomycetemcomitans. It is unclear at what point in the infection and subsequent disease process initial seroconversion occurs, and it is also unknown how long serum titters remain elevated after the infection has subsided.

Recent evidence has also pointed to the presence of natural killer (NK) cells within the periodontal tissues in health and disease. They constitute between 3 and 7% of the total mononuclear cell infiltrate in periodontitis and are virtually absent in healthy gingiva. Although being associated with the active B-cell lesion, their role in periodontal disease is unknown.

Effector systems

Complement systems, immunoglobulins and antibodies
Host protection against pathogenic plaque micro-organisms is generally considered to heavily rely upon the constant migration of phagocytic cells, and exudation of complement fragments and specific antibodies into the sulcus or pocket. Several lines of evidence indicate that crevicular phagocytic function is particularly efficient in the presence of both complement fragments and specific opsonic antibodies. *In vitro* studies have shown that PMN phagocytosis on suspected gram negative pathogens is impaired in the absence of serum. Complement fragments have been detected and quantitatively described in gingival fluid from different clinical conditions, ranging from health to advanced breakdown[22]. These studies indicated that the concentration of most complement fragments was in the 75 to 85% range with respect to serum. The amount of C3 was significantly decreased (about 25% of serum concentrations), accounted for its activation breakdown product C3b, thus indicating complement activation in the periodontal pocket. Presence of specific immunoglobulins to periodontal micro-organisms has also been reported in serum and gingival fluid. IgG

and IgA are the predominant classes. As a consequence of chronic antigen exposure, an isotype shift has been observed in antibody production against certain antigens, with increased levels of IgG4 and IgA2 in periodontitis lesions[23].

Cytokines
Regulation of lymphocyte proliferation and differentiation into effector cells occurs via a cascade of soluble factors (cytokines) that interact with specific surface receptors, each factor inducing receptor expression for the next cytokine in the cascade. Cytokines were first named on the basis of their activity in biological assays. With the cloning of different cytokine genes and the determination of the nucleotide and amino acid sequences, it is now evident that a variety of biological activities can be attributed to the same protein. The term "interleukin" was introduced to apply to factors with multiple overlapping biological activities.

Cytokines are protein cell regulators produced by a wide range of cells that play important roles in many physiological responses. They are low molecular weight proteins involved in the immune and inflammatory responses, where they regulate the amplitude and duration of this response. They are extremely potent and are produced transiently and interact with high-affinity specific cell receptors, that are usually expressed in relatively small numbers. By acting as intercellular communicators between cells in the immune system, cytokines are central to the way in which helper T cells regulate the immune response[24]. The majority of immune responses occur locally rather than systemically within a small area of tissue. Different cytokines induce different subset of T cells or have different effects on proliferation within a particular subset.

Interleukin 1 is a principal mediator of inflammatory responses acting on many cell types other than those of the immune system and itself produced by many cells, including macrophages, endothelial cells, B cells, fibroblasts, epithelial cells and osteoblasts in response to micro-organisms, bacterial endo or exotoxins, complement components, or tissue injury. One of the most important actions of IL-1 is its induction capacity on other cytokines in what appears to be part of a network of cytokines with self-regulating and self suppressing properties. IL-1 has a central role in T-cell activation resulting in transcription of various genes, including IL-2 and CD25 (IL-2 receptors), and the activated T-cell then secretes a number of cytokines that affect the cells of the immune system. It appears to act by means of priming B cells to respond to subsequent activation by potentiating their proliferation and/or differentiation. IL-1 plays an important role in bone resorption, which is an important feature in periodontal diseases. B-cells, which are present in increased numbers in progressive periodontal lesions, have shown to produce IL-1 and IL-1 collected in gingival crevicular fluid has shown to have a direct correlation with periodontal attachment loss[25,26].

Interleukin 2 is synthesised and secreted by T cells after activation by antigen or mitogen and plays an essential role in T cell division. It also induces T cell cytotoxicity and natural killer (NK) cell activity. IL-2 also acts as a growth factor for activated B-blast cells inducing increased IgG secretion.

Interferon gamma (IFN-gamma) is produced during an immune response by antigen-specific T cells and NK cells recruited by IL-2. Its regulatory effect include the activation of macrophages to enhance their phagocytosis as well as activation of NK cells. IFN-Gamma upregulates class I MHC antigen expression and induces class II MHC and FcaR expression on macrophages and other cells influencing its capacity to present antigens. It also plays a major role in the control of immunoglobulin isotypes produced during the immune response, enhancing the expression of IgG2 and suppressing other isotypes. IgG2 is very effective in fixing complement and promoting NK-cell mediated killing so that IFN-Gamma promotes the ability of the humoral system to destroy microbial pathogens. IFN-Gamma inhibits most of the activities induced by IL-4 and its presence appears to be a requisite for the induction of the Th1 subset.

Interleukin 4 is produced by T-cells, mast cells and basophils and is an important factor in the clonal expansion of antigen-specific B-cells. It appears that IL-4 modulates humoral responses to different antigen stimuli. It inhibits IL-2 and IFN-gamma-induced activities, including the activation of macrophages and antimicrobial activity. It induces the differentiation of Th0 clones toward a Th2 phenotype.

Interleukin 5 has several effects on B cells, including the induction of IgM and IgA production. It is chemotactic and a potent stimulator for the growth and differentiation of eosinophils.

Interleukin 6 is produced by both hemopoietic and non-hemopoietic cells and induces immunoglobulin secretion in B cells inducing their final maturation. Like IL-1 it has a major role in the mediation of inflammatory and immune responses initiated by infection or injury. IL-6 activates T and B cells and together with IL-1 seem to mediate most of the effects ascribed to macrophages in lymphocyte activation. It also seem to mediate in bone destruction and its levels in gingival crevicular fluid have also correlated with periodontal destruction in the course of periodontal infections.

Interleukin 10 plays a major role in suppressing immune and inflammatory responses. It is produced by T cells, B cells and macrophages after activation. IL-10 mediates the suppression of antigen-specific T-cell responses by down regulating class II MHC expression. It also contributes to the suppression of IFN-Gamma-induced macrophage-mediated immune destruction of pathogens. IL-10 significantly reduces proliferation and cytokine production by activated T-cells and other Th1 cell-mediated responses.

Interleukin 12 is produced by macrophages, B cells and other accessory cells in response to bacteria, bacterial products or parasites. It stimulates the growth and cytotoxic activity of NK cells and T cells. It also induces IFN-gamma production and it is an essential factor for Th1 induction.

Interleukin 13 is a newly described protein produced by activated T-cells and is a potent modulator of monocytes and B cell function. Like IL-4, IL-13 may favour the development of Th2 responses and downregulates the production of IL-12. It induces B cell growth and differentiation.

A number of studies have reported the presence of cytokines in periodontal disease. These results indicate possible lower levels of both IFN-Gamma and IL-2 in periodontitis lesions suggesting decreased Th1 responses. IL-1 have been shown to be elevated in the gingiva of adult periodontitis subjects and from active sites as compared with healthy or stable sites. These increased amounts of IL-1 may lead to the proliferation of IL-4 secreting T-cells, which in turn contribute to the expansion of activated B cells.

With the increased plaque accumulation a shift from a Gram-positive population to one where Gram negative bacteria such as *P. gingivalis*, *F. nucleatum*, *P. intermedia*, *Capnocytophaga* and spirochaetes may play a major role in the progression of periodontal disease. If the nature of the antigen is important in the selection of a particular T cell cytokine profile, then it is possible that the host may respond to the Gram-positive organisms in gingivits subjects by inducing a protective Th1 response. In contrast, genetically susceptible individuals may respond to antigens such as LPS from Gram-negative micro-organisms by mounting a non-protective Th2 response. Studies have established the B cell nature of the progressive lesion, suggesting an increase in the Th2 B cell proliferation and differentiation cytokines. B cells produce IL-1, which acts as a co-stimulatory signal for Th2 T cells as well as mediating tissue destruction via the inflammatory pathway. If the result of B cell differentiation was protective antibody production, elimination of the causative organism would ensue and disease progression would stop, but production of non protective antibodies to antigens such as LPS in susceptible subjects, could on the other hand, result in continual connective tissue breakdown.

Inflammatory mediators
Besides cytokines, other regulatory mechanisms may also play important roles in the induction, amplification, persistence, control and resolution of localised inflammatory and immune responses. Growth factors, prostaglandins, leukotrienes, tromboxanes, anaphylotoxins, kinins and biologically active amines intervene at different levels in this local cascade of biological activity. Presence of these immune and inflammatory modulators has been evidenced both in gingival fluid and in extracts from gingival biopsies[27]. Among other mediators, prostaglandins, PGE-2 in particular, have received considerable attention. Offenbacher *et al.* were able not only to detect PGE-2 in gingival crevicular fluid, but to associate increased levels of this mediator with impending periodontal tissue breakdown. Besides, PGE-2 has been directly associated with the bone destruction occurring in periodontitis and the use of non-steroidal antiinflammatory drugs which specifically inhibit this protein has demonstrated inhibition of this bone breakdown.

In summary, the concept of functional T-cell subsets makes possible to construct a cellular and molecular model of the pathogenesis of periodontal disease[28]. According to Seymour[29,30], the basis of this hypohesis is the concept that some individuals are susceptible to periodontal breakdown, whereas other manifest a disease that over their life time progresses very slowly. Further, even in susceptible individuals, the disease may follow a cyclic pattern, with periods of progression and periods of relative stability[31]. Data indicates a depression of IL-2 and IFN-Gamma levels in adult periodontitis suggesting a depression of Th1 cells in the progressive lesion. B cells activate Th2 cells to produce IL-4 and IL-6, which induce clonal expansion and differentiation of B-cell clones. Studies have established the B-cell nature of the progressive periodontal lesion. In the presence of polyclonal B-cell activation with the subsequent production of large amounts of B-cell IL-1, tissue destruction will take place via a number of different pathways. If the result of B-cell differentiation was protective antibody production, elimination of the causative organism would ensue and disease progression would stop.

The nature of the initial innate immune response may also have a crucial influence in the type of subsequent adaptive immune response. A strong innate response with the production of IL-12 may induce a Th1 T-cell response[32]. These T-cells are involved in the recruitment and activation of PMNs at the site of infection, thus representing a positive feedback between T-cells and PMNs resulting in an efficient microbial defence mechanism.

References

1. Van Dyke TE, Lester MA, Shapira L. The role of host response in periodontal disease progression, Implications for future treatment strategies. *J Periodontol* 1993; **64** (Suppl), 792-806.
2. Genco R. Host Responses in Periodontal Disease: Current Concepts. *J Periodontol* 1992; **63**, 338-355.
3. Genco R, Hamada S, Lehner T, McGhee J, Mergenhagen S. *Molecular Pathogenesis of Periodontal Disease*. Washington, ASM Press, 1994,
4. Seymour GJ. Importance of the Host Response in the Periodontium. *J Clin Periodontol* 1991; **18**, 421-426.
5. Crawford JM, Watanabe K. Cell Adhesion Molecules in Inflammation and Immunity, Relevance to Periodontal Diseases. *Crit Rev Oral Biol Med* 1994; **5**, 91-123.
6. Van Dyke TE, Hoop GA. Neutrophil Function and Oral Disease. *Crit Rev Oral Biol Med* 1990; **1**, 117-133.
7. Van Dyke TE, Vaikuntam J. Neutrophil function and dysfunction in periodontal disease. *Current Opinion Periodontol* 1994; 19-27.
8. Ashkenazi M, White RR, Denisson DK. Neutrophil Modulation by Actinobacillus actinomycetemcomitans I: Chemotaxis: Surface Receptor Expression and F-Acin Polymerization. *J Periodontal Res* 1992; **27**, 264-273.
9. Daniel MA, McDonald G, Offenbacher S, Van Dyke TE. Defective Chemotaxis and Calcium Response in Localized Juvenile Periodontitis Neutrophils. *J Periodontol* 1993; **64**, 617-621.
10. Kurihara H, Murayama Y, Warbington M, Chanpagne C, Van Dyke TE. Calcium Dependent Protein Kinase C Activity of Neutrophils in Localized Juvenile Periodontitis. *Infect Immun* 1993; **61**, 3137-3142.
11. Sjthetastrthetam K, Darveau R, Page R, Whitney C, Engel D. Opsonic Antibody Activity Against Actinobacillus actinomycetemcomitans in Patiens With Rapidly Progressive Periodontitis. *Infect Immun* 1992; **60**, 4819-4825.
12. Socransky SS, Haffajje AD. Microbial Mechanisms in the Pathogenesis of Destructive Periodontal Disease: A Critical Assessment. *J Periodontal Res* 1991; **62**, 195-212.
13. MacFarlane GD, Herzberg MC, Wolff LF, Hardie NA. Refractory Periodontitis Associated with abnormal polymorphonuclear leukocyte phagocytosis and cigarette smoking. *J Periodontol* 1992; **63**, 908-913.
14. Lamster IB, Novak JM. Host Mediators in Gingival Crevicular Fluid, Implication for the Pathogenesis of Periodontal Disease. *Crit Rev Oral Biol Med* 1992; **3**, 31-60.

15. LLoyd AR, Oppenheim JJ. Poly's Lament, The neglected role of the polymorphonuclear neutrophil in the afferent limb of the Immune Response. *Immunol Today* 1992; **13**, 169-172.
16. Mahanonda R, Seymour GJ, Powell LW, Good MF, Halliday JW. Effect of initial treatment of chronic inflammatory periodontal disease on the frequency of peripheral blood T-lymphocytes specific to periodontopathic bacteria . *Oral Microbiol Immunol* 1991; **6**, 221-227.
17. Bloom BR, Salgame P, Diamond B. Revisiting and revising suppressor T cells. *Immunol Today* 1992; **13**, 131-136.
18. Scott P. Selective differentiation of CD4+ T helper cell subsets. *Curr Opin Immunol* 1993; **5**, 391-397.
19. Gemmell E, Feldner B, Seymour GJ. CD45RA and CD45RO positivr CD4 cells in human peripheral blood and periodontal disease tissue before and after stimulation with periodontopatic bacteria. *Oral Microbiol Immunol* 1992; **7**, 84-88.
20. Gemmell E, Seymour GJ. Phenotypic analysis of B-cells extracted from human periodontal disease tissue. *Oral Microbiol Immunol* 1991; **6**, 356-362.
21. Ebersole JL, Taubman MA. The protective nature of host responses in periodontal diseases. *Periodontology 2000* 1994; **5**, 112-141.
22. Schenkein HA. The Role of Complement in Periodontal Diseases. *Crit Rev Oral Biol Med* 1991; **2**, 65-81.
23. Reinhardt RA, McDonald TL, Bolton RW, Dubois LM, Kaldahl KW. IgG subclasses in gingival crevicular fluid from acive versus stable periodontal sites. *J Periodontol* 1989; **60**, 44-50.
24. Gemmell E, Seymour GJ. Cytokines and T Cells switching. *Crit Rev Oral Biol Med* 1994; **5**, 249-279.
25. Masada MP, Persson R, Kenney JS, Lee SW, Page RC, Allison AC. Measurement of Interleukin-1 alfa and -1 beta in gingival crevicular fluid, Implication for pathogenesis of periodontal disease. *J Periodontal Res* 1990; **25**, 156-163.
26. Stashenko P, Fujiyoshie P, Obernesser MS, Prostak L, Haffajje AD, Socransky SS. Levels of Interleukin 1 Beta in tissue from sites of active periodontal disease . *J Clin Periodontol* 1991; **18**, 548-554.
27. Page RC. The role of inflammatory mediators in the pathogenesis of Periodontal Disease. *J Periodont Res* 1991; **26**, 230-242.
28. Taubman MA. Immunological aspects of periodontal diseases. In: Slots J, Taubman MA, eds. *Contemporary Oral Microbiology and Immunology*. St. Louis, Mosby Year Book, 1992, 542-554.
29. Gemmell E, Seymour GJ. Modulation of immune responses to periodontal bacteria. *Current Opinion Periodontol* 1994; 28-38.
30. Seymour GJ, Gemmell E, Reinhardt RA, Eastcott J, Taubman MA. Immunopathogenesis of Chronic Inflammatory Periodontal Disease: Cellular and Molecular Mechanisms. *J Periodontal Res* 1993; **28**, 478-486.
31. Tonetti MS. Etiology and Pathogenesis. In: Lang NP, Karring T, eds. *Proceedings of the 1st European Workshop on Periodontology*. London, Quintessence Publishing, 1994, 54-89.
32. Trinchieri G. Interleukin-12 and its role in the generation of Th1 cells. *Immunol Today* 1993; **14,** 193-198.

9   Pre- and post- surgical approach to periodontal treatment

Martin Addy

Division of Restorative Dentistry, Bristol Dental School and Hospital, Bristol BS1 2LY, UK

The long term successful treatment of the periodontal patient depends as much on the pre and post treatment care as the actual treatment phase itself. Indeed, the mainstay of periodontal disease management is the control of supragingival plaque. Plaque at or below the gingival margin is the major aetiological factor in chronic gingivitis. Moreover, subgingival plaque which is derived from supragingival plaque is intimately associated with the advancing lesions of chronic periodontal diseases. Factors which control the conversion of chronic gingivitis to chronic periodontitis are not clearly understood and at present are vaguely described as a pathogenic microflora acting on a susceptible host. This makes widespread prevention of the disease difficult, since what constitutes a pathogenic flora is not established. Thus over 300 micro-organisms have been identified from the diseased subgingival environment and at least a further 100 have yet to be isolated and identified.

The list of potential pathogens appears to lengthen with each year of scientific publications such that the breadth of the specific plaque hypothesis has widened considerably. The predictive value of microbiological diagnosis has not really been studied on a longitudinal basis and would obviously be a massive task complicated by the fact that apparent pathogens are commonly found in periodontally healthy mouths and healthy sites in diseased mouths.

Microbiological diagnosis in the management of established disease is fraught with problems, which will be discussed further, but at this juncture, mainly for the reasons alluded to already, namely their specificity. Similarly, susceptibility cannot be predicted at an early age. For example, an epidemiological study of periodontal disease prevalence and severity in two Indonesian populations, which differed only in socio-economic status, was performed recently. The 20-30 year old tea pickers had poorer oral hygiene and approximately twice the level of gingivitis compared to a similarly aged university population yet both groups had the same levels of periodontitis and loss of attachment. This indicates that gingivitis existing for 10 or more years is a poor predictor of future periodontal disease. Proven markers of susceptibility are at present few, have been determined retrospectively and account for a tiny proportion of the variance observed for the disease. As such they provide minimal predictive power for the disease in the at present unaffected individual. Nevertheless, as will be discussed, such markers are relevant to the management of the individual with disease, and include smoking and diabetes.

Other markers are suspected but as yet unproven. The determination of genetic markers, such as HLA typing, is in its infancy, has minimal predictive power and is of course only of academic interest in the already diseased individual.

Despite the problems of disease prediction it is nevertheless true that a large proportion of middle aged adults will have some periodontal disease although this will be mainly of the slowly progressive adult type and of questionable significance to the longevity of their dentitions. Only a very small proportion of individuals will show advanced disease and then only at some sites. Prevention of periodontal disease is therefore compromised and on a population level must be overprescribed and directed at maintaining gingival health. This is logical since although chronic gingivitis is not a direct threat to tooth survival, nor a good predictor of future periodontal breakdown or disease recurrence, chronic periodontitis is considered to be always preceded by chronic gingivitis. The concept that plaque will cause gingivitis and given time will inextricably progress to periodontitis and tooth loss no longer holds true. However, the individual who presents with periodontal disease can be considered as susceptible and has been exposed already to the relevant bacterial pathogen(s). For these individuals the concept of the disease process has in part been fulfilled, namely plaque has caused gingivitis and gingivitis has at one or more sites progressed to periodontitis. The residual aspect of the scenario that the disease will progress to tooth loss is an important aspect of diagnosis and treatment planning. Unfortunately, determining prognosis for teeth or a dentition afflicted by periodontal disease is often difficult or impossible to predict accurately, certainly in the short term. Nonetheless, it is known that in those individuals treated for periodontal disease, lack of bleeding on probing or gingivitis is highly predictive of no further loss of attachment. This is most relevant to the pre and post surgical approach to periodontal management. The diagnosis of chronic periodontitis is not difficult and has been aptly described as noting chronic gingivitis associated with loss of attachment. Indeed, chronic gingivitis associated with loss of attachment may be a more accurate definition of periodontal disease than others that have been recommended over the years. The more important aspect of periodontal disease is the qualification of the diagnosis. Such qualification requires an identification of aetiological and predisposing factors, disease severity and finally patient factors. Only with such qualification can treatment planning be effectively tailored for the individual patient.

The major aetiological factor in the initiation of chronic gingivitis is supragingival plaque. Also, it is from supragingival plaque that the subgingival plaque associated with chronic periodontitis is derived. There is still debate as to whether good supragingival plaque control can alone modify subgingival plaque sufficiently to benefit established chronic periodontitis. However, as stated good supragingival plaque control must be established in the pretreatment phase and maintained in the post treatment years of periodontal management. Predisposing factors may be considered under two headings, namely those which predispose to plaque accumulation and those which predispose the individual to gingivitis and/or periodontal disease by modifying the host response. Factors predisposing to plaque accumulation are potentially numerous and vary greatly in their influence. To debate the importance of all possible predisposing factors is outside the remit of this review and the reader is referred to standard old and new texts on the subject. However, to summarise: the importance of local factors predisposing to plaque accumulation appear much less important than was once considered. Crowded teeth, shallow sulci, high fraenal attachments, narrow or absent attached gingivae all appear to have limited impact on oral hygiene and gingival health and there are no data to suggest an influence on the initiation or progress of periodontal disease.

Restorative dentistry on the other hand can have an adverse effect on gingival health via a plaque retention effect. Thus, partial dentures predispose to plaque accumulation and without suitable advice, instruction and maintenance are a detrimental to dental and periodontal health of the individual. Subgingival restorations are associated with increased gingivitis and there is evidence that overhanging restorations are associated with loss of attachment. Whether the latter represents the initiation of periodontitis or acceleration of existing disease is not established. Inadequate contact points and food packing are suspected to cause loss of attachment, a contention supported by studies on germ free animals but not thus far proven. Occlusal trauma appears irrelevant to plaque accumulation and gingivitis or the conversion of gingivitis to periodontitis but may be a co-destructive factor in further breakdown in established disease, a possibility of considerable importance to planning of orthodontic treatment in adults.

Of more importance to plaque control, gingivitis and therefore periodontal treatment appears to relate to the individual as a whole. At the extremes of social class oral hygiene and gingivitis vary enormously. Gender appears to influence toothcleaning with females overall having better oral hygiene than males. Age affects oral hygiene significantly, albeit over a short age span with marked improvements overall in individuals between ages 12 to 16 years with small improvements thenceforth to 20 years. Toothbrushing hand is only important as far as tooth sites are concerned with for example right handers in general cleaning the right buccal quadrants less well than the left. Most individuals clean lingual and palatal surfaces very poorly, spending little or no proportion of the cleaning cycle at these surfaces. This clearly has relevance to provision of oral hygiene instruction. Toothbrushing frequency is relevant to oral hygiene with significant benefits up to twice a day but not thereafter. Perhaps the first and most important approach to oral hygiene is to persuade individuals to brush twice per day. In general approximately 40% of populations brush once a day or less frequently. Increasing brushing to more than twice a day may have detrimental affects including gingival recession and tooth abrasion. As all world workshops have concluded it would appear that it is the compliance and dexterity of the individual with regular toothcleaning that are most important at least to gingival health. Except at the extremes, namely of physical and/or mental handicap it is not known why some individuals tooth clean well and others not. This led Frandsen (1986) at the workshop on Plaque Control and Oral

Hygiene Practices to suggest that it was time to determine what factors influenced oral hygiene practices of an individual rather than continue to research toothcleaning aids and devices.

Host modifying factors are probably numerous but most appear to affect the gingival response to plaque rather than the rate of periodontal breakdown. For example, in juveniles incompetent lips and/or mouth breathing increases gingival inflammation although it is still debated whether this is through increased plaque or a modified gingival response. The often seen gingival enlargement anteriorly is nevertheless of interest. Hormonal influences on the gingival response to plaque in females at the menarch and during pregnancy also are noteworthy as is the gingival fibroblast response to a number of drugs such as phenytoin, nifedipine and cyclosporin A. Those conditions which modify the rate of periodontal destruction, usually increasing it, include diabetes type I and II, polymorph defects or depletions such as Chediak-Higashi syndrome and cyclical neutropaenia, and smoking. Others are suspected including stress, HIV etc. but remain unproven.

The qualification of disease by severity clearly is fundamental to determining prognosis. Most reliance to date has been placed on clinical and radiographic measurements. Probing depth, loss of attachment, type and extent of bone loss, including furcation involvement are all important recordings as are mobility assessments to determine degree and whether physiological or pathological in origin. The importance of correlating all of these severity measures to the age of the patient cannot be overemphasised. Clinical and radiographic assessments are also necessary to determine the presence of other dental disease as this can have direct impact upon periodontal treatment planning. Ideally, diagnostic aids which give reliable information on the activity of the disease or the specificity of the infection would be of value. This is an important area of research and thus far has been aimed at test kits which identify the presence of certain marker bacteria, albeit with only modest precision, bacterial activity, host response or tissue breakdown. In diagnostic terms they provide little or no further information relevant to treatment planning than clinical and radiographic diagnostic methods. Even more detailed microbiological methods are of questionable value because of lack of specificity to the disease process. None of these methods can be convincingly shown to influence treatment options in a positive or negative way, including the use of antimicrobial adjunctive therapy. It would appear that at present technology is in advance of knowledge and one is reminded of "Simon's Law" "Science is true don't be misled by the facts". Nevertheless, to continue research towards reliable diagnostic tests for periodontal disease susceptibility, activity and response to therapy is important. It is probable that such tests will first prove of value in assessing the response to treatment and last in predicting susceptibility.

Patient factors in diagnosis and treatment planning are important. Clearly, some relate to disease susceptibility and have been discussed. Others influence directly or indirectly the ability and willingness of the individual with periodontal disease to be involved in the management programme. Important questions are, firstly, can the individual fulfil the long term commitment to the all important prevention phase of disease management alone or with assistance from third parties. Secondly can they actually receive the ideal treatment for the disease. Answers to these questions lie mainly in the psycho-social and medical histories of individuals which are complex to say the least and poorly understood in the most part as far as periodontal disease management is concerned.

Obvious factors, however, can be taken into account in respect of the first question, namely whether the individual is capable physically or mentally to achieve a satisfactory level of oral hygiene. At the extremes of physical and mental abnormalities the answer is obvious, but many other medical, physical and mental states can influence the possible co-operation provided by the individual. All may require considerable changes to the provision of advice and instruction in oral hygiene to the patient or the planned treatment for the patient.

Factors which influence the receipt of treatment and therefore the treatment are numerous and vary enormously in their impact. The age and general medical and psychological health of an individual are most important. For example, in the aged it is possible retrospectively to judge susceptibility and balance the treatment accordingly which in general is more likely to be conservate even palliative. Also certain medical conditions which put the patient at risk from periodontal treatment will influence treatment planning. These include, congenital and acquired heart valve defects, bleeding diatheses and other acute haematological disorders.

A range of other medical disorders, conditions and pharmocotherapies will also influence the type of treatment prescribed and the timing of the treatment ranging from anticoagulant therapy to pregnancy. Willingness or ability to receive periodontal treatment can also be influenced by apparently simple things such as distance to travel and availability of transport. Moreover, depending on the health and health insurance services of a particular country financial status may have a major impact on receipt of treatment. In summary, the qualification of the diagnosis of chronic periodontitis can be influenced by numerous aetiological, predisposing, modifying and patient factors which along with a disease severity assessment can affect treatment planning.

At this juncture it is important to realise that periodontal disease is a chronic disease and where susceptibility cannot be changed. It is therefore important to realise that before the treatment is commenced that the management for many patients involves along term commitment by themselves and by professionals.

Periodontal disease as stated appears to arise when a suitable pathogen acts on a susceptible host. This provides hypothetically three quite diffcrent treatment approaches namely; remove the pathogens, alter the host response or change the individual susceptibility. The latter is at present impossible, although attempts to alter the host response to advantage can be achieved in part by using drugs such as non-steroidal anti-inflammatory agents. The exact role of such agents in periodontal therapy is not established, and is at present more of interest in researching the pathogenesis of periodontal disease. Thus, the main stream approach to periodontal therapy has and remains the elimination of pathogens from the periodontal environment. The modern text book treatment plan is as follows:.

(1) Advice and instruction in supra gingival plaque control.
(2) Thorough debridement of the root surface.

(3) The use of surgery primarily to improve access.

(4) The adjunctive use of antimicrobials.

(5) Recall and maintenance.

Although considered a modern treatment plan, such can be found in periodontal textbooks of the early part of this century, having re-emerged after an interim period when periodontology appeared to become a surgical speciality more concerned with the results of the disease than the cause. Within the remit of this text it is the former and latter parts of the treatment plan which need to be debated. Nevertheless, at this juncture it is important to again stress that periodontal disease is a chronic disease where susceptibility cannot be changed. As with other chronic diseases " Once a periodontal patient always a periodontal patient". It must be therefore emphasised that for many patients periodontal disease management requires a long term commitment to prevention by the individual and the professional.

Advice and instruction in oral hygiene methods must be tailored to the individual needs of patients. There is no scientific basis for how such advice and instruction should be given but it would seem reasonable for patients to understand their own problem. This requires information upon the diseases of gingivitis and periodontitis and the causal agent namely plaque. Such information should be both verbal and written. The primary aim is for the patients to achieve for themselves a level of supragingival plaque control compatible with gingival health. The mainstay of supragingival plaque control is mechanical cleaning with a toothbrush and toothpaste. Numerous toothbrush designs are available with no clear cut evidence that any one is clinically significantly better than another. It would seem reasonable to suggest that head sizes are not too large, filaments are soft to medium and end rounded. However, as noted previously it is the individual who is the major variable in what can be achieved by mechanical cleaning.

The debate concerning electric toothbrushes vs manual brushes has re-emerged. The 1986 world workshop on plaque control considered that electric brushes offered no significant benefits compared to manual brushes except in the handicapped individual. Since this time a number of new generation devices have appeared for which there is growing evidence of modest superiority over manual brushes. Although there is no clear cut difference in favour of any one particular electric device. Recommendation of such devices thus rests with the professional who will have to consider the needs of the individual and of course the cost of the products which is considerably higher than that of manual brushes.

In providing oral hygiene instruction it would seem reasonable to monitor the response and plaque and bleeding indices are particularly useful. There are numerous indices and essentially any can be used for the purpose. If plaque indices are scored using disclosing solutions there is the added advantage for the professional and the patient to appreciate areas which are not cleaned effectively. Both the scoring and visualisation of plaque also provide an educational element for patients. Because of the nature of the disease some form of interdental cleaning is necessary. Such devices include woodsticks, interdental cleaning brushes or floss. Again there are no data proving any one method is better than another and recommendation should be based on the needs and ability of individual patients rather than the often blanket recommendation of one device. Whatever, instruction in correct use is essential.

In the pre-treatment preparation phase the value of chemical plaque control agents is controversial. The most effective agent, chlorhexidine, usually employed as a 18-20 mg dose mouthrinse twice a day has been recommended as an adjunct to toothcleaning in the pre-treatment preparatory phase of periodontal care. However, there are drawbacks. Firstly, chlorhexidine in a mouthrinse has poor therapeutic potential and is very slow to produce benefits to established gingival inflammation and no benefit to periodontal disease. Even when irrigated directly into pockets the results are equivocal and possibly little better than can be produced by water irrigation. Some professional intervention to remove established plaque and calculus deposits are therefore required before the use of chlorhexidine in order to facilitate its considerable plaque prevention activity. Secondly, even in the latter situation, chlorhexidine will tend to mask the mechanical cleaning ability of the individual and therefore monitoring becomes impossible. This clearly has long term implications since, as will be discussed, chlorhexidine is unlikely to be used for long periods for plaque control because of the well known local side effects. The recommendation of "antiplaque" toothpastes is conceptually a better idea, the problem is the present evidence for efficacy of such products. To date some toothpastes containing triclosan combined with a copolymer or a zinc salt have proven useful in patients with moderate gingivitis. Unfortunately there is no evidence as yet to prove their value in the pre-treatment phase of periodontal therapy or more particularly in the long term maintenance of treated periodontal patients. Similar conclusions can be drawn concerning stannous fluoride toothpaste which have recently re-emerged as potential antiplaque products.

The professional responsibility in pre-treatment patient preparation is not only accurate diagnosis, treatment planning and advice and instruction but the removal or modification where possible of predisposing or aggravating factors. This includes a thorough prophylaxis, removal and replacement or modification of poor restorations and appliances *e.g.* partial dentures. Finally, before commencing the treatment phase it is essential that supragingival plaque control is satisfactory. Whatever the quality and success of treatment, long term success is dependant on supragingival plaque control and there is no evidence that this will further improve post operatively.

The choice of non-surgical or surgical therapies is outside the remit of this review. However it is worth stating that systemic antimicrobial therapy has no place in the pre-treatment phase of patient preparation. Most reviews on the subject consider both local and systemic chemotherapy as adjuncts and not replacements for mechanical therapy and should follow debridement. Moreover, reports and clinical experience indicate that systemic antimicrobial therapy alone can lead to multiple abscess formation in the periodontal patient.

Immediate pre-operative patient preparation is rarely debated but two procedures have been independently recommended. Firstly, prior to any mechanical instrumentation particularly where ultra sonic instruments are to be used chlorhexidine rinsing may be considered. This markedly reduces the bacterial contamination of the operatory area and is a simple precaution to the likelihood of cross-infection. Secondly, and particularly for the at risk, chlorhexidine irrigation around the gingival margin area reduces the incidence of bacteremia.

The post operative care and preparation of the periodontal patient can be divided into short term and long term management. Short term management is primarily concerned with firstly the comfort of the patient and the healing of the operation site. Discomfort following most periodontal procedures is usually not great but consideration may be given to the provision of analgesics. Aspirin or paracetamol usually suffice and some practitioners provide this pre or immediately post operatively on the basis that it should be easier to prevent pain than stop it once it has been initiated. The pain pattern appears greatest within the first 48 hours. The facilitation of healing and therefore in part the prevention of pain is usually concerned with preventing bacterial contamination of the operation site. Periodontal dressings were in common usage and have apparent values namely physical protection for an open wound such as following a gingivectomy, stabilisation of a flap and obturation of spaces. Dressings do have disadvantages; most do not provide antimicrobial protection and rapidly become contaminated, they are occlusive and following flap procedures are associated with increased discomfort compared to chlorhexidine rinses, often dressings are poorly retained, they isolate the operative site from antimicrobial rinses and most are unaesthetic. As a result dressings have now limited use and after most surgical and non-surgical procedures antimicrobial rinses, usually chlorhexidine, are prescribed. Regimens of use vary and will depend on the number and interval between appointments. The prime aim of such rinses is to provide optimum plaque control when mechanical cleaning may be difficult or impossible due to local discomfort. To this end rinsing is usually prescribed for two to four weeks after each surgical or non-surgical procedure. Importantly, patients need to be advised of local side effects of chlorhexidine relating to taste and staining and reassured that these can be resolved at the end of rinsing.

In the short term it is important to remember that dentine hypersensitivity may follow non surgical and surgical periodontal procedures as dentine becomes exposed to the oral environment. It is unlikely that instrumentation of the root surface directly causes sensitivity as such procedures leave a smear layer on dentine. This is however very labile to dietary acid and even toothpaste detergents and will disappear to leave tubules open. The incidence of this problem is not well researched nor is the management based on sound science. Frequently the condition appears to resolve spontaneously however desensitising toothpaste products are usually prescribed. Additionally and anecdotally fluoride rinses are reported effective. This would not seem surprising since they would be expected to reduce the acid solubility of the exposed dentine.

Long term patient management to reaffirm advice is first and foremost based on effective supragingival plaque control by the patient. This however needs professional support and there is a need to recall, reassess and remotivate patients. Where necessary professional prophylaxes should be given. The exact timing of recall appears arbitrary and should be based on patient needs rather than applying the same regimen for everyone. Essentially, the aim should be to re-establish a gingivitis free patient by the combined effects of the patient and the professional since under these circumstances recurrence of disease is most unlikely.

There are two factors that should be balanced. Patients unable to maintain satisfactory oral hygiene or who are not followed up post operatively tend to breakdown again, whilst on the other hand, patients subjected to frequent and repeat scaling of teeth show iatrogenic loss of attachment. In essence care and maintenance are essential but should not be overprescribed. The value of long term chemical plaque control for the susceptible periodontal patient who has been treated is not established. For reasons stated, the long term use of mouthrinses is not viable on the grounds that few are efficacious as adjuncts, those that are efficacious have local side effects and none are particularly cost effective. Antiplaque toothpastes would appear ideal but remain unproven as any more beneficial than conventional products in the susceptible periodontal patient.

In conclusion, the main aspect of pre and post treatment management or preparation of the periodontal patient is the achievement and maintenance of satisfactory supragingival plaque control. This is dependant on professional and personal involvement in a disease which is chronic in nature and for which susceptibility cannot be altered by means available to date. "Once a periodontal patient always a periodontal patient".

10 New horizons in periodontology

Roy C. Page

Department of Periodontics, School of Dentistry; Department of Pathology, School of Medicine, and the Regional Clinical Dental Research Center, Health Sciences Center, University of Washington, Seattle, WA 98195, USA

Introduction

Periodontology is currently a very rapidly developing field. Research is the driving force behind this change. The rapid rate of progress is reflected in a recent statement by Dr. Harald Löe, former director of the National Institute for Dental Research in Bethesda, Maryland: "The clinical discipline we call periodontology has come a long way. Concepts and procedures for treatment of periodontal diseases are scientifically based, well defined and generally adopted and applied by clinicians. Rational measures to prevent these diseases are available and widely practiced in industrialized societies. The goal of virtually eliminating periodontal disease as a public health problem seems not only feasible but probable for the large majority of most populations." [1]. It has not always been so. Indeed, the rapid pace of change goes unrecognized by most of us in Periodontics today, and there is almost no memory of what periodontics and dentistry were like only a few decades ago.

The purpose of this paper is to point out the role that research and related factors have played in the rapid change now occurring in Periodontology and Clinical Periodontics, to describe the oral health status of populations in industrialized societies prior to the research revolution, and to summarize information on the major milestones that have been achieved and the developments now on the horizon.

Periodontology prior to the research revolution

The modern era of research in Periodontology began roughly 50 years ago. At mid century, Periodontology and dentistry in general had not substantively changed since the 1890s, when W. D. Miller wrote his landmark book, Microorganisms of the Human Mouth. Oral health of the general public was extremely bad.[2] Caries was rampant, affecting 97% of all children in the U. S. by age fourteen. Lesions began soon after eruption of the primary teeth and continued unabated as the permanent teeth erupted. Frequently, the first permanent molars were lost to caries before the

129

second molars erupted at the age of 12 years. Drifting teeth and collapse of the occlusion hastened the onset of periodontal disease. Those teeth that escaped the ravages of caries during youth fell victim to periodontitis in later years. Periodontitis afflicted virtually 100% of the population by early middle age. More than 50% of the population age 65 and older were edentulous.[3] Practicing dentists were overwhelmed by the universal prevalence and severity of caries and periodontal disease. Even in 1974, half of older persons in the U. S. either had not seen a dentist for five years or had never visited a dentist.[4] At that time there was no generally accepted understanding of the cause of periodontitis, nor did there exist any generally acceptable treatments. It was widely accepted that periodontitis was an untreatable condition, and for the major portion of the population in most countries, treatment consisted of tooth extraction.

Periodontology was a stagnant field in which no research had been done other than elementary histopathologic observations. There was no understanding of the pathogenesis of periodontitis. There were no programs aimed at disease prevention and improvement of oral health. Dental practice was characterized by empiricism. The diagnostic procedures and the treatments used were the result of decades of trial and error on patients. In the 1950s, with the exception of a few individuals in the Scandinavian countries, virtually no dentists received research training and few trained scientists knew anything about dentistry. Membership in the International Association for Dental Research, a reasonable measure of world-wide research activity in dentistry, in 1960 was about 1000, and that number had changed very little since the 1930s (Figure 1). Almost all of the members were from the United States. Similarly, the number of research papers presented at the annual IADR meeting was fewer than 500 (Figure 2). It was into this environment that dental research was born.

The birth of dental research

The terrible oral health status of the American people became dramatically apparent in the 1940s during World War II when it was learned that more than 10% of the nations young men could not qualify for the military draft because they did not have six occluding teeth. Although not as well documented, oral health conditions were about the same or worse in other industrialized countries. On June 24, 1948, the Congress of the United States created the National Institute of Dental Research and charged it with developing and leading a research effort aimed at improving oral health. During the same time period, dental research began to flourish in the Scandinavian countries and by the 1960s in some parts of Western Europe. These were seminal events which were to have a dramatic, world-wide effect on periodontology and dentistry.

Thus, a major portion of the 1950s and 1960s was expended in development of new training programs and production of a cadre of competent investigators trained in the rigors, concepts and technologies of basic research, as well as in clinical dentistry. By the end of the 1960s sufficient numbers of trained investigators existed to begin to conduct a productive research effort. Subsequently, research in

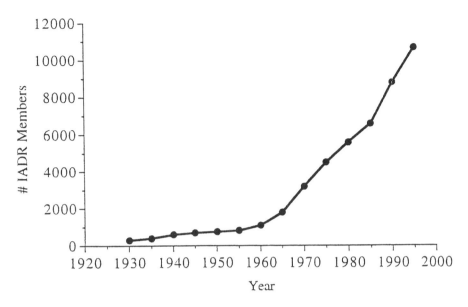

Figure 1 *Membership in the International Association for Dental Research (IADR), 1930 - 1994.*

Papers Presented

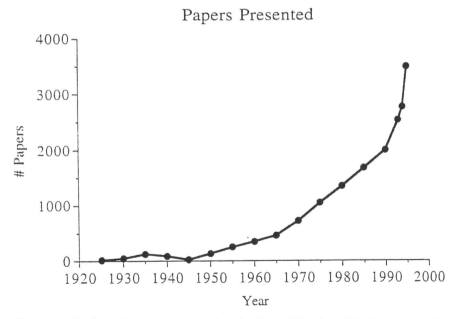

Figure 2 *Number of papers presented at the Annual Session of the International and American Associations for Dental Research.*

periodontology and in dentistry in generally grew rapidly. The growth of dental research since the 1960s has been phenomenal. Membership in the IADR now stands at a record high of about 10,600 and the number of papers presented at the annual IADR/AADR sessions totals more than 3,400 (Figures 1 and 2).

The modern era of periodontal research has had three distinct phases. The first phase occurred in the 1950s and 1960s and was the period when significant numbers of competent researchers were trained. The second phase was the golden age of basic periodontal research, which occurred in the 1970s and 1980s. During this period, an enormous wealth of new information about the basic causes and pathogenesis of periodontitis was acquired. The third phase is now occurring. In the 1990s we have witnessed a major change in the focus of periodontal research from basic investigations into the etiology and mechanisms of tissue destruction to clinical research documenting the efficacy, safety, and clinical utility of new diagnostics and treatments, and new approaches to prevention. This change of focus has resulted from several factors. First, we have acquired the basic information essential for successful clinical research. For example, microbial etiology of periodontitis and the pathways of soft tissue and bone destruction have been elucidated. Studies on untreated patients permitted a better understanding of the natural history and characteristics of progression of disease. Epidemiology studies demonstrated that the prevalence of periodontitis is relatively low, affecting roughly 10 to 15 percent of most populations. The relatively low prevalence led to elucidation of several risk factors and indicators related to susceptibility. Second, there is a rapidly growing involvement of biotechnology and industry in periodontology with the consequent application of the wealth of new information and development of many new products for prevention, diagnosis and treatment. Third, the partnership essential for progress in periodontology, which includes clinical periodontists and dentists, investigators, industry, and third-party payers, has finally evolved. These developments account for the unusually rapid rate of change in periodontics that we are now witnessing. We can expect the rate of change to accelerate in the future.

Milestones in periodontology

The modern era of periodontal research began about 35 years ago in the 1960s. Many milestones have been achieved since that time. The major advances are listed by decade in Tables 1-4, and they are discussed below.

The 1950s and 1960s (Table 1)
Numerous epidemiology studies were performed in the 1950s and 1960s in many countries around the world. A large proportion of these were performed using the Periodontal Index of Russell[5] or the Periodontal Disease Index of Ramfjord[6], both of which have methodological flaws, although others utilized a more complete periodontal examination including radiographs and were performed on relatively large numbers of subjects (86). The results of a typical study are shown in Figure 3. Gingivitis was observed to begin at a very early age and to decrease to low levels by the third decade of life. Periodontitis began in the teenage years, increased in an almost linear fashion until virtually 100% of the population was affected by early

Table 1 *Milestones in periodontology.*

1950s and 1960s
Prevalence is universal in adults
Destruction is continuous
Infectious and transmissible in rodents
Periodontitis is an infectious disease
Treatment focused on pocket elimination

Table 2 *Milestones in periodontology*

1970s
Pathogenesis of disease elucidated
Role of immune and other host responses
Identification of specific pathogens
Resective surgical therapeutic techniques perfected
Bone and gingival grafts first used
Studies comparing various therapies

Table 3 *Milestones in periodontology*

1980s
Disease prevalence is low
Disease progression is episodic and infrequent
Periodontitis is a family of diseases
Additional pathogens identified
Mechanism of tissue destruction elucidated
Root planing and conservative therapies effective
Beginning use of antimicrobials
Regenerative periodontics born
(bone and gingival grafts; GTR)
Decrease in resective surgery.

middle age. The concurrent appearance of periodontitis and disappearance of gingivitis gave rise to dogma that untreated gingivitis became periodontitis. Tooth loss began early in the third decade of life and continued in an almost linear manner. Once a periodontal pocket was established, disease progression without treatment was considered to occur in a continuous manner until tooth loss.

Early in the decade of the 1960s, the cause of periodontitis was not understood, and this lack of understanding greatly hampered development of effective treatments. One of the major discoveries in periodontology was made by Keyes and Jordan in 1964[8], when they demonstrated that periodontitis in rodents is infectious and transmissible. This observation motivated investigators to begin to suspect the same may be true for periodontitis in humans. In 1965 Harald Löe and his coworkers published their study demonstrating that gingivitis in humans is caused by microbial

Table 4 *Milestones in periodontology*

1990s
Decreased prevalence
New diagnostic methods
Risk indicators and factors
Link between periodontitis and systemic diseases
P. gingivalis and *B. forsythus* in adult periodontitis
Birth and rise of aesthetic periodontitis
Widespread use of guided tissue regeneration
New therapies based on host responses
Progress on a vaccine
Osseointegrated implants

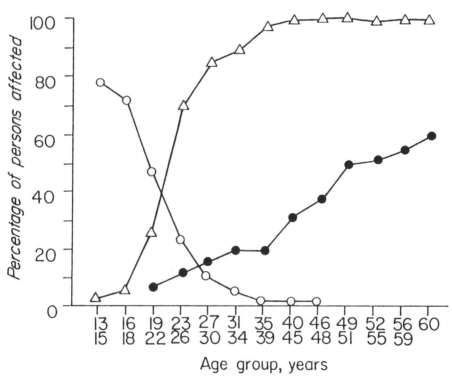

Figure 3 *Prevalence of gingivitis and periodontitis. Gingivitis (0); Periodontitis (Δ); Tooth mortality (●). Adapted from Marshall-Day et al. 1995.*

plaque and that it can be alleviated by effective removal of microbial plaque [9]. These observations were followed by studies in beagle dogs [10] and subsequently in humans, demonstrating the seminal fact that human periodontitis is an infectious disease process. By the end of the decade, the idea was widely accepted that microbial plaque of any composition could cause periodontitis.

With regard to treatment, the presence of periodontal pockets was considered to be tantamount to disease and the goal of therapy was to achieve zero pocket depth. To attain this goal, initial therapy consisting of scaling and root planing was performed and followed by osseous surgery, and this continued to be the dominant therapy used into the 1980s.

The 1970s
While the decade of the 1960s is notable for documentation of the infectious nature of periodontitis, investigators in the 1970s focused on host aspects of periodontitis (Table 2). Page and Schroeder[11] clarified for the first time stages in the pathogenesis of periodontitis and Ivanyi and Lehner[12] documented the fact that host defense mechanism are activated by microbial plaque bacteria. They demonstrated that peripheral blood mononuclear cells exposed to plaque bacteria in vitro respond by undergoing blast transformation and production of cytokines. T-lymphocyte blastogenesis was considered to be the in vitro correlate of cell mediated hypersensitivity. As a consequence, cell mediated hypersensitivity was erroneously thought to be an important component in the pathogenesis of periodontitis. This idea ignored the fact that the advanced periodontitis lesion is predominated by B cells and plasma cells and macrophages, not T lymphocytes. These observations and ideas led investigators to focus on various aspects of host response for the remainder of the decade. In 1975, Lavine and coworkers reported a defect in PMNs from patients with localized juvenile periodontitis (LJP) which resulted in impaired chemotaxis [13]. This observation was quickly confirmed by others[14,15]. This observation changed the direction of host response investigations from the lymphoid cells and the immune system to the PMN and acute inflammation. Large numbers of studies were performed documenting that the PMN defect could be detected in about 70 to 75 percent of all LJP patients[16]. More recently, Van Dyke and coworkers demonstrated additional abnormalities in PMNs from LJP including abnormal cell surface protein GP110 and intracellular signaling defects[17].

Significant advances were also made in defining the bacterial etiology of periodontitis. Newman *et al.*[18] demonstrated an association between the presence of a specific bacterial species and LJP and thereby demonstrated for the first time the involvement of specific bacterial species with periodontitis. Other investigators provided evidence for a role for several other species in severe adult periodontitis [19]. These species included *Bacteroides assachrolyticus* (*Porphyromonas gingivalis*), *Actinobacillus actinomycetemcomitans*, *Bacteroides intermedius* (*Prevotella intermedia*), *Eikenella corrodens*, fusoform bacteroides (*Bacteroides forsythus*), *Fusobacterium nucleatum* and anaerobic vibrios.

During the 1970s, resective surgical therapy techniques were honed to perfection and grafting procedures using bone, bone substitutes, and gingival tissue were tried. Also during that decade, the idea arose that while osseous surgery was an effective treatment for periodontitis, more conservative therapies might be equally effective in the long term. This idea motivated Ramfjord and coworkers [20] and others to begin to perform studies comparing various therapeutic modalities. These studies demonstrated that more conservative therapies including scaling and root planing, the Widman flap, and elevation of microperiodontal flaps to gain access to the teeth roots without recontouring bone could successfully arrest the progression of periodontitis. These observations resulted in the beginning of a decline in the use of osseous surgery as the predominant therapy.

The 1980s

The decade of the 1980s was an unusually productive period for periodontal research, with major advances made in all aspects of the field (Table 3).Numerous populations in many a countries were studied to measure the prevalence of periodontitis[7]. A picture very different from that of the 1950s and 1960s began to emerge. In a national survey of Americans aged 18 to 65 years conducted in 1981, only about 14% to 16% of individuals 45 years and older had one or more pockets 6mm or greater in depth[21,22]. When present, periodontitis was not extensive. Less than 4% of the population had three or more pockets 6m or greater in depth. Low levels of prevalence were also observed in the national survey of working adults aged 18 to 65 years and senior citizens 65 years and older[23]. Attachment loss of 5mm or more at one or more sites was observed in less than 1% of all sites studied, and in less than 13% of persons. Periodontal pockets from 4mm to 6mm deep were observed in slightly less than 14%, and deep pockets in less than 1% of the sample studied. These studies demonstrated a prevalence much lower than expected with severe periodontitis observed in a very small portion of the population. Low levels of prevalence were also observed for several other countries[24-28]. The realization that periodontitis was not a universally occurring affliction, but rather that it afflicted only a relatively small proportion of the adult population led to the identification of risk factors and indicators to be discussed later.

Another unexpected observation came from studies of populations in developing countries. It had been widely accepted, and evidence had been presented indicating that individuals with low plaque and calculus levels have little or no periodontitis, compared with individuals with chronically high levels of plaque and calculus who have much higher levels of more severe periodontitis. The situation may not be that simple. The study by Baelum *et al.*[29] on villagers the Zanzibar and Pemba Islands region of Tanzania who have had little or no access to dental care and who manifested extremely high levels of plaque and calculus serves to illustrate. In spite of unusually high levels of tooth deposits, periodontitis and tooth loss were very low. Fewer than 10% of individuals had attachment loss exceeding 6mm, and the mean number of teeth present in the oldest members of the study population was 23.9. Pockets deeper than 3mm were present fewer than 10% of all surfaces studied. Very similar results were observed in South Africa [30].

Several longitudinal studies on the progression of periodontal disease in untreated patients were conducted in the 1980s and shed new light on the natural history of periodontitis. In a 6-year study of 64 patients with untreated early to moderately severe periodontitis, only 11.6% of the sites had lost 2 mm or more of attachment, 34 of the patients had no attachment loss at any site, and 5 of the patients accounted for over 50% of the deteriorating sites. In another group of 36 patients with advanced untreated periodontitis evaluated over a period of 1 year, only 3.2% of the sites deteriorated and 5 of the 36 patients accounted for 41% of the active sites[31]. Very similar results were reported for populations in Japan[33,34] and by Jenkins *et al.* [34] for a population in Scotland. Hirschfeld and Wasserman[35] and McFall[36] found that about 5% to 8% of treated patients continued on a downhill course regardless of the type or frequency of treatment. The data demonstrate clearly that prevalence of periodontitis is low; disease-active and disease-inactive pockets exist, and in most, although not all, patients manifesting periodontal pockets, most sites at any given time are disease-inactive. Disease progression is infrequent and episodic, and its causes are unclear. Periodontal conditions deteriorate in a small portion of treated patients regardless of the treatment rendered.

During the 1970s many investigators began attempting to define and identify different kinds of periodontitis. These efforts culminated in the publication by Page and Schroeder of a proposed new classification with diagnostic criteria in 1982[37], and more recently, recognition of the existence of multiple kinds of periodontitis by the American Academy of Periodontology[38]. Periodontitis can be separated into two general types on the basis of age of onset, teeth affected, and rates of progression. These are early-onset aggressive periodontitis, a form that begins before the age of 35 years and progresses rather rapidly, and adult periodontitis, a more common form that begins later than age 35 and progresses more slowly. The early-onset form has been subdivided into prepubertal, juvenile, and rapidly progressive periodontitis. Prepubertal periodontitis begins soon after eruption of the primary dentition and occurs in localized and generalized forms[39]. Juvenile periodontitis begins during the circumpubertal period and is usually confined to the permanent first molars and/or incisors. Rapidly progressive periodontitis, also known as generalized juvenile periodontitis and severe periodontitis in young adults, begins between puberty and 35 years of age, affects most if not all of the teeth, and can progress at a rapid rate[40]. On rare occasions, periodontitis worsens regardless of the type or frequency of treatment provided; such cases are referred to as refractory. Two additional types of periodontitis are known, although they have not been well characterized. Severe periodontal destruction may be observed in individuals who have recurrent bouts of acute necrotizing ulcerative gingivitis, and a unique form of periodontitis is seen in some patients with HIV infection.

Significant progress was also made in the microbiologic etiology of periodontal diseases. Additional specific species were implicated in the cause of the disease including *A. actinomycetemcomitans*, *P. gingivalis*, *Bacteroides forsythus*, *Prevotella intermedia*, *Campylobacter rectus*, *Eubacterium nodatum*, and *Treponema* species. Several additional species were moderately associated and several more were under investigation. Two hundred or more species and serotypes were shown to exist in periodontal pockets.[41]

While in the 1970s investigators interested in the role of host defense mechanisms focused on T cells and possible cell-mediated hypersensitivity mechanisms, in the 1980s the possible role and importance of B cells and the humoral immune response

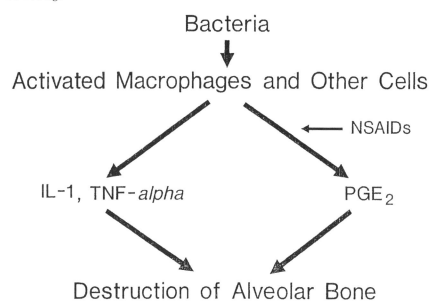

Figure 4 *Pathway where cells are activated by lipopolysaccharide and other bacterial substances to produce the mediators interleukin-1 (IL-1), Tumor Necrosis Factor-alpha (TNF-α), and Prostaglandin E2 (PGE2) that cause destruction of*

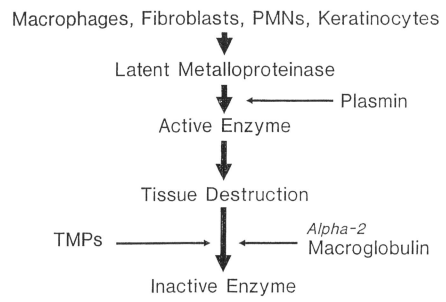

Figure 5 *Diagrammatic representation of the production of metalloproteinases by macrophages, fibroblasts, and other cells following activation by bacterial substances or cytokines and enzyme destruction of the extracellular matrix.*

became a focus. This was made possible in part by the application of the enzyme-linked immunosorbent assay (ELISA) to periodontal research[42]. Using ELISA various investigators demonstrated that some periodontitis patients mount an immune response to antigens of their infecting bacteria. The role these antibodies may play in the pathogenesis of the disease process remained uninvestigated until the decade of the 1990s.

Enormous advances were made in the 1980s in our understanding of mechanisms of tissue destruction and the role of inflammatory mediators in periodontitis. The mechanisms by which bone and the extracellular matrix of periodontal tissues are destroyed became reasonably well understood. Macrophages and fibroblasts present in the inflamed gingival tissue become activated, probably by bacterial substances such as lipopolysaccharide, to produce and secrete prostaglandin E (PGE-2), interleukin-1 (IL-1), and tumor necrosis factor-alpha (TNF-α), and these molecules mediate osteoclastic destruction of the alveolar bone (Figure 4) [43]. These same cells, as well as keratinocytes of the pocket epithelium, are similarly activated to produce a family of enzymes known as the metalloproteinases, which collectively have the capacity to degrade and destroy the gingival tissue and periodontal ligament (Figure 5). These enzymes are produced in latent form and activated by plasmin-like enzymes after which they can degrade connective tissue matrix. Enzyme activity is dependent upon the presence of divalent cations. The active enzymes can be inactivated by alpha-2-macroglobulin and by tissue inhibitors of metalloproteinases (TIMPs).[44-47] A recent development has been the realization that fibroblasts can play a major role in destruction of the very tissues they produce and maintain. When fibroblasts are located in normal, healthy gingiva, their genes for production of collagen and other extracellular matrix proteins and those for inhibitors of the activity of the metalloproteinases are turned on, while the genes for the metalloproteinases are turned off. Under these conditions, normal connective tissue is produced and maintained, and wound healing and tissue regeneration can occur. As periodontitis develops, the cells undergo a change in shape. The genes for collagen and other proteins normally produced are turned off, and the genes for metalloproteinases are activated, resulting in degradation. Following successful treatment by scaling and root planing, the reverse occurs and healing and regeneration can proceed [43-47]. Advances in our understanding of pathogenesis of periodontitis served as their basis for development of new methods for prevention and new diagnostics and therapies that began to occur in the 1990s.

Numerous advances were made in the 1980s in the area of periodontal therapy. Some clinicians and investigators began to suspect that pocket elimination was not essential to the success of periodontal therapy; that control of subgingival infection was sufficient [20]. This approach became known as non-surgical therapy. The idea that an appropriate goal for periodontal therapy was not zero pocket depth but rather conversion of infected diseased periodontal pockets to healthy periodontal sites maintained free of pathogenic bacteria was at first enormously controversial. As a consequence, large numbers of longitudinal studies were conducted comparing the outcome of various therapeutic modalities such as surgical pocket elimination versus scaling and root planing with or without the use of chemotherapy[29,48-51]. These studies demonstrated clearly that the quality of the subgingival debridement and infection control, not the presence or absence of the periodontal pocket, was the major determinant of successful periodontal therapy. Such therapy may result in resolution of the inflammatory response, cessation of the progress of periodontal destruction, a small gain in periodontal attachment, significant reduction in probing depth and formation of a long junctional epithelium. These studies set in motion a worldwide trend toward more widespread use of nonsurgical therapies that still continues today.

The decade of the 1980s also heralded the birth of regenerative periodontics with the use of grafting materials and development of an entirely new approach known as guided tissue regeneration (GTR). The goals of therapy were redefined. No longer were we content with a reduced but healthy periodontium with or without healthy periodontal pockets. The goal became not only arresting the progress of periodontal tissue destruction, but also regenerating previously destroyed tissues and restoring a normal periodontal status. Procedures for covering denuded root surfaces using free and pedical gingival grafts and grafts of palatal connective tissue were developed. A wide variety of bone and bone substitute materials became available and came into use. Studies demonstrated that the use of osseoconductive and osseoinductive graft materials could, under favorable conditions, induce roughly 60% to 70% regeneration of bone lesion height or volume with concomitant improvement in the clinical conditions.

Our ability to regenerate previously destroyed periodontal tissues was advanced enormously when Nyman and coworkers[52-54] demonstrated that exclusion of gingival epithelium and fibroblasts from the periodontal wound site by placement of a barrier over the wound allowed cells, presumably from the periodontal ligament and the adjacent bone marrow to populate the wound and these cells gave rise to new cementum, periodontal ligament, and alveolar bone. Extensive studies performed in experimental animals and in humans have demonstrated that the procedure, known as guided tissue regeneration, results in periodontal regeneration in 2- and 3-wall intrabony defects and in class II furcations, especially on lower molars. A wide variety of barrier materials has been evaluated.

The 1990s (Table 4)
By the decade of the 1990s large numbers of epidemiologic studies had been performed in countries around the world[7]. Indeed, the World Health Organization data bank in Geneva has the largest set of epidemiologic data on periodontal disease ever assembled. Prevalence of moderate to severe periodontitis in the United States, Canada, Scandinavia and Europe appears to be approximately 15%. With some exceptions, where the validity of the data is questionable, the prevalences in other countries also seem relatively low, although there is evidence for a higher prevalence in some Asian countries, such as Japan and China[27,55].

The major question we are facing in the 1990s is whether or not prevalence is decreasing. There is anecdotal evidence in the United States that this is indeed the case. Many dental schools have difficulties in obtaining sufficient numbers of patients with moderate to severe periodontitis. The same seems to be true for many practicing periodontists. The recently acquired epidemiologic data is difficult to

reconcile with studies performed in the 1950s and 1960s, it would appear that either the earlier studies were flawed or the prevalence of periodontitis has changed. Although the recent studies may have been performed with more precision and better methods, the populations used the earlier studies were large and the methods in many cases sufficiently adequate that the resulting conclusions cannot be ignored. When all of the data are considered, there appears to have been a decrease of major proportions in the prevalence of periodontitis in adults in Western industrialized countries, especially for populations in the United States for whom the data are most complete[7]. This conclusion is supported by the observation reported by Douglass *et al.* [56] that the proportion of Americans without gingivitis or periodontitis increased from roughly 25% in the 1960s to 50% a decade later. More definitive data will not become available until the next national survey is conducted in the United States, possibly in 1996 or 1997.

The longitudinal studies of the progression of periodontitis in untreated patients already described, clearly documented that disease progression at individual tooth sites in most patients is episodic and infrequent; disease-active and disease-inactive periodontal pockets exist. For most patients at any given point in time, most of periodontal pockets are disease inactive and therefore do not require intervention. Traditional diagnostic procedures including visual examination of the gingival tissues, assessment of pocket depth, bleeding on probing, attachment level and radiographic assessment of alveolar bone status when used in a cross-sectional manner cannot distinguish between disease-active and -inactive periodontal sites. This constitutes a diagnostic problem that is central to periodontics today. As a result, we treat all sites in a given mouth.

A major research effort is underway to resolve our diagnostic dilemma. Numerous objective tests designed to gain information about disease activity at given periodontal sites are under development in many university and industrial laboratories. These tests fall into two general categories: those measuring specific components of gingival crevicular fluid (GCF) that may be indicators of disease activity, and tests designed to detect periodontopathic bacterial species in the subgingival microflora. More than forty components of GCF have been studied[57]; those most studied are listed in Table 5. A few of these appear to be related to disease activity, and may serve as the basis for tests that permit detection of disease-active sites. Among these are alkaline phosphatase, beta-glucuronidase, prostaglandin E2, interleukin 1-beta, aspartate aminotransferase, and the IgG4 antibody body subclass. Clinical trials of safety, efficacy and clinical utility for tests based on some of these components are nearing completion and FDA submission, and some of the tests will undoubtedly come to market in the near future. Tests designed to detect and roughly quantify pathogenic bacteria in the sub-gingival microflora also show considerable promise. These include culture techniques using various standard and selective media, tests based on the use of specific monoclonal antibodies and DNA probes.

Another aspect of diagnosis and prognosis upon which investigators are currently focusing is assessment of risk. Once the relatively low prevalence of moderate to severe periodontitis was established, the next logical step was to attempt to identify

Table 5 *Gingival crevicular fluid components that have been most studied*

Collagenase and related molecules
Cathepsin-like activities and other proteases
Alkaline phosphatase
β-glucuronidase and arylsulfatase
Aspartate aminotransferase
Cytokines
Metabolites of arachidonic acid
Antibodies
Lysozyme and lactoferrin
Tissue components and degradation products
Factors influencing microbial growth
Myeloperoxidase
Complement components

Table 6 *Risk factors and indicators for periodontitis*

Cigarette Smoking
Advancing age
Past history of periodontitis
Presence of periodontopathic bacteria
Compromised host defense
Race and ethnicity
Low income and educational levels
Poor oral hygiene
Infrequent visits to the dentist
Family history of periodontitis

characteristics of individuals in the subpopulation a high probability of having or developing disease. This approach has led to one of the major recent advances in periodontology, the identification of several risk factors or indicators. Risk factors are participants in the causation of disease, such as smoking and lung cancer, while risk indicators may be associated with a disease but have not been proven to be linked to causation. Risk factors and indicators associated with the probability of developing severe periodontitis are listed in Table 6.

Cigarette smoking is the most well documented risk indicator for severe periodontitis now known [58-62]. Smokers are two to five times more likely to develop severe attachment loss than non-smokers. The majority of patients with refractory periodontitis are smokers. The periodontal status of former smokers ranks between that of current smokers and those who have never smoked. Smoking secession is rapidly becoming an integral part of treatment for advanced periodontitis. Smoking has both local and systemic effects. Tobacco smoke inhibits gingival inflammation by causing constriction of blood vessels, and this may mask gingival inflammation. Components present in tobacco smoke inhibit the functional activity of macrophages and the other leukocytes, and there is recent evidence that smoking inhibits the production of the IgG2 subclass of immunoglobulin (Tew, personal communication). IgG2 is the major serum antibody subclass produced in response to periodontal infection. Some experts believe that advancing age is a risk indicator for severe periodontitis[61,62], although this seems questionable. Since periodontal pockets once formed do not disappear, they accumulate over time. As a consequence, older individuals may be expected to manifest more pockets than younger individuals and this may account for the idea that older persons are more susceptible. Past history of periodontitis places a patient at risk for future periodontal deterioration; the more severe the disease the more likely there will continue to be disease in the future[58,63-65]. The presence of certain putative periodontal pathogens such as *Porphyromonas gingivalis* in the subgingival flora at levels of 2% or greater is a risk indicator[61,62,66-68].

Diseases states and other factors that compromise the body's defense against infection can increase the risk of developing periodontitis. Examples of such diseases include diabetes mellitus[69], HIV infection[70], any of several abnormalities in the phagocytic cells such as neutropenia[16,17,71], and several hereditary diseases such as Down's Syndrome[72,73]. Other predisposing factors include drugs that inhibit immune responsiveness and irradiation. Race and ethnicity also appear to play a role. African Americans and, to a lesser extent, Hispanic Americans are more susceptible to severe periodontitis than European Americans. Those with low income and low educational levels manifest more periodontitis than others, as do individuals who visit the dentist infrequently[58,63,74]. Oral hygiene also plays a role; those with higher plaque levels manifest more risk for periodontitis than individuals with low levels[63,75,76].

There is an increasing body of evidence supporting a role for hereditary as an important determinant of disease susceptibility[73]. Periodontitis, especially the early onset forms, is known to be familial. In fact, the existence of an autosomal dominant major genetic locus for these forms of periodontitis has recently been reported[77]. Similarly, several studies of dizygotic and monozygotic twins have demonstrated an important role for heredity in adult periodontitis[73,78]. The studies of Michalowicz *et al.*[79] indicates that roughly half of the variance for severe periodontitis can be accounted for be heredity alone.

The discovery of risk factors and indicators has major implications for management of periodontitis. While having only a single positive risk indicator may not be very meaningful, being positive for multiple indicators is highly meaningful. Beck *et al.*[50] have shown that if four of the risk indicators they studied were positive, risk for disease increased 160-fold. Furthermore, for individuals who smoked, had *P. gingivalis* in their subgingival flora, were BANA test-positive (a colorimetric test for certain periodontal pathogens), and had not visited the dentist for three or more years, risk was enhanced 500-fold. Our ability to identify patients with risks of this magnitude will aid greatly in diagnosing, treatment planning, and establishing a prognosis and maintenance programs for our patients. Assessment of risk is rapidly becoming integrated into the practice of periodontics and dentistry in general.

Although it has been clear for many years that any of several systemic diseases such as diabetes mellitus can place individuals who have them at risk for severe periodontitis, only recently have investigators become concerned with the possibility that having periodontitis may predispose other systemic diseases[80-83]. Clearly that is the case. DeSteffano *et al.* [80] recently reported the results of a study of approximately 10,000 Americans who were monitored for 17 years. Those with periodontitis had a 25% increased risk for coronary heart disease. This enhanced risk was associated with poor oral hygiene but not with caries or missing teeth. Individuals having periodontitis at a relatively young age (under 50 years) manifested a 50% risk for coronary disease and a risk of dying was enhanced 300%. It must be noted, however, that those with severe periodontitis were also older, non-white men, who were less educated, unmarried, and smoked. These are also factors risk indicators for heart disease.

An observation of great importance to practitioners was recently reported by Offenbacher and his coworkers[82]. They observed a very strong association between the presence of severe periodontitis in the mother and spontaneous abortion, premature labor, and low birth-weight infants. Additional studies indicated that *P. gingivalis* infection results in elevated circulating levels of TNF-alpha and prostaglandin E2, and these may be related to the effect on the fetus[82,83]. Because of observations such as these, the interface between periodontics and general medicine is of growing importance.Significant advances have been recently made in understanding the microbiology of periodontitis. Throughout the 1970s and 1980s, the list of putative periodontal pathogens continued to lengthen. Indeed, in a recent review, 14 species were listed as strongly or moderately associated with periodontitis[41]. Current studies are tending to draw focus to a smaller number. For example, Grossi *et al.* [62] recently reported the results of a study on almost 1400 patients. Using stepwise logistic regression, they found that only *P. gingivalis* and *Bacteroides forsythus* to be associated with adult periodontitis. Another significant advance has been resolution of the question about transmission of periodontal pathogens. There is strong evidence that putative periodontal pathogens can be found at periodontally nomal sites in patients with periodontitis [84] and at sites in periodontally nomal individuals[85,86]. These observations support the idea that with sufficiently sensititive techniques, pathogenic species can be found commonly in peridontally normal individuals. On the other hand, there is also strong evidence that *Actinobacillus* and *P. gingivalis* are transmitted among family members[87-90] and between spouses [91,92]. One report suggests transmission of *A. actinomycetemcomitans* from the family pet dog to a child [93]. These observations argue in favor of transmission, but much additional evidence is needed. If transmission is an essential step in the spread of disease and disease onset, our approach to treatment may have to change from focus on a given patient to focus on infected families, with the aim of eliminating disease-causing pathogens.

The enormous amount of new information about the pathways of tissue destruction obtained in the 1970s and 1980s now serves as the basis for entirely new

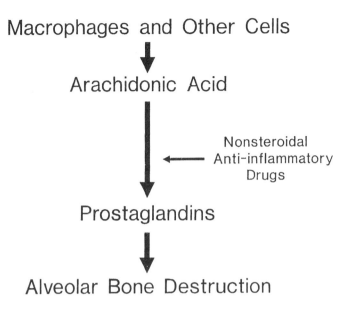

Macrophages and Other Cells

⬇

Arachidonic Acid

Nonsteroidal
Anti-inflammatory
Drugs

Prostaglandins

⬇

Alveolar Bone Destruction

Figure 6 *Diagrammatic representation of the inhibition of alveolar bone loss by inhibition of cyclooxygenase activity and PGE2 production by activated macrophages and other cells.*

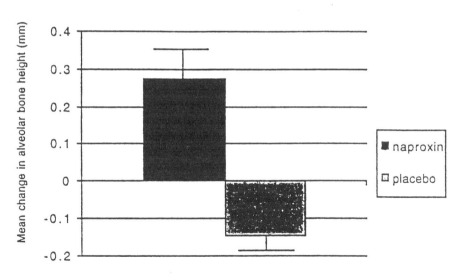

Figure 7 *Mean change in alveolar bone height measured using standardized digital radiography. There was significantly less bone loss during the treatment period in naprosen-treated patients compared with placebo patients (p=0.001, test). (From Jeffcoat et al. 1991, with permission).*

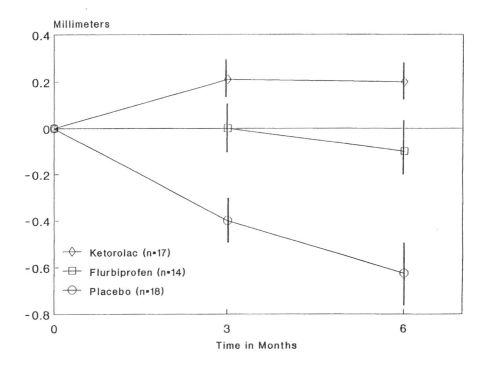

Figure 8 *Mean cumulative change in bone height. Topical ketorolac and systemic flurbiprofin preserved significantly more alveolar bone height than placebo (p<0.001; p<0.002, respectively). Ketorolac treatment preserved 0.30 mm more alveolar bone height than systemic flurbiprofin (p=0.066).*

approaches to periodontal therapy, such as drugs which modify host responses. As noted previously, tissue macrophages, activated by pocket bacteria and their products, produce large quantities of arachidonic acid metabolites known as the prostaglandins and these, especially PGE2 mediate pathologic alveolar bone resorption [94]. The non-steroidal anti-inflammatory family of drugs (NSAIDS) can suppress or block prostaglandin production, and could be expected to block or suppress alveolar bone destruction (Figure 6). Clinical trials have demonstrated that this is indeed the case [95,96]. As shown in Figure 7, administration of the anti-inflammatory drug naproxen as an adjunct to scaling and root planing not only blocks alveolar bone loss, but also results in a significant bone gain relative to placebo. However, these drugs, when administered systemically, can have significant undesirable side effects, especially when taken over long time periods. A clinical trial has been conducted using an oral rinse containing the NSAID ketorolac

146

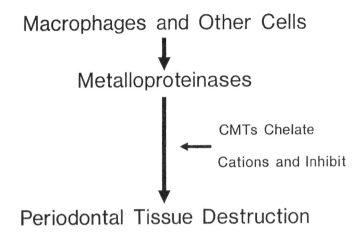

Figure 9 *Diagrammatic representation of the inhibition of metalloproteinase degradation of extracellular matrix components by chemically modified tetracyclines (CMTs) that act by chelating divalent cations.*

tromethamine as the active agent. The rinse was used twice each day over a period of six months in a randomized, double blind, parallel placebo-controlled study. The positive control consisted of a 50 mg flurbiprofen capsule twice daily. Alveolar bone status was monitored by digital subtraction radiography [96]. A significant loss in bone height was observed at 3 and 6 months in the placebo group with no significant bone loss in the positive control, and an actual bone gain in the oral rinse group (Figure 8). On the basis of this study, topical application of this anti-inflammatory drug appears to arrest the progress of alveolar bone loss. If the observations made in this study can be confirmed, topical application of anti-inflammatory drugs may provide a new, simple, and inexpensive way to arrest the progression of periodontal destruction.

It is now clear that the connective tissue matrix of the gingiva and periodontal ligament is destroyed by the metalloproteinase family of enzymes that are produced by macrophages and fibroblasts following their activation by bacterial substances[44-47]. The activity of these enzymes is dependent upon the presence of divalent cations. Golub and his colleagues[97] have demonstrated that antibiotics of the tetracycline class are not only detrimental to bacteria, but they also chelate divalent cations and thereby suppress or block metalloproteinase activity. Chemically modified tetracyclines that do not have antibacterial activity, but that still chelate divalent cations have been synthesized. These drugs are effective at reducing collagenase and other metalloproteinases in experimental animal model systems and in humans with periodontitis, and in suppressing destruction of collagenous tissue (Figure 9).

Thus, in the 1990s periodontal therapy has three central components, each approaching the disease from a different direction: first, scaling and root planing with

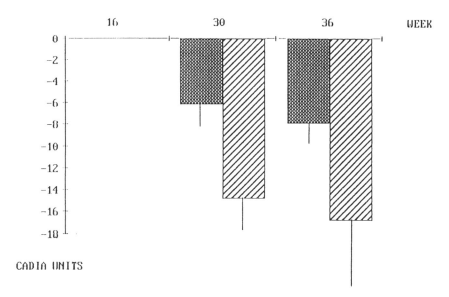

Figure 10 *Mean change and standard error bars in alveolar bone housing mandibular test teeth, reported in terms of CADIA units from week 16 when ligatures were placed to week 36; (values at week 16 were considered as zero). (From Persson* et al. *1994, with permission).*

or without opening mucoperiosteal flaps aimed at debridement of the surfaces of the tooth roots; second, antibiotics and other antimicrobials aimed directly at destruction of the bacteria present in the periodontal pockets and in the periodontal tissues; and third, drugs aimed at modification of host-response mechanisms to suppress or inhibit prostaglandin-mediated alveolar bone resorption and metalloproteinase-mediated tissue destruction. Using these therapies, we can be remarkably successful in arresting the progress of periodontal destruction in most patients with or without osseous resection and with or without pocket elimination.

An additional approach at modification of host response pathways is development of a vaccine to enhance immune responsiveness to antigens of periodontopathic bacteria. My colleagues and I have shown that a vaccine containing whole killed *P. gingivalis* as antigen can effectively suppress alveolar bone loss in experimental periodontitis in the nonhuman primate *Macaca fascicularis* (Figure 10) [98,99]. This observation suggests that development of a vaccine for prevention and possible treatment of periodontitis in humans is likely to be possible.

Of all the advances made in Periodontology and Clinical Periodontics in the 1990s, those in the area of surgical periodontal therapy may be the most significant. Regenerative therapies are rapidly replacing resective approaches. Bone morphogenic proteins and various other growth factors are being used with and without various barrier membranes[100-102]. The placement of osseointegrated implants and use of guided tissue regeneration are the most rapidly growing aspects of clinical periodontics. Indeed, the use of these procedures permits periodontists to address and successfully resolve problems that could not be dealt with only a few years ago. Among these are placement of fixed prostheses in locations where previously only full or partial removable dentures could be used, rebuilding edentulous ridges using GTR and grafts of bone or other material, and regeneration of bone over denuded tooth roots[103]. Such procedures are now a day-to-day component of periodontal practice, and they have greatly broadened the scope of periodontics. Their use has given birth to aesthetic periodontics. Therapists and patients now see as their goals a full complement of well aligned teeth, natural or otherwise, with a normal amount of alveolar bone support and normal gingival color, texture and contour with gingival margins located at or near the cementoenamel junction and papillae filling the interproximal embrasure spaces. Periodontics is approaching the time in which these goals can be achieved.

References

1. Löe, H. Periodontal disease: A brief historical perspective. *Periodontology 2000* 2, 7-12, 1993.
2. Finn, SB. Prevalence of dental caries. In: A *Survey of the literature of dental caries*, pp. 117-173. Washington, DC, National Academy of Sciences / National Research Council, 1952.
3. *Edentulous persons in the United States.* DHEW Publication No. (HRA) 74-1516, Vital Health Statistics, Series 10, No. 89, 1971.
4. *Facts about older Americans.* DHEW Publication No. (OHD) 77-20006, Office of Human Development, Administration on Aging, National Clearinghouse on Aging, 1976.
5. Russell, AL. The periodontal index. *J. Periodontol.* **38** (part II), 585-591, 1967.
6. Ramfjord, SP. Periodontal disease index (PDI). *J. Periodontol.* **38** (Part II), 602-610, 1967.
7. Page, RC. Severe forms of periodontitis in children, juveniles and adults. World-Wide prevalence. In: *Proceedings of a Symposium, Markers of disease susceptibility and activity in periodontal diseases.* Royal Society of Medicine, London, England, pp. 76-105, 1989.
8. Keyes, PH, Jordan HV. Periodontal lesions in the a Syrian hamster . III. Findings related to an infectious and transmissible component. *Arch. Oral Biol.* **9**, 377-400, 1964.
9. Löe, H, Theilade ,E, Jensen, SB. Experimental gingivitis in man. *J. Periodontol.* **36**, 177-187, 1965.
10. Lindhe, J, Hamp, S-E, Löe, H. Plaque induced periodontal disease in beagle dogs. 4-year clinical, roentgenographical and histometrical study. *J. Periodont. Res.* **10**, 243-255,1975.

11. Page, RC , Schroeder, HE. Pathogenesis of chronic inflammatory periodontal disease, A summary of current work. *Lab. Invest.* **33**, 235-249, 1976.

12. Ivanyi, L, Lehner, T. Stimulation of lymphocyte transformation by bacterial antigens in patients with periodontal disease. *Arch. Oral Biol.* **15**, 1089-1096, 1970.

13. Lavine, WS, Stolman J, Maderazo, EG, Ward, P, Cogen, RC. Defective neutrophil chemotaxis in patients with early onset periodontitis. *54th Gen. Meeting*, IADR, Miami, Abstract 603,1976.

14. Cianciola, LJ, Genco, RJ, Patters, MR, McKenna, J, Van Oss, CJ. Defective polymorphonuclear leukocyte function in a human periodontal disease. Nature, London **265**, 445-447, 1977.

15. Clark , RA, Page, RC, Wilde, G. Defective neutrophil chemotaxis in juvenile periodontitis. *Infect. Immun.* **18**, 694-700, 1977

16. Van Dyke, TE, Levine, MJ, Genco, RJ. Neutrophil function and oral disease. *J. Oral Pathol.* **14**, 95-120, 1985.

17. Daniel, MA, McDonald, G, Offenbacher, S, Van Dyke, TE. Defective signal transduction in localized juvenile periodontitis. *J. Periodontol.* **64**, 617-621, 1993.

18. Newman, MG, Socransky, SS, Savitt, ED, Propas, DA, Crawford, A. Studies of the microbiology of periodontosis. *J. Periodontol.* **47**, 373-379, 1976.

19. Tanner, ACR, Haffer, C, Bratthal, GT, Visconti, RA, Socransky, SS. A study of the bacteria associated with advancing periodontitis in man. *J. Clin. Periodontol.* **6**, 278-307, 1979.

20. Knowles, JW, Burgett, FG, Niddle, RR, Schick, RA, Morrison, EC, Ramfjord, SP. Results of periodontal treatment related to pocket depth and attachment level. Eight years. *J. Periodontol* **50**, 225-233, 1979.

21. Miller, AJ, Brunelle, JA, Carlos, JP, Brown, LJ, Löe, H. Oral Health of United States Adults. U. S. Department of Health and Human Services, National Institute of Dental Research, NIH Publication No. 87-2868, 1987.

22. Brown JL, Löe, H Prevalence, extent, severity, and progression of periodontal disease. *Periodontology 2000*, **2**, 57-71, 1993.

23. Brown, JL, Oliver, RC, Löe, H. Evaluating periodontal status of US employed adults. *J. Am Dent. Assoc.* **121**, 226-232, 1990.

24. Gaengler, P., Goebel, G., Kurbad, A., and Kosa, W. Assessment of periodontal disease and dental caries in a population survey using the CPITN, GPM/T and DMF/T indices. *Comm. Dent. Oral Epidemiol.* **16**, 236-239, 1988.

25. Gaengler, P., Gobel, B., Kurbad, A., and Kosa, W. *Local epidemiological profile of periodontal disease and dental caries of the Districts of Erfurt and Suhl, German Democratic Republic, 1985-1986.* 100 pages, 1986.

26. Hugoson, A., and Jordan, T. Frequency distribution of individuals aged 20-70 years according to severity of periodontal disease. *Comm. Dent. Oral Epidemiol.* **10**, 187-192, 1982.

27. Miyazaki, H., Hanada, M., Andoh, N.I., Yamashita, Y., Saito, T., Sogame,. A., Goto, K., Shirahama, R., and Takehara, T. Periodontal disease prevalence in different age groups in Japan as assessed according to the CPITN. *Comm. Dent. Oral Epidemiol.* **17**, 71-74, 1989.

28. Papapanou, P.N. Patterns of alveolar bone loss in the assessment of periodontal treatment priorities. *Swedish Dent. J.* (Suppl. 66), 1989 (pages not numbered).

29. Baelum, V., Fejerskov, O., and Karring, T. Oral hygiene, gingivitis and periodontal breakdown in adult Tanzanians. *J. Periodont. Res.* **21**, 221-232, 1986.

30. Africa, C.W., Parker, J.R. and Reddy, J. Bacteriological studies of subgingival plaque in a periodontal disease-resistant population. I. Darkfield microscopic studies. *J. Periodont. Res.* **20**, 1-7, 1985.

31. Lindhe, J., Haffajee, AD, and Socransky, SS. Progression of periodontal disease in adult subjects in the absence of periodontal therapy. *J. Clin. Periodontol.* **10**, 433-442, 1983.

32. Lindhe, J., Okamoto, H., Yoneyama, T., Haffajee, A. and Socransky, S.S. Longitudinal changes in periodontal disease in untreated subjects. *J. Clin. Periodontol.* **16**, 662-670, 1989a.

33. Lindhe, J, Okamoto, H, Yoneyna, T., Haffajee, A. and Socransky, S.S. Periodontal loser sites in untreated adult subjects. *J. Clin. Periodontol.* **16,** 671-678, 1989b.

34. Jenkins, W.H.M., MacFarlane, T.W., and Gilmour, W.H. Longitudinal study of untreated periodontitis. Clinical findings. *J. Clin. Periodontol.* **15**, 324-330, 1988.

35. Hirschfeld, L., and Wasserman, B. A long-term survey of tooth loss in 600 treated periodontal patients. *J. Periodontol.* **49**, 225-237, 1978.

36. McFall, W.T. Tooth loss in 100 treated patients with periodontal disease. A long-term study. *J. Periodontol.* **53**, 539-549, 1982.

37. Page, RC, Schroeder HE. *Periodontitis in Man and Other Animals. A Comparative Review.* S. Karger, Basel, 1982, 330 pages.

38. *Proceedings of the World Workshop in Clinical Periodontics*, Consensus Report Discussion Section 1, pages 1-23 - I24, 1989.

39. Page, RC, Bowen T, Altman LC, Vandesteen GE, Ochs H, Mackenzie P, Osterberg SK, Engel, LD, Williams, BL. Prepubertal periodontitis I. Definition of a clinical disease entity. *J. Periodontol.* **54**, 257-271, 1983a.

40. Page RC. Bowen T, Altman LC, Vandesteen GE, Dahlberg WH, Williams BL, Osterberg SK. Rapidly progressive periodontitis, A distinct clinical condition. *J. Periodontol.* **54,** 197-209, 1983.

41. Hafffajee, AD, Socransky, SS. Microbial etiological agents of destructive periodontal diseases. *Periodontology 2000* **5**, 78-111, 1994.

42. Ebersole, JL, Taubman, Ma, Smith, DJ, Goodson, JM. Gingival crevicular fluid antibody to oral microorganisms. I. Methods of collection and analysis of antibody. J. *Periodont. Res.* **19**, 124-132, 1984.

43. Page, RC. The role of inflammatory mediators in the pathogenesis of periodontal disease. *J. Periodontal Res.* **26**, 230-242, 1991.

44. Heath, JK, Atkinson, SJ, Hembry, RM, Reynolds, JJ, Meikle, MC. Bacterial antigens induce collagenase and prostaglandin E2 synthesis in human gingival fibroblasts through a primary effect on circulating mononuclear cells. *Infect. Immun.* **55**, 2148-2154, 1987.

45. Heath, JK, Gowen, M, Meikle, MC, Reynolds, JJ. Human gingival tissues in culture synthesize three metalloproteinases and a metalloproteinase inhibitor. *J. Periodont. Res.* **17**, 183-190, 1982.

46. Meikle, MC, Atkinson, SJ, Ward, RV, Murphy, G, Reynolds, JJ. Gingival fibroblasts degrade type I. Collagen films when stimulated with tumor necrosis factor and inter-leukin 1, Evidence that breakdown is mediated by metalloproteinases. *J. Periodont. Res.* **24**, 207-213, 1989.

47. Birkedal-Hansen, H. Role of cytokines and inflammatory mediators in tissue destruction. *J. Periodontol. Res.* **28** (Part 2), 500-510, 1993.

48. Pihlstrom, BL, McHugh, RB, Oliphant, TH, Ortiz-Campos, C. Comparison of surgical and non-surgical treatment of periodontal disease. A review of current studies and additional results after 6 1/2 years. *J. Clin. Periodontol.* **10**, 524-541, 1983.

49. Baderstein, A, Nilveus, R, Egelberg, J. Effect of non-surgical periodontal therapy. III. Single versus repeated instrumentation. *J. Clin. Periodontol.* **11**, 114-124, 1984.
50. Beck, JD, Koch, GG, Rozier, RG, Tudor, GE. Prevalence and risk indicators for periodontal attachment loss in a population of older community-dwelling blacks and whites. *J. Periodontol.* **61**, 521-528, 1990.
51. Renvert, S, Nilveus, R, Dahlen, G, Slots, J, Edelberg, J. Five-year follow-up of periodontal intraosseous defects treated by root planing or flap surgery. *J. Clin. Periodontol.* **17**, 356-363, 1990.
52. Nyman S, Gottlow J, Lindhe J, Karring T, Wennestrôm, J. New attachment formation by guided tissue regeneration. *J. Periodontol Res.* **22**, 252-254, 1987.
53. Nyman, S, Gottlow, J, Karring, T, Lindhe, J. The regenerative potential of the periodontal ligament . *J. Clin Periodontol.* **17**, 257-262, 1982.
54. Nyman, S, Lindhe, J, Karring, T, Rylander, H. New attachment following surgical treatment of human periodontal disease. *J. Clin. Periodontol.* **9**, 290-296, 1982.
55. Wang, WJ, Liu, CY, Liu, CZ, Lee, CJ. Survey of periodontal disease among workers in Tianjin using RamfjordÕs Periodontal Diseases Index (PDI). *Comm. Dent. Oral Epidemiol.* **15**, 98-99, 1987.
56. Douglass, C.W., Gelling, D., Sollocito, W., and Gamn, M. National trends in the prevalence and severity of the periodontal diseases. *J. Am. Dent. Assoc.* **107**, 403-412, 1983.
57. Page, RC. Host response tests for diagnosing periodontal diseases. *J. Periodontol.* **63**, 356-366, 1992.
58. Beck, J. Methods of assessing risk for periodontitis and developing multifactorial models. *J. Periodontol.* **65**, 468-478, 1994.
59. Bergstrom, J. Preber, H. Tobacco use as a risk factor. *J. Periodontol.* **65**, 545-550, 1994.
60. Haber J. Cigarette smoking, A major risk factor for periodontitis. *Compendium of Continuing Education* **25**, 1002-1012, 1994.
61. Grossi, S, Zambon J, Ho A, Koch G, Dunford, R, Machtei, E, Norderyd, O, Genco, RJ. Assessment of risk for periodontal disease. Risk indicators for attachment loss. *J. Periodontol.* **65**, 260-267, 1994.
62. Grossi, SG, Genco, RJ, Machtei, EE, Ho, AW, Koch, G, Dunford, R, Zambon, JJ, Hausmann, E. Assessment of risk for periodontal disease. II. Risk indicators for alveolar bone loss. *J. Periodontol.* **66**, 23-29, 1995.
63. Hansen, BF, Bjertness, E, Cronnesby, JK. A socio-ecologic model for periodontal diseases. *J. Clin. Periodontol.* **20**, 584-590, 1993.
64. Grbic, J, Lamster, I. Risk indicators for future clinical attachment loss in adult periodontitis. Tooth and site variables. *J. Periodontol.* **63**, 262-269, 1992.
65. Horning, G, Hatch, C, Cohen, M. Risk indicators for periodontitis in a military treatment population. *J. Periodontol.* **63**, 297-302, 1992.
66. Petit, MDA, van Steenbergen, TJM, Timmerman, MF, de Graaff, J, Jr., van der Velden U. Prevalence of periodontitis and suspected periodontal pathogens in families of adult periodontitis patients. *J. Clin Periodontol.* **21**, 76-85, 1994.
67. Beck, J, Koch, G, Zambon, J, Genco, R, Tudor, G. Evaluation of oral bacteria as risk indicators for periodontitis in older adults. *J. Periodontol.* **63**, 93-99, 1992.
68. Wolff, L., Dahlan, G, Aeppli, D. Bacteria as risk markers for periodontitis. *J. Periodontol.* **65**, 498-510, 1994.
70. Murray, P. HIV disease as a risk factor for periodontal disease. *Compendium of Continuing Education* **25**, 1052-1063, 1994.

71. Van Dyke, TE, Wilson-Burrows, C, Offenbacher, S, Henson, P. Association of abnormality of neutrophil chemotaxis in human periodontal disease with a cell surface protein. *Infect Immun* **55**, 2262-2267, 1987.

72. Hart, T, Shapira, L, Van Dyke, T. Neutrophil defects as risk factors for periodontal diseases. *J. Periodontol.* 521-529, 1994b.

73. Hart, TC. Genetic considerations of risk in human periodontal disease. *Current Opinion in Periodontol.* **2**, 3-11, 1994a.

74. Brown, LJ, Garcia, R. Utilization of dental services as a risk factor for periodontitis. *J. Periodontol.* **65**, 551-563, 1994.

75. Newman, M, Kornman, K Holtzman, S. Association of clinical factors with treatment out comes . *J. Periodontol.* **65**, 489-497, 1994.

76.. Corbet, EF, Davis, WIR. The role of supragingival plaque in the control of progressive periodontal disease. A review. *J. Clin. Periodontol.* **20**, 3-7-313, 1993.

77. Marazita, ML, Burmeister, JA, Gonsolley, JC, Koertge, TE , Lake, K. Shenkein, HA. Evidence for autosomal dominant inheritance and race-specific heterogeneity in early-onset periodontitis. *J. Periodontol.* **65**, 623-630, 1994.

78. Michalowicz, B. Genetic and heritable risk factors in periodontal disease. *J. Periodontol.* **65**, 479-488, 1994.

79. Michalowicz, BS, Aeppli, D, Virag, JG, Klump, DG, Hinrichs, JE, Segal, NL *et al.* Periodontal findings in adult twins. *J. Periodontol* **62**, 293-299, 1991.

80. DeStefano, R, Anda, RF, Kahn, HS, Williamson, DF, Russell, CM. Dental disease and risk of coronary heart disease and mortality. *Br. Dent. J.* **306**, 688-691, 1993.

81. Beck, J, Garcia, R, Heiss, G, Vockonas, P, Offenbacher, S. Periodontal disease and cardiovascular disease. *J. Periodont.* **67**, 1123-1127, 1996.

82. Offenbacher, S, Katz, V, Fertik, G, Collins, J, Boyd, D, Maynor, G, McKaig, K, Beck, J. Periodontal infection as a possible risk factor for preterm low birth weight. *J. Periodont.* **67**, 1103-1113, 1996.

83. Collins, IG, Kirtland, BC, Arnold, RR, Offenbacher, S. Experimental periodontitis retards hamster fetal growth. *Annual Meeting of the AADR*, San Antonio, TX, Abst. #1171, 1995.

84. Socransky, SS, Haffajee, AD, Smith, C, Dibart, S. Relation of counts of microbial species to clinical status at the site. *J. Clin. Periodontol.* **18**, 766-775, 1991.

85. Dahlen, G, Manji, F, Baelum, V, Fejerskov, O. Black-pigmented Bacteroides species and Actinobacillus actinomycetemcomitans in subgingival plaque of adult Kenyans. *J. Clin. Periodontol.* **16**, 305-310, 1989.

86. McNabb, H, Mombelli, AS, Gmur, R, Mathey-Din, S, Lang, NP. Periodontal pathogens in the shallow pockets of immigrants from developing countries. *Oral Microbiol. Immunol.* **7**, 267-272, 1992.

87. DiRienzo, JM , Slots, J. Genetic approach to the study of epidemiology and pathogenesis of Actinobacillus actinomycetemcomitans in localized juvenile periodontitis. *Arch. Oral Biol.* **35** (suppl), 79S-84S, 1990.

88. Alaluusua, S, Saarela, M. Jousimies-Somer, H, Asikainen, S. Ribotyping shows intrafamiliar similarity in Actinobacillus actinomycetemcomitans isolates. *Oral Microbiol. Immunol.* **8**, 225-229, 1993.

89. Petit, MDA, Van Steenbergen, TJM, DeGraff, J, van der Velden, U. Actinobacillus actinomycetemcomitans in families of adult periodontitis patients. *J. Periodontal Res.* **28**, 335-345, 1993a.

90. Petit, MDA, Van Steenbergen, TJM, Scholte, LMH, van der Velden, U, DeGraff, J. Epidemiology and transmission of Porphyromonas gingivalis and Actinobacillus

actinomycetemcomitans among children and their family members. *J. Clin. Periodontol.* **20**, 641-650, 1993b.

91. Saarela, M, von Troll-Linden, B, Torkko, H, Stucki, A-M, Alaluusua, S, Jousimies-Somer, H., *et al.* Transmission of oral bacterial species between spouses. *Oral Microbiol. Immunol.* **8**, 349-354, 1993.

92. Van Steenbergen, TJM, Petit, MD, Scholte, LH, van der Velden, U, DeGraff J. Transmission of Porphyromonas gingivalis between spouses. *J. Clin. Periodontol.* **20**, 340-345, 1993.

93. Preus, HR, Olson, I. Possible transmittance of *A. actinomycetemcomitans* from a dog to a child with rapidly destructive periodontitis. *J. Periodontal Res.* **23**, 68-71, 1988.

94. Offenbacher, S, Heasman, PA, Collins, JG. Modulation of host PGE2 secretion as a determinant of periodontal disease expression. *J. Periodontol.* **64**, 432-444, 1993.

95. Jeffcoat, MK, Page, R, Reddy, M, Wannawisute, A, Waite, P, Palcanis, K, Cogen, R, Williams, RC, Basch, C. Use of digital radiography to demonstrate the potential of naproxen as an adjunct in the treatment of rapidly progressive periodontitis. *J. Periodont. Res.* **26**, 415-421, 1991.

96. Jeffcoat, MK, Reddy, MS, Haigh, S, Buchanan, W, Doyle, MJ, Meredith, MP, Nelson, SL, Goodale, MB, Wehmeyer, KR. A comparison of topical ketorolac, systemic flurbiprofen and placebo for the inhibition of bone loss in adult periodontitis. *J. Periodontol.* **66**, 329-338, 1995.

97. Golub, LM, Ramamurthy, NS, McNamara, TF, Greenwald, RA, Rifkin, BR. Tetracyclines inhibit connective tissue breakdown, New therapeutic implications for an old family of drugs. *Crit. Rev. Oral Biol. Med.* **2**, 297-322, 1991.

98. Page, RC. Humoral response in patients with periodontitis, Effects of treatment and propects for a vaccine. *Compen. Contin. Dent. Educ.* **15** (suppl. 18), S666-S671, 1994.

99. Persson, GR, Engel, D, Whitney, C, Darveau, R, Weinberg, A, Brunsvold, M, Page, RC. Immunization against Porphyromonas gingivalis inhibits progression of experimental periodontitis in nonhuman primates. *Infect. Immun.* **62**, 1026-1031, 1994.

100. Wozney, JM. The potential role of bone morphogenetic proteins in periodontal reconstruction. *J. Periodontol.* **66**, 506-510, 1995.

101. Sigurdsson, TJ, Tatakis, DN, Lee, MB, Wikesjo, UME. Periodontal regenerative potential of space-providing expanded poyltetrafluorethylene membranes and recombinant human bone morphogenetic proteins. *J. Periodontol.* **66**, 511-521, 1995.

102. Cho, M-H, Lin, W-L, Genco, RJ. Platelet-derived growth factor-modulated guided tissue regenerative therapy. *J. Periodontol.* **66**, 522-530, 1995.

103. Hardwick, R, Hayes, BK, Flynn, C. Devices for dentoalveolar regeneration, An up-to-date literature review. *J. Periodontol.* **66**, 495-505, 1995.

Acknowledgement

Supported in part by grants from the National Institutes of Health Number 5 P01 DE08555, 5 P50 DE08229 and T32 DE07063. The author is grateful to Anne Kastel for the preparation of this manuscript.

11 Microbial specificity and virulence factors in periodontitis

Jørgen Slots, Casey Chen and Homa Zadeh

University of Southern California, School of Dentistry, MC-0641, Los Angeles, CA 90089-0641, USA

The bacterial specificity in periodontitis is becoming increasing clear. The proportion of subgingival Actinobacillus actinomycetemcomitans increase markedly before initiation of localized juvenile periodontitis. Adults on supportive periodontal therapy with elevated proportions of Actinobacillus actinomycetemcomitans and Porphyromonas gingivalis *exhibit an increased relative risk for periodontitis recurrence. A sensitive polymerase chain reaction assays found Actinobacillus actinomycetemcomitans and Porphyromonas gingivalis to be relatively rare inhabitants of the healthy mouth. These organisms also evoke strong antibody responses that are comparable with those of classic medical infections. DNA fingerprinting studies have suggested transmission of Actinobacillus actinomycetemcomitans between adults and children, and of* Porphyromonas gingivalis *between adults. Studies in families with localized juvenile periodontitis and adult periodontitis suggest that transmission of these organisms can cause disease in the recipient. Based on the characteristic occurrence and host immune response of Actinobacillus actinomycetemcomitans and* Porphyromonas gingivalis, *these two species may be considered exogenous pathogens in the human mouth. Major virulence factors of Actinobacillus actinomycetemcomitans and* Porphyromonas gingivalis *include fimbriae and other surface structures that are important in the initial attachment to host tissues and microbial plaque. Fimbrillin proteins of Actinobacillus actinomycetemcomitans and* Porphyromonas gingivalis *constitute interesting candidates for vaccine development against oral colonization of these bacteria. Porphyromonas gingivalis also expresses several proteolytic enzymes that may play roles in adherence, nutrient acquisition, evasion of host immune defense, and host tissue destruction. In addition, Actinobacillus actinomycetemcomitans and Porphyromonas gingivalis induce superantigen-like proliferation of T-cells in vitro. Superantigens may play a role in periodontitis by inducing immune dysfunction as a result of altering the T cell repertoire and disrupting the normal homeostasis of immunoregulatory T cells. This may dilute the antigen-specific response and eventually paralyze the immune response and/or induce tissue injury mediated by effector cytokines. Thus, periodontopathic microorganisms may induce their pathogenic effects either directly or indirectly by manipulating the host.*

Introduction

Periodontal diseases result from bacterial infections. Conventional mechanical debridement and possibly adjunctive antimicrobial therapy are effective in limiting or arresting the progression of periodontal disease. However, the virtually asymptomatic course of periodontal disease causes many affected subjects not to seek therapy before major damage to the dentition has occurred.

Much research has been directed toward development of simple and effective means to diagnose and treat periodontal disease. Unfortunately, destructive periodontal disease represents one of the most difficult challenges facing scientists interested in infectious diseases. A variety of very different microorganisms can produce periodontal disease. The subgingival microbiota exists in a deeply anaerobic environment of the periodontal pocket that may compromise important antimicrobial mechanisms of polymorphonuclear leukocytes and other protective host cells. Several suspected periodontal pathogens have evolved devastating strategies to avoid host immune response.

Despite the complex parasite-host interactions in human periodontal disease, a considerable body of information has been gathered about important periodontopathic organisms, microbial mechanisms of virulence, and antimicrobial host reactions. This paper describes new insights into how *Actinobacillus actinomycetemcomitans* and *Porphyromonas gingivalis*, which probably constitute the two most important periodontal pathogens in humans, may give rise to destructive periodontal disease. The possible importance of bacterial superantigens in the pathogenesis of periodontal disease is emphasized.

Disease association

Research in the 1980s related the levels of subgingival *A. actinomycetemcomitans* and *P. gingivalis* and systemic and local antibodies against these species to progressive periodontitis.[1] *A. actinomycetemcomitans* tends to be associated with periodontitis in children and adolescents,[2] and *P. gingivalis* with adult forms of periodontitis[3] but these pathogens can be associated with periodontal disease in all age groups.

Recent studies have focused on the utility of periodontal pathogens as predictors for periodontal tissue breakdown. In prospective studies, subgingival *A. actinomycetemcomitans* proportions tended to increase markedly at 6 months or less prior to initiation of localized juvenile periodontitis.[4] Black-pigmented anaerobic rods as a group (mainly *P. gingivalis* and *Prevotella intermedia/nigrescens*) were not able to reliably predict periodontitis progression in untreated patients.[5] Wennström *et al.*[6] demonstrated that the absence of *A. actinomycetemcomitans, P. gingivalis* and *P. intermedia* was a better predictor of no further loss of attachment than the presence of these species was for disease progression. Listgarten *et al.*[7] showed that these three bacteria by themselves were not reliably predictors of future disease; however, the organisms coupled with increased pocket probing depth seemed to imply an increased risk of periodontal breakdown. Haffajee *et al.*[8] used the proportional

Table 1 *Utility of 5 major putative pathogens and clinical parameters to predict periodontal breakdown.*[a]

Baseline	Disease	Stable	*p*-Value
No. of subjetcs	25	53	
Mean pocket depth in mm	2.6	2.2	0.008
Mean % sites>4 mm depth	6.0	1.5	0.001
Mean no. of teeth with furcation involvement	3.5	2.1	0.02
% subjects with critical test microorganisms	80	53	0.02

No relationship between disease activity and sex, race, current smoking, mean number of missing teeth, mean plaque index or mean gingival index.
[a]Data obtained from Rams *et al.*[10]

recovery of *P. gingivalis, Campylobacter rectus, Veillonella parvula* (health-associated species) and *Capnocytophaga ochracea* (health-associated species) to correctly identify disease activity over a period of 2 months in 28 of 38 subjects. Brown *et al.*[9] showed *P. gingivalis* and *P. intermedia* in subgingival proportions greater than 2% to be significant predictors of periodontitis progression over an 18-month period in older adults.

Rams *et al.*[10] studied the predictive utility of 5 major putative periodontopathic species, "superinfecting" organisms, and several clinical parameters relative to periodontitis recurrence over a 12-month period. 78 treated adult patients enrolled in a 3-month maintenance care program participated in the study. A 2.5 relative risk for periodontitis recurrence was found for subjects yielding at baseline cultivable subgingival proportions of either 0.01% *A. actinomycetemcomitans,* 0.1% *P. gingivalis,* 2.5% *P. intermedia,* 2.0% *C. rectus* or 3.0% *Peptostreptococcus micros.* The best predictive capability for periodontitis recurrence was a combination of the recovery of one or more of the 5 test species in elevated subgingival proportions, the proportion of 5 mm probing depths, and the mean whole-mouth probing depth (Table 1). The study found no relationship between baseline plaque and gingival indices and subsequent periodontitis disease activity. Overall, the findings indicate that elevated subgingival proportions of major putative periodontal pathogens together with increased probing pocket depths predispose adults on maintenance care to increased risk of recurrent periodontitis disease-activity.

Future approaches to predict periodontal disease activity should focus on high risk patient groups[11] and include a combination of microbiological parameters, representing the infectious component of periodontal disease breakdown, and clinical parameters mirroring host susceptibility. With increased knowledge about critical host factors in periodontal disease, direct measurement of host susceptibility might be possible as well.

Epidemiology

The epidemiology of *A. actinomycetemcomitans* and *P. gingivalis* in various populations have been studied using DNA fingerprinting techniques such as arbitrarily primed polymerase chain reaction (AP-PCR),[12] restriction fragment length polymorphism (RFLP),[13] and restriction endonuclease analysis.[14] *A. actinomycetemcomitans* is transmitted between adults and children[12,14,15] and *P. gingivalis* between adults.[12,16,17] That the transmission of these organisms may cause disease in the recipient has been implied in families with localized juvenile periodontitis[15] and adult periodontitis.[18]

A. actinomycetemcomitans and *P. gingivalis* may constitute exogenous organisms in the human oral cavity.[19] These species are relatively rare inhabitants of the healthy mouth. Sensitive PCR-based diagnostic assays detected subgingival *A. actinomycetemcomitans* and *P. gingivalis* in, respectively, 14% and 10% of healthy young adults[20] and the two species comprised less than 1% of the subgingival microbiota in culture-positive healthy individuals.[1] Also, *A. actinomycetemcomitans* and *P. gingivalis* evoke strong systemic and local antibody responses that are comparable with those of classic medical infections.[1] Moreover, systemic antibiotic therapy can eradicate or suppress these organisms to below detectable levels for at least 2 years.[21] In contrast, treatment of endogenous infections merely reduces opportunistic indigenous pathogens.

The realization of a possible exogenous nature of periodontal *A. actinomycetemcomitans* and *P. gingivalis* infections may be exploited in the prevention and treatment of destructive periodontal disease. Classical means for managing infectious diseases, including antibiotic or vaccination strategies, might be employed to control periodontal pathogens in a family/cohabitant setting.

Virulent clones

A clone of microbial organisms denotes a collection of isolates that are recovered from different sources but are phenotypically and genetically similar, suggesting a common origin of the isolates.[22] Bacterial clonality has been delineated using polyacrylamide gel electrophoretic analysis of membrane proteins and lipopolysaccharides, multilocus enzyme electrophoretic typing, restriction endonuclease analysis, DNA sequence analysis, RFLP analysis, and AP-PCR analysis. Studies show that most medical pathogens comprise discrete clones, and a few clones are responsible for the majority of the disease caused by the species.[23] The pathogenic clones are those that are successful in competing for an ecological niche and in producing pathologic changes. Similarly, relatively few *A. actinomycetemcomitans* and *P. gingivalis* clones may cause the majority of the periodontitis associated with these species. Also, different clones of *A. actinomycetemcomitans* and *P. gingivalis* may cause distinct types of periodontitis. If so, periodontal microbial diagnostics should aim at identifying not only the species recovered, but also the specific clones of the species involved.

Strains of *A. actinomycetemcomitans* vary in pathogenic potential. *In vitro* studies have shown that *A. actinomycetemcomitans* strains differ in production of leukotoxin[24] and in adhesion and invasion of epithelial cells,[25,26] suggesting a clonal difference in the pathogenicity of this species.

Slots *et al.*[27] used AP-PCR and RFLP analyses to identify 30 distinct clones among 73 *A. actinomycetemcomitans* strains from different geographic areas in the USA; five major clones comprised 41 strains. A recent study from our laboratory found similar clones and clonal distribution among *A. actinomycetemcomitans* strains from Finland, further supporting the existence of a clonal structure within the *A. actinomycetemcomitans* species.[28] Caugant *et al.*[29] identified 11 electrophoretic types among 17 *A. actinomycetemcomitans* isolates.

DiRienzo *et al.*[30] used a randomly cloned probe for RFLP analysis of *A. actinomycetemcomitans* isolates from localized juvenile periodontitis patients and their healthy family members, as well as from unrelated healthy controls in a 5-year longitudinal study. Of 15 *A. actinomycetemcomitans* RFLP types, genotype II occurred with high prevalence in subjects converting from periodontally healthy status to periodontitis. The RFLP type II clone was absent in non-converting, *A. actinomycetemcomitans*-positive individuals. On the basis of AP-PCR analysis and serotyping of 93 *A. actinomycetemcomitans* strains, Asikainen *et al.*[31] identified clones within serogroup b that were preferentially associated with either adult periodontitis or localized juvenile periodontitis. Apparently, the *A. actinomycetemcomitans* species includes clones of particularly high periodontopathic potential.

P. gingivalis strains inoculated subcutaneously in animals demonstrate a considerable strain-to-strain variation in pathogenicity.[3] The more virulent strains cause disseminated infections with severe tissue damage or death, whereas less virulent or non-invasive strains produce localized abscess with milder tissue damage. Similarly, *P. gingivalis* strains produce different severity of disease in subcutaneous tissue chamber in animal studies.[3] Quantative or qualitative variations in the production of virulence factors among individual strains may explain differences in pathogenicity.

Chen and Slots,[32] using the AP-PCR method, identified 59 genotypes among 73 *P. gingivalis* strains from adult periodontitis patients. Loos *et al.*[33] examined the electrophoretic types of 88 human *P. gingivalis* strains and 12 animal strains from 11 countries over 5 continents. Most strains originated from periodontitis sites and a few were from other odontogenic infections. 78 distinct electrophoretic types in three major divisions were identified. All human strains were assigned to division I. The disease-associated *P. gingivalis* strains were widely distributed over different electrophoretic types and no distinct virulent clones were identified. However, the study included relatively few strains from periodontally healthy subjects. Furthermore, difficulties in defining clinically distinct periodontal disease types and

Table 2 *Virulence factors of A. actinomycetemcomitans and P. gingivalis .*

Virulence factor or trait	Possible role in pathogenesis
A. actinomycetemcomitans	
Fimbriae	Adherence
Extracellular vesicle	Adherence
Extracellular amorphous material	Adherence
Leukotoxin	Avoidance of host defense
Tissue invasion	Avoidance of host defense, tissue damage
Intracellular invasion	Avoidance of host defense, tissue damage
Superantigen(s)	Distraction of host defense, tissue damage
P. gingivalis	
Fimbriae	Adherence
Proteolytic enzymes	Adherence, avoidance of host defense, tissue damage
Haemagglutinin	Adherence
Lipopolysaccharide	Tissue damage
Capsule	Avoidance of host defense
Fibroblast activating factor	Tissue damage
Intracellular invasion	Avoidance of host defense, tissue damage
Superantigen(s)	Distraction of host defense, tissue damege

in assessing disease activity might have hampered determination of the association between virulent *P. gingivalis* clones and disease severity.

Virulence factors

A microbial virulence factor is defined as a trait that contributes to the pathogenesis of the an organism. Virulence factors are loosely classified into three categories; adherence, avoidance of host defense, and tissue damage.[34] Table 2 lists potential virulence factors of *A. actinomycetemcomitans* and *P. gingivalis.*

Microbial adherence is an important part of the early events in host-pathogen interaction. Many bacterial species have fimbriae (pili), hair-like surface projections which may mediate adherence to either the host tissue or to other bacteria. Interactions between fimbriae and receptors on eukaryotic cells have been characterized for many bacterial species including *Escherichia coli,*[35] *Neisseria gonorrheae,*[36] and *Haemophilus influenzae.*[37]

Freshly isolated *A. actinomycetemcomitans* strains demonstrate fimbriae that may not be expressed after several *in vitro* passages. Fimbriated strains of *A. actinomycetemcomitans* have shown 3-4 folds greater adherence to hydroxyapatite, saliva-coated hydroxyapatite[38] and to mouse skin epithelial cells[39] than non-fimbriated variants. The structural composition of *A. actinomycetemcomitans* fimbriae has not been defined. Gillespie *et al.*[40] found that crude preparations of fimbriae from a *A. actinomycetemcomitans* strain consisted of 11 kDa, 29 kDa and 63 kDa proteins and suggested that the 11 kDa protein may be an important adhesin for *A. actinomycetemcomitans.* Inouye *et al.*[41] identified a 54 kDa fimbrial protein from an *A. actinomycetemcomitans* clinical isolate. Synthetic peptide analogues of the protein were used to generate rabbit anti-fimbrillin sera.[42] The anti-fimbrillin sera reacted with other *A. actinomycetemcomitans* strains and inhibited the adherence of *A. actinomycetemcomitans* to buccal epithelial cells.[42] Meyer and Fives-Taylor[39] showed that fimbriae, along with two other surface structures (extracellular vesicles and extracellular amorphous material), mediate the adherence of *A. actinomycetemcomitans* to epithelial cells. Little information is available on the non-fimbrial adhesins of *A. actinomycetemcomitans*.

Following adherence to host tissue or preexisting microbial plaque, *A. actinomycetemcomitans* is able to enter host tissue either extracellularly or intracellularly. Christersson *et al.*[43] using immunofluorescence and culture methods provided evidence for the presence of extracellular *A. actinomycetemcomitans* in periodontal gingival tissue of juvenile periodontitis patients. Meyer *et al.*[32] demonstrated intracellular invasion of *A. actinomycetemcomitans* in epithelial cell lines *in vitro*. The internalization was an active process, requiring modulation of both *A. actinomycetemcomitans* and host cells, similar to the invasion mechanism utilized by other invasive microorganisms.[25,44] It is conceivable that *A. actinomycetemcomitans* uses both extracellular and intracellular strategies to evade the host defense and produce greater host tissue damage.

P. gingivalis fimbriae was initially identified and purified by Yoshimura *et al.*[45] The monomeric subunit of the fimbriae (fimbrillin) was estimated to be 43 kDa[45] and the gene encoding fimbrillin (*fimA*) has been cloned and sequenced.[46] Fimbriae and synthetic peptide analogue of fimbrillin inhibit binding of *P. gingivalis* to saliva-coated hydroxyapatite[47] and anti-fimbriae monoclonal antibody inhibits adherence of *P. gingivalis* to epithelial cells.[48] *FimA* gene-inactivated *P. gingivalis* mutant expresses lower binding capacity to saliva-coated hydroxyapatite[49] and to human gingival fibroblasts[50] than the wild type. Collectively, these findings suggest that *P. gingivalis* fimbriae mediate adherence of the organism to host tissue. *P. gingivalis* fimbriae may also be involved in other phases of the pathogenesis, as evidenced by an diminished ability of the *fimA*-inactivated mutant to cause periodontal bone loss in a gnotobiotic rat model of periodontal disease.[49] There are conflicting reports on the relationship between fimbriae and haemagglutination activity.[45,51] However, it appears that at least some types of fimbriae may not possess haemagglutination activity, since inactivation of *fimA* expression does not influence the haemagglutination activity in the mutant strain.[49,50] Other surface molecules such as proteolytic enzymes may in part be responsible for the haemagglutination activity of *P. gingivalis*.

P. gingivalis expresses a variety of distinct proteolytic enzymes that may play roles in adherence, nutrient acquisition, evasion of host immune defense, and host tissue destruction. Most *P. gingivalis* enzymes have been characterized by their enzyme activity and apparent molecular weights. However, the use of different study strains, different growth conditions and different enzymatic assays in studies makes it difficult to determine the relationship between the various proteases.

Madden *et al.*[52] cloned and sequenced the *prtT* gene from *P. gingivalis* ATCC 53977. The 96-99 kDA PrtT protein is a cysteine protease and hemagglutinin. Sequence analysis indicated a close relationship between the PrtT protein and streptococcal pyrogenic exotoxin B and streptococcal proteinase. Bourgeau *et al.*[53] cloned and sequenced the *tpr* gene from *P. gingivalis* which appeared to be a unique thiol protease. Kato *et al.*[54] isolated and sequenced the collagenase gene *prtC* from *P. gingivalis*. The collagenase is a 35 kDa protein and the active enzyme behaved as a dimer, and exhibited proteolytic activity against type I collagen. Pike *et al.*[55] identified a 50 kDa arginine-specific preoteinase and a 60 kDa lysine-specific cysteine proteinase, referred to as Arg-gingipain (RGP-1) and Lys-gingipain proteinases. Both enzymes complexed non-covalently with a 44 kDa haemagglutinin. The gene for RGP-1 was cloned and sequenced.[56] The gene coded for a polyprotein of 185.4 kDa containing the RGP-1 and four adhesion proteins of 44, 27, 17 and 15 kDa previously identified in the high molecular mass gingipain. Since the high molecular mass gingipain was 95 kDa, it was suggested that the 50 kDa RGP-1 was complexed noncovalently with different components of the individual adhesion proteins. Kirszbaum *et al*[57] reported cloning and sequencing of the *prtR* gene encoding a 132 kDa protein that contained an arginine-specific thiol protease and a hemagglutinin. The arg-specific protease was essentially identical to the RGP-1 and the 44 kDa adhesion component of the high molecular mass gingipain.[55,56,58] Okamoto *et al.*[59] also cloned and sequenced a arginine-specific cysteine protease gene that exhibited a nearly identical sequence to the 50 kDa RGP-1 protease and the 44 kDa adhesion protein.

Other proteolytic enzymes with no published sequence data include a 70 kDa Lys-gingivain thiol protease,[60] a 94 kDa collagenase with mode of action resembling cysteine protease,[61] three proteases identified by Hinode *et al.*,[62] a 44 kDa cysteine protease/haemagglutinin identified by Nishikata and Yoshimura,[63] a 105-110 kD serine protease, a 72-80 kDa arg-specific thiol protease, a 44 kDa thiol protease with activity against both arginine and lysine, and a 47 kDa trypsin-like protease I identified by Curtis *et al.*,[64] and a 80 kDa trypsin-like protease with ability to inactivate complement-dependent bactericidal activity.[65] These proteases need to be further characterized.

Immunopathogenicity

Immunomodulatory effects of bacteria in periodontal disease
The pathogenic effects of periodontopathic bacteria is mediated in part by their ability to manipulate the host, a property referred to as immunomodulation. The immune response has been likened to a double-edged sword, on the one hand fighting microorganisms that it comes in contact with and on the other hand it may mediate injury to the very host it is charged with protecting. Maintaining a balance between these two conflicting properties is assured by proper immunoregulation which preserves health. Conversely, a breakdown of this immunoregulation may lead to disease. Critical to an understanding of the pathogenesis of periodontitis, have been efforts to dissect the protective immune mechanisms from those that mediate localized tissue injury. The prevailing concept that has emerged from research in this area appears to be that periodontal disease is initiated as a consequence of immunoregulatory dysfunctions that tip the balance between

protective and destructive immune mechanisms toward the latter.[66] There are phenotypic, as well as functional indications of immunoregulatory imbalance in periodontitis.[66] The idea that periodontopathic bacteria may use immunomodulation as a virulence factor, thus giving rise to the immunoregulatory dysfunction has been around for several decades. A number of periodontitis-associated bacteria have been shown to possess immunomodulatory properties including, immunoproliferation,[67, 68] immunoadjuvant effects,[69] immunosuppression[67-70] and polyclonal B cell activation.[71] The best-characterized immunomodulatory bacterial products are the lipopolysaccharides of gram-negative bacteria, which can activate B cells, monocytes/macrophages, and polymorphonuclear leukocytes.[72] In addition, polyclonal B cell activators are produced by many of the periodontitis-associated bacteria, and can activate B cells in an antigen-independent fashion.[71] However, in most cases, the bacterial components that mediate the immunomodulatory effects have not been defined.

The review of the literature in this area reveals that progress in identifying bacterial components that initiate the T cell response in periodontal disease has not kept at equal pace with the other areas. This is partly due to early reports that suggested that the predominant cell type of the inflammatory infiltrate in advanced periodontitis sites is B cells.[73] However, we have since learned that there is a large population of T cells in the inflammatory infiltrate[74-77] and that these cells are a key component of the immune response.[78] T lymphocytes are generally believed to be the regulators of the immune response; therefore, information about how the T cell response is initiated and the components of the dental plaque that moderate this response is critical to the understanding of the pathogenesis of periodontal disease.

Immunomodulation by superantigens
Recently, a component of bacteria and viruses has been described which modulate the T cell response in a dramatic fashion. These products, referred to as superantigens, are defined by the unique manner in which they modulate the immune response.[79] Their immunomodulatory properties also appear to be of significance in periodontitis. Superantigens are potent stimulators of T cells, yet ironically they are ultimately thought to be immunosuppressive.[80] Superantigens are believed to cause immune dysfunction by (1) massive antigen-independent T cell stimulation which disrupts the delicate homeostasis that is maintained by having specific proportions of immunoregulatory T cell subsets relative to other cells;[81] (2) following the initial T cell proliferation, there is eventual deletion of T cell subsets, as well as anergy (functional inactivation of T cells); (3) superantigen-activated T cells elaborate tremendous quantities of cytokines that can paralyze the local immune system and induce tissue injury[82, 83] followed by underexpression of other cytokines due to T cell depletion and/or anergy; and (4) the antigen-independent T cell stimulation can potentially lead to the activation of quiescent autoreactive T cells.[84] These autoreactive T cells can either directly induce tissue injury by cell-mediated cytotoxicity or act as helper T cells, activating B cells that produce autoantibodies. Furthermore, long-term stimulation of T cells with superantigens *in vivo*, leads to functional inactivation or cell death.[85, 86] In extreme cases, such as in AIDS, it has been proposed that superantigens encoded by the HIV virus, initially cause

Table 3 *Summary of the properties of conventional antigens, mitogens and superantigens*

Property	Conventional antigens	Mitogens	Superantigens
Domain of TCR critical for recognition	Vβ Jβ Dβ / Vα Jα[a]	α/β	Vβ
Frequency of responder cells	1,106 to 1,104	1,10 to 1,1	1,20 to 1,4
Requirement for processing by APC[b]	Yes	No	No
Presenting molecule on APC	MHC Class I & II[c]	N/A[d]	MHC Class II
MHC Class II binding	Yes	No	Yes
MHC restriction	Yes	No	No

[a] Variable segment of T cell antigen receptor β-chain
[b] Antigen presenting cells
[c] Major histocompatibility antigen
[d] Not applicable

large-scale T cell expansion and lymphadenopathy followed by progressive depletion of the superantigen-stimulated T cell subsets.[87-90] Thus, the superantigen-induced local immune paralysis is a clever virulence factor of microorganisms to exploit the immune response to their advantage and increase their survival.

Superantigens and medical disease
Bacterial infections have been known to be followed by autoimmune disease, *e.g.* streptococcal infections are sometimes followed by rheumatic fever;[91] however, the mechanism of that has only been investigated recently. The availability of reagents with which to study the various domains of the T cell antigen receptor (TCR) has enabled investigators to define the molecular mechanism behind the interactions of microbial products with T cells. As a result, a novel pathway of disease induction by microorganisms has been proposed. The role of microbial superantigens in a number of disease states has been studied, and there are varying strengths of evidence in support of their role in diseases such as rheumatoid arthritis,[92-94] toxic shock syndrome,[95] diabetes mellitus,[96] tuberculosis,[97] Kawasaki disease,[98] multiple sclerosis,[84] systemic lupus erythematosus,[84] inflammatory bowel disease,[99] sarcoidosis[100], and acquired immunodeficiency syndrome (AIDS).[87-90]

A number of microorganisms have been shown to produce superantigens, and their list is gradually growing and includes *Yersinia enterocolitica*[101] *Yersinia pseudotuberculosis*,[102] *Mycoplasma arthritidis*,[103] *Staphylococcus aureus*,[80] *Streptococcus pyogenes*,[80] *Pseudomonas aeroginosa*,[104] *Clostridium perfringens*,[105] *Borrelia burgdorferi*,[106] and *Mycobacterium tuberculosis*.[97] In addition, we have recently shown that some of the periodontopathic bacteria have superantigenic properties.

Mechanism of action of superantigens
Superantigens differ from conventional antigens in several important respects (summarized in Table 3). Some of these differences will be briefly reviewed. T cells recognize exogenous conventional antigens only after being processed by antigen

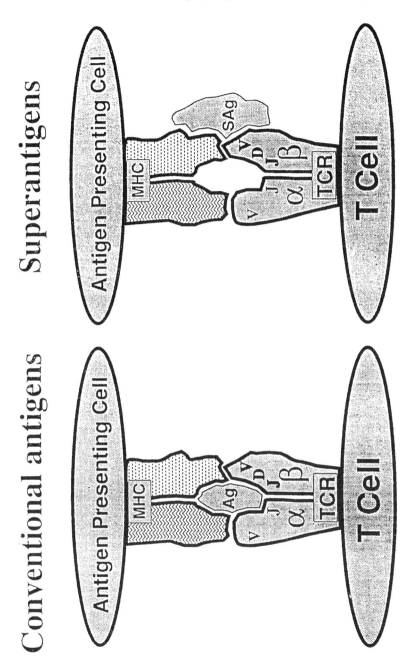

Figure 1 *Molecular mechanism of recognition of conventional antigens (Ag) and superantigens (SAg) by T cells. Variable (V), Joining (J) and Diversity (D) domains of α- and β-chains of the T cell receptor (TCR) are illustrated.*

presenting cells (APC).[107] During antigen processing molecules are taken up by APC and broken into smaller fragments, bound to major histocompatibility (MHC) molecules and transported to the surface. T cells are then able to recognize the complex between antigen and MHC molecule by their T cell antigen receptors (TCR), which is analogous to immunoglobulin on B cells. Two classes of TCR's are expressed by human T cells: TCRαβ which is expressed by approximately 95% and TCRγδ expressed by approximately 5% of peripheral T cells. The TCRαβ is composed of two chains (α and β), each of which has a constant (C), variable (V) and joining (J) domain.[108] The β-chain also contains a diversity region (D). There are multiple C, V, D, and J families of genes, for example there are 25 different Vβ genes, ie Vβ1, Vβ2, Vβ3, etc. The diversity of T cells is generated by random rearrangement of the various C, V, J and D gene segments to code for a unique TCR molecule. A model for the recognition of conventional antigens is presented in Figure 1.

In contrast, superantigens bypass some of these steps and bind to the more common components of the MHC and TCR molecules. As a result, superantigens react with T cells at a higher frequency leading to a much more widespread response. Superantigens do not require processing by APC and they can be presented by APC after merely binding to MHC molecules.[81] Superantigens also do not require binding to the antigen combining site on TCR. For each conventional antigen there is a specific TCR which is present on very few T cells (*i.e.* 1 in a million T cells). Conversely, superantigens bind to the Vβ domain of TCR, outside of the antigen combining site (Figure 1). Each superantigen can bind to one or few of the 25 different Vβ families and activate nearly all of the T cells that express that Vβ family, irrespective of the antigen specificity of the TCR. The immune response to superantigens is characterized by T cells that express a limited number of Vβ's, eg the superantigen toxic shock syndrome toxin is specific for the Vβ2 region and in toxic shock syndrome nearly half of all peripheral blood T cells are Vβ2$^+$. Thus, superantigens are potent stimulators of T cell proliferation, capable of activating and expanding a large number of T cells.

Superantigens and periodontitis
Studies in our laboratory have focused on determining the expression of superantigens associated with *A. actinomycetemcomitans* and *P. gingivalis.*[109,110] To investigate whether these microorganisms express superantigens, it was assessed whether they can stimulate T cells *in vitro* that display dominance of a limited number of Vβ's. To that end, peripheral blood mononuclear cells from healthy volunteers were cultured *in vitro* with sonic extracts of *A. actinomycetemcomitans*, *P. gingivalis*, known superantigens as positive control or media alone for 3 days and recultured with interleukin-2 for an additional day. The cultured cells were harvested, immunofluorescently labeled with anti-TCRαβ which measures the proportion of all T cells and Vβ-specific monoclonal antibodies and analyzed by multivariate flow cytometry (Figure 2).

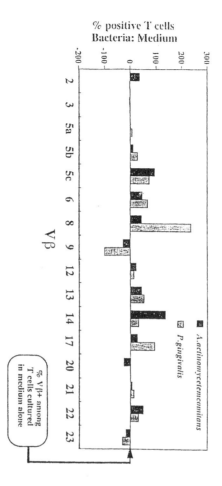

Figure 2 *Alteration of the repertoire of T cells expressing various Vb regions induced by periodontopathic bacteria. T cells were cultured in the presence of* A. actinomycetemcomitans, P. gingivalis *or media. The percentages of T cell subsets expressing each of the Vβ regions in the presence or absence of the bacteria were determined by immunofluorescent labeling of cells with specific monoclonal antibodies against each Vβ region, in conjunction with a pan T cell marker (anti-TCRαβ) followed by multivariate flow cytometry. The X axis represents the Vβ's examined. The Y axis represents percentage of Vβ regions in cultures containing* A. actinomycetemcomitans *or* P. gingivalis *normalized relative to control cultures using the formula, 100 X [(%Vβ+ T cells in cultures containing bacteria / %Vβ+ T cells in control cultures) - 100]. In this manner, the % of T cell subsets expressing each Vβ in control cultures was normalized to zero. This data is representative of five experiments with individual donors.*

T cell cultures containing *A. actinomycetemcomitans* are characterized by a TCR Vβ repertoire that is different than that of control cultures not containing any bacterial sonicates. Specifically, in cultures containing *A. actinomycetemcomitans* higher proportions of T cells expressing Vβ2, Vβ5c, Vβ6, Vβ8, Vβ13, Vβ14, and Vβ22 are detected. Similarly, a skewing in the proportion of T cells expressing Vβ5c, Vβ6, Vβ8, Vβ9, Vβ13, and Vβ17 is noted among T cells stimulated by *P. gingivalis* compared with T cells cultured in media alone. Stimulation of T cells with the microorganisms induces a 25-200% skewing of these Vβ's compared with media. These results suggest that *A. actinomycetemcomitans* and *P. gingivalis* induce perturbation of TCR Vβ repertoire *in vitro*, a key characteristic of superantigens.

Evidence for the presence of superantigen-stimulated T cells in periodontitis sites
Since superantigens recognize Vβ and expand T cell subsets based on their particular Vβ, this is the strongest evidence for the *in vivo* action of superantigens. To provide evidence for the existence of T cells activated and expanded by superantigens in periodontitis lesion sites, the proportion of T cells that express various TCR Vβ families in isolated gingival leukocyte preparations was determined. To that end, the expression of various Vβ's in gingiva and peripheral blood of five adult periodontitis and three rapidly progressive periodontitis patients were compared. The results in Figure 3 illustrate the differences between the Vβ's in gingiva and peripheral blood lymphocytes.[111] In this graph, the proportion of T cells expressing each Vβ is considered the baseline for that individual (zero value) and the percentage of Vβ+ T cells in gingiva of those subjects that is below or above the peripheral blood lymphocytes value is shown here. These results underscore the marked differences between the repertoire of Vβ families expressed in gingiva and peripheral blood lymphocytes. Some of the Vβ regions such as Vβ2 were very similar in peripheral blood lymphocytes and gingiva of the periodontitis patients. On the other hand, most of the other Vβ regions were markedly different in the two sites. It is notable that although many Vβ's appear to be elevated in gingiva, some are apparently underrepresented.

When the proportion of various Vβ families in gingiva of periodontitis and non-periodontitis patients is plotted, it is evident that two or three Vβ families account for up to 50% of all T cells in periodontitis patients.112 In comparison, gingival and peripheral blood T cells of non-periodontitis subjects use the various Vβ families more evenly. Hence, our data support the hypothesis that superantigen-stimulation in periodontitis patients constitutes a major pathway of T cell activation in gingiva.

Immunointervention of superantigen-induced diseases
Recent advances in molecular interactions of the antigens/superantigens, TCR and MHC trimolecular complex have contributed to the development of new treatment strategies of T cell-mediated diseases. These include (1) peptide immunotherapy, which entails addition of peptides that act as competitive inhibitors of the trimolecular complex[113] and (2) T cell vaccination, which involves vaccinating with

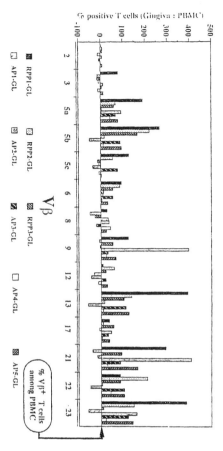

Figure 3 *Comparison of the expression of T cell receptor Vβ regions among isolated gingival T cells and peripheral blood mononuclear cells (PBMC) of periodontitis patients. Gingival specimens were obtained from three rapidly progressive periodontitis (RPP) and five adult periodontitis (AP) patients. Gingival leukocytes (GL) were isolated by digestion of the gingiva with type IV collagenase[112]. The expression of various Vβ regions was measured by immunofluorescent labeling of cells with specific monoclonal antibodies against each Vβ region, in conjunction with a pan T cell marker (anti-TCRαβ) followed by multivariate flow cytometry. Each column represents one patient. The X axis represents the Vβ's examined. The Y axis represents percentage of gingival T cells that are positive for each given Vβ relative to that among PBMC. The values are calculated as, 100 X [(%Vβ+ gingival T cells / %Vβ+ PBMC T cells) - 100]. According to this formula, the percentage of T cells positive for each Vβ in PBMC is considered zero. Note that the T cell receptor Vβ repertoire in gingiva varies significantly from that of peripheral blood. Where no bars are shown, the proportion of Vβ in gingiva is the same as that of peripheral blood.*

T cell clones that bear specificity to the target antigens/superantigens, leading to the generation of anti-idiotypic antibodies, ie antibodies specific for the T cell antigen receptor molecules.[114] Both of these strategies have been successful in preventing and reversing disease in animal models, such as those for rheumatoid arthritis and multiple sclerosis. It is conceivable to devise similar strategies in the treatment of periodontitis, if the molecular mediators of disease are identified. Therefore, defining the domains of the T cell receptor molecules important in periodontitis and the bacterial components that interact with the TCR may lay the foundation for devising new diagnostic and therapeutic modalities.

References

1. Slots J, Listgarten MA. *Bacteroides gingivalis, Bacteroides intermedius* and *Actinobacillus actinomycetemcomitans* in human periodontal diseases. *J Clin Periodontol* 1988, **15**, 85-93.
2. Dougherty MA, Slots J. Periodontal diseases in young individuals. *J Calif Dent Assoc* 1993, **21** (January issue), 55-69.
3. Slots J, Rams TE. Pathogenicity of *Porphyromonas gingivalis*. 1993, 127-138. In: HN Shah, D Mayrand, RJ Genco (eds). *Biology of the species* Porphyromonas gingivalis. CRC Press, Inc., Boca Raton, FL.
4. Slots J, Schonfeld SE. *Actinobacillus actinomycetemcomitans* in localized juvenile periodontitis. 1991, 53-64. In: S Hamada, SC Holt, JR McGhee (eds). *Periodontal disease, pathogens & host immune responses.* Quintessence Publishing Co., Ltd., Tokyo, Japan.
5. MacFarlane TW, Jenkins WMM., Gilmour WH, McCourtie J, McKenzie D. Longitudinal study of untreated periodontitis. *J Clin Periodontol* 1988, **15**, 331-337.
6. Wennström JL, Dahlén G, Svensson J, Nyman S. *Actinobacillus actinomycetemcomitans, Bacteroides gingivalis* and *Bacteroides intermedius*, predictors of attachment loss? *Oral Microbiol Immunol* 1987, **2**, 158-163.
7. Listgarten MA, Slots J, Nowotny AH, Oler J, Rosenberg J, Gregor B, Sullivan P. Incidence of periodontitis recurrence in treated patients with and without cultivable *Actinobacillus actinomycetemcomitans, Prevotella intermedia* and *Porphyromonas gingivalis*, A prospective study. *J Periodontol* 1991, **62**, 377-386.
8. Haffejee AD, Socransky SS, Smith C, Dibart S. Relation of baseline microbial parameters to future periodontal attachment loss. *J Clin Periodontol* 1991, **18**, 744-750.
9. Brown LF, Beck JD, Rozier RG. Incidence of attachment loss in community-dwelling older adults. *J Periodontol* 1994, **65**, 316-323.
10. Rams TE, Listgarten MA, Slots J. Utility of 5 major putative periodontal pathogens and selected clinical parameters to predict periodontal breakdown in patients on maintenance care. *J Clin Periodontol* 1996, **23**, 346-354.
11. Slots J, Taichman NS, Oler J, Listgarten MA. Does the analysis of the subgingival flora have value in predicting periodontal breakdown? 1988, 132-140. In: B Guggenheim (ed). *ERGOB proceedings on the conference "Periodontology Today".* S. Karger AG, Basel, Switzerland.
12. Asikainen S, Chen C, Slots J. Likelihood of transmitting *Actinobacillus actinomycetemcomitans* and *Porphyromonas gingivalis* in families with periodontitis. *Oral Microbiol Immunol* 1996, **11**, 387-394.

13. DiRienzo JM, Cornell S, Kazoroski L, Slots J. Probe-specific DNA fingerprinting applied to the epidemiology of localized juvenile periodontitis. *Oral Microbiol Immunol* 1990, **5**, 49-56.
14. Petit MDA, van Steenbergen TJM, de Graff J, van der Velden U. Transmission of *Actinobacillus actinomycetemcomitans* in families of adult periodontitis patients. *J Periodont Res* 1993, **28**, 335-345.
15. DiRienzo JM, Slots J, Sixou M, Sol M-A, Harmon R, McKay TL. Specific genetic variants of *A. actinomycetemcomitans* correlate with disease and health in a regional population of localized juvenile periodontitis families. *Infect Immun* 1994, **62**, 3058-3065.
16. van Steenbergen TJM, Petit MDA, Scholte LHM, van der Velden U, de Graaff J. Transmission of *Porphyromonas gingivalis* between spouses. *J Clin Periodontol* 1993, **20**, 340-345.
17. Saarela M, von Troil-Lindén B, Torkko H, Stucki A-M, Alaluusua S, Jousimies-Somer H, Asikainen S. Transmission of oral species between spouses. *Oral Microbiol Immunol* 1993, **8**, 349-354.
18. Von Troil-Lindén B, Torkko H, Alaluusua S, Wolf J, Jousimies-Somer H, Asikainen S. Periodontal findings in spouses. A clinical, radiologic and microbiological study. *J Clin Periodontol* 1995, **22**, 93-99.
19. Slots J, van Winkelhoff AJ. Antimicrobial therapy in periodontics. *J Calif Dent Assoc* 1993, **21** (November issue), 51-56.
20. Ashimoto A, Chen C, Bakker I, Slots J. Polymerase chain reaction detection of 8 putative periodontal pathogens in subgingival plaque of gingivitis and advanced periodontitis lesions. *Oral Microbiol Immunol* 1996, **11**, 266-273.
21. Pavicic MJAMP, van Winkelhoff AJ, Douqué NH, Steures RWR, de Graaff J. Microbiological and clinical effects of metronidazole and amoxicillin in *Actinobacillus actinomycetemcomitans* associated periodontitis, a 2-year evaluation. *J Clin Periodontol* 1994, **21**, 107-112.
22. Ørskov F, Ørskov I. Summary of a workshop on the clone concept in the epidemiology, taxonomy, and evolution of the *Enterobacteriaceae* and other bacteria. *J Infect Dis* 1983, **148**, 346-357.
23. Finlay BB, Falkow S. Common themes in microbial pathogenicity. *Microbiol Rev* 1989, **53**, 210-230.
24. Zambon JJ. *Actinobacillus actinomycetemcomitans* in human periodontal disease. *J Clin Periodontol* 1985, **12**, 1-20.
25. Mintz KP, Fives-Taylor PM. Adhesion of *Actinobacillus actinomycetemcomitans* to a human oral cell line. *Infect Immun* 1994, **62**, 3672-3678.
26. Meyer DH, Sreenivasan PK, Fives-Taylor PM. Evidence for invasion of a human oral cell line by *Actinobacillus actinomycetemcomitans*. *Infect Immun* 1991, **59**, 2719-2726.
27. Slots J, Liu YB, DiRienzo JM, Chen C. Evaluating two methods for fingerprinting genomes of *Actinobacillus actinomycetemcomitans*. *Oral Microbiol Immunol* 1993, **8**, 337-343.
28. Chen C, Asikainen S, Slots J. AP-PCR analysis shows transmission of periodontal pathogens between cohabiting adults. *Annual meeting of the American Society for Microbiology* 1994, 142 (Abstract # D-261).
29. Caugant DA, Selander RK, Olsen I. Differentiation between *Actinobacillus* (*Haemophilus*) *actinomycetemcomitans*, *Haemophilus aphrophilus* and *Haemophilus paraphrophilus* by multilocus enzyme electrophoresis. *J Gen Microbiol* 1990, **361**, 2135-2141.

30. DiRienzo JM, Slots J, Sixou M, Sol M-A, Harmon R, McKay TL. Specific genetic variants of *Actinobacillus actinomycetemcomitans* correlate with disease and health in a regional population of families with localized juvenile periodontitis. *Infect Immun* 1994, **62**, 3058-3065.

31. Asikainen S, Chen C, Slots J. *Actinobacillus actinomycetemcomitans* genotypes in relation to serotypes and periodontal status. *Oral Microbiol Immunol* 1995, **10**, 65-68.

32. Chen C, Slots J. Clonal analysis of *Porphyromonas gingivalis* by the arbitrarily primed polymerase chain reaction. *Oral Microbiol Immunol* 1994, **9**, 99-103.

33. Loos BG, Dyer DW, Whittam TS, Selander RK. Genetic structure of populations of *Porphyromonas gingivalis* associated with periodontitis and other oral infections. *Infect Immun* 1993, **61**, 204-212.

34. Slots J, Genco RJ. Black-pigmented *Bacteroides* species, *Capnocytophaga* species, and *Actinobacillus actinomycetemcomitans* in human periodontal disease, virulence factors in colonization, survival, and tissue destruction. *J Dent Res* 1984, **63**, 412-421.

35. Hacker J. Genetic determinants coding for fimbriae and adhesins of extraintestinal *Escherichia coli*. *Curr Topics Microbiol Immunol* 1990, **151**, 1-27.

36. Heckels JE. Structure and function of pili of pathogenic *Neisseria* species. *Clin Microbiol Rev* 1989, **2** (Suppl), S66-S73.

37. Guerina NG, Langermann S, Schoolnik GK, Kessler TW, Goldmann DA. Purification and characterization of *Haemophilus influenzae* pili, and their structural and serological relatedness to *Escherichia coli* P and mannose-sensitive pili. *J Exp Med* 1985, **161**, 145-159.

38. Rosan B, Slots J, Lamont RJ, Listgarten MA, Nelson GM. *Actinobacillus actinomycetemcomitans* fimbriae. *Oral Microbiol Immunol* 1988, **3**, 58-63.

39. Meyer DH, Fives-Taylor PM. Characteristics of adherence of *Actinobacillus actinomycetemcomitans* to epithelial cells. *Infect Immun* 1994, **62**, 928-935.

40. Gillespie MJ, DeNardin E, Cho MI, Zambon JJ. Isolation and characterization of fimbrial proteins from *Actinobacillus actinomycetemcomitans*. *J Dent Res* 1990, **69**, 297.

41. Inouye T, Ohta H, Kokeguchi S, Fukui K, Kato K. Colonial variation and fimbriation of *Actinobacillus actinomycetemcomitans*. *FEMS Microbiol Lett* 1990, **69**, 13-18.

42. Harano K, Yamanaka A, Kato T, Okuda K. Molecular biological study of *A. actinomycetemcomitans* fimbriae. *J Dent Res* 1994, **73**, 899.

43. Christersson LA, Albini B, Zambon JJ, Wikesjo UME, Genco RJ. Tissue localization of *Actinobacillus actinomycetemcomitans* in human periodontitis. I. Light, immunofluorescence and electron microscopic studies. *J Periodontol* 1987, **58**, 529-539.

44. Sreenivasan PK, Meyer DH, Fives-Taylor PM. Requirements for invasion of epithelial cells by *Actinobacillus actinomycetemcomitans*. *Infect Immun* 1993, **61**, 1239-1245.

45. Yoshimura F, Takahashi K, Nodasaka Y, Suzuki T. Purification and characterization of a novel type of fimbriae from the oral anaerobe *Bacteroides gingivalis*. *J Bacteriol* 1984, **160**, 949-957.

46. Dickinson DP, Kubiniec MA, Yoshimura F, Genco RJ. Molecular cloning and sequencing of the gene encoding the fimbrial subunit protein of *Bacteroides gingivalis*. *J Bacteriol* 1988, **170**, 1658-1665.

47. Lee J-Y, Sojar HT, Bedi GS, Genco RJ. Synthetic peptides analogous to the fimbrillin sequence inhibit adherence of *Porphyromonas gingivalis*. *Infect Immun* 1992, **60**, 1662-1670.

48. Isogai H, Siogai E, Yoshimura F, Suzuki T, Kagota W, Takano K. Specific inhibition of adherence of an oral strain of *Bacteroides gingivalis* 381 to epithelial cells by monoclonal antibodies against the bacterial fimbriae. *Arch Oral Biol* 1988, **33**, 479-485.

49. Malek R, Fisher JG, Caleca A, Stinson M, van Oss CJ, Lee J-Y, Cho M-I, Genco RJ, Evans RT, Dyer DW. Inactivation of the *Porphyromonas gingivalis fimA* gene blocks periodontal damage in gnotobiotic rats. *J Bacteriol* 1994, **176**, 1052-1059.

50. Hamada N, Watanabe K, Sasakawa C, Yoshikawa M, Yoshimura F, Umemoto T. Construction and characterization of a *fimA* mutant of *Porphyromonas gingivalis*. *Infect Immun* 1994, **62**, 1696-1704.

51. Ogawa T, Hamada S. Hemagglutinating and chemotactic properties of synthetic peptide segments of fimbrial protein from *Porphyromonas gingivalis*. *Infect Immun* 1994, **62**, 3305-3310.

52. Madden TE, Clark VL, Kuramitsu HK. Revised sequence of the *Porphyromonas gingivalis PrtT* cysteine protease/hemagglutinin gene, homology with streptococcal pyrogenic exotoxin B/streptococcal proteinase. *Infect Immun* 1995, **63**, 238-247.

53. Bourgeau G, Lapointe H, Peloquin P, Mayrand D. Cloning, expression, and sequencing of a protease gene (*tpr*) from *Porphyromonas gingivalis* W83 in *Escherichia coli*. *Infect Immun* 1992, **60**, 3186-3192.

54. Kato T, Takahshi N, Kuramitsu HK. Sequence analysis and characterization of the *Porphyromonas gingivalis prtC* gene, which expresses a novel collagenase activity. *J Bacteriol* 1992, **174**, 3889-3895.

55. Pike R, McGraw W, Potempa J, Travis J. Lysine- and arginine-specific proteinases from *Porphyromonas gingivalis*. *J Biol Chem* 1994, **269**, 406-411.

56. Pavloff N, Potempa J, Pike RN, Prochazka V, Kiefer MC, Travis J, Barr PJ. Molecular cloning and structural characterization of the arg-gingipain proteinase of *Porphyromonas gingivalis*. *J Biol Chem* 1995, **270**, 1007-1010.

57. Kirszbaum L, Sotiropoulos C, Jackson C, Cleal S, Slakeski N, Reynolds EC. Complete nucleotide sequence of a gene *prtR* of *Porphyromonas gingivalis* W50 encoding a 132 kDa protein that contains an arginine-specific thiol endopeptidase domain and a haemagglutinin domain. *Biochem Biophys Res Comm* 1995, **207**, 424-431.

58. Chen Z, Potempa J, Polanowski A, Wikstrom M, Travis J. Purification and characterization of a 50-kDa cysteine proteinase (gingipain) from *Porphyromonas gingivalis*. *J Biol Chem* 1992, **267**, 18896-18901.

59. Okamoto K, Misumi Y, Kadowaki T, Yoneda M, Yamamoto K, Ikehara Y. Structural characterization of argingipain, a novel arginine-specific cysteine proteinase as a major periodontal pathogenic factor from *Porphyromonas gingivalis*. *Arch Biochem Biophys* 1995, **316**, 917-925.

60. Scott CF, Whitaker EJ, Hammond BF, Colman RW. Purification and characterization of a potent 70 kDa thiol lysyl-proteinase (Lys-gingivain) from *Porphyromonas gingivalis* that cleaves kininogens and fibrinogen. *J Biol Chem* 1993, **268**, 7935-7942.

61. Lawson DA, Meyer TF. Biochemical characterization of *Porphyromonas* (*Bacteroides*) *gingivalis* collagenase. *Infect Immun* 1992, **60**, 1524-1529.

62. Hinode D, Hayashi H, Nakamura R. Purification and characterization of three types of proteases from culture supernatants of *Porphyromonas gingivalis*. *Infect Immun* 1991, **59**, 3060-3068.

63. Nishikata M, Yoshimura F. Characterization of *Porphyromonas* (*Bacteroides*) *gingivalis* haemagglutinin as a protease. *Biochem Biophys Res Comm* 1991, **178**, 336-342.

64. Curtis MA, Macey M, Slaney JM, Howells GL. Platelet activation by protease I of *Porphyromonas gingivalis* W83. *FEMS Microbiol Lett* 1993, **110**, 167-174.

65. Grenier D. Inactivation of human serum bactericidal activity by a trypsinlike protease isolated from *Porphyromonas gingivalis*. *Infect Immun* 1992, **60**, 1854-1857.

66. Taubman MA, Wang HY, Lundqvist CA, Seymour GJ, Eastcott JW, Smith DJ. The cellular basis of host response in periodontal diseases. 1991, 199-208. In: S Hamada, SC Holt, JR McGhee (eds). *Periodontal disease, pathogens & host immune responses*. Quintessence Publishing Co., Ltd., Tokyo, Japan.

67. Shenker BJ, Slots J. Immunomodulatory effects of *Bacteroides* products on in vitro human lymphocyte functions. *Oral Microbiol Immunol* 1989, **4**, 24-29.

68. Shenker BJ, Vitale L, Slots J. Immunosuppressive effects of *Prevotella intermedia* on *in vitro* human lymphocyte activation. *Infect Immun* 1991, **59**, 4583-4589.

69. Ochiai K, Kurita T, Nishimura K, Ikeda T. Immunoadjuvant effects of periodontitis-associated bacteria. *J Periodont Res* 1989, **24**, 322-328.

70. Kurita-Ochiai T, Ochiai K, Ikeda T. Immunosuppressive effect induced by *Actinobacillus actinomycetemcomitans*: effect on immunoglobulin production and lymphokine synthesis. *Oral Microbiol Immunol* 1992, **7**, 338-343.

71. Tew J, Engel D, Mangan D. Polyclonal B-cell activation in periodontitis. *J Periodont Res* 1989, **24,** 225-241.

72. Ranney RR. Immunologic mechanisms of pathogenesis in periodontal diseases: An assessment. *J Periodont Res* 1991, **26**, 243-254.

73. Seymour GJ, Powell RN, Davies WIR. Conversion of a stable T-cell lesion to a progressive B-cell lesion in the pathogenesis of chronic inflammatory periodontal disease: an hypothesis. *J Clin Periodontol* 1979, **6**, 267-277.

74. Stoufi ED, Taubman MA, Ebersole JL, Smith DJ. Preparation and characterization of human gingival cells. *J Periodont Res* 1987, **22**, 144-149.

75. Stoufi ED, Taubman MA, Ebersole JL, Smith DJ, Stashenko PP. Phenotypic analyses of mononuclear cells recovered from healthy and diseased periodontal tissues. *J Clin Immunol* 1987, **7**, 235-245.

76. Malberg K, Mülle A, Streuer D, Gängler P. Determination of lymphocyte populations and subpopulations extracted from chronically inflamed human periodontal tissues. *J Clin Periodontol* 1992, **19**, 155-158.

77. Meng HX, Zheng LF. T cells and T cell subsets in periodontal disease. *J Periodont Res* 1989, **24**, 121-126.

78. Seymour GJ, Gemmel E, Reinhardt R, Eastcott J, Taubman M. Immunopathogenesis of chronic inflammatory periodontal disease: cellular and molecular mechanisms. *J Periodont Res* 1993, **28**, 478-486.

79. Kotzin BL, Satyanarayana H, Chou YK, Lafferty J, Forrester JM, Better M, Nedwin GE, Offner H, Vandenbark AA. Preferential T-cell receptor β-chain variable gene use in myelin basic protein-reactive T-cell clones from patients with multiple sclerosis. *Proc Natl Acad Sci USA* 1991, **88**, 9161-9165.

80. Kotzin B, Leung D, Kappler J, Marrack PC. Superantigens and their potential role in human disease. *Adv Immunol* 1993, **54**, 99-149.

81. Herman A, Kappler JW, Marrack P, Pullen AM. Superantigens, Mechanism of T-cell stimulation and role in immune responses. *Ann Rev Immunol* 1991, **9**, 745-772.

82. Brand J, Kirchner H, Neustock P, Kruse A. Induction of cytokines in human whole blood cultures by a mitogen derived from mycoplasma arthritidis and by staphylococcal enterotoxin B. *Immunobiology* 1992, **186**, 246-253.

83. Mourad W, Mehindate K, Schall TJ, McColl SR. Engagement of major histocompatibility complex class II molecules by superantigen induces inflammatory cytokine gene expression in human rheumatoid fibroblast-like synoviocytes. *J Exp Med* 1992, **175**, 613-616.

84. Freidman SM, Posnett DN, Tumang JR, Cole BC, Crow MK. A potential role for microbial superantigens in the pathogenesis of systemic autoimmune disease. *Arthritis Rheumatol* 1991, **34**, 468-480.

85. Huang L, Crispe IN. Superantigen-driven peripheral deletion of T cells. Apoptosis occurs in cells that have lost the alpha/beta T cell receptor. *J Immunol* 1993, **151**, 1844-51.

86. McCormack JE, Callahan JE, Kappler J, Marrack PC. Profound deletion of mature T cells in vivo by chronic exposure to exogenous superantigen. *J Immunol* 1993, **150**, 3785-92.

87. Laurence J, Hodtsev AS, Posnett DN. Superantigen implicated in dependence of HIV-1 replication in T cells on TCR V beta expression. *Nature* 1992, **358**, 255-259.

88. Laurence J, Hodtsev AS, Posnett DN. Superantigens in infectious diseases, including AIDS. *Ann NY Acad Sci* 1993, **685**,746-755.

89. Bisste L R. Looking for a 'superantigen' in AIDS, a possible role for *Mycoplasma*? *Med Hypothesis* 1993, **40**, 146-53.

90. Soudeyns H, Rebai N, Pantaleo G, Ciurli C, Boghossian T, Sekaly RP, Fauci A. The T cell receptor V-beta repertoire in HIV-1 infection and diseases. *Immunology* 1993, **5**, 175-185.

91. Zulma A. Superantigens, T cells, and microbes. *Clin Infect Dis* 1992, 15, 313-20.

92. Broker B, Korthauer U, Heppt P, Weseloh G, de la Camp R, Kroczek A, Emmirch E. Biased T cell receptor V gene usage in rheumatiod arthtitis. *Arthritis Rheumat* 1993, **36**, 1234-1243.

93. Paliard X, West SG, Lafferty JA, Kappler JW, Marrack P, Kotzin BL. Evidence for the effects of a superantigen in rheumatoid arthritis. *Science* 1991, **253**, 325-329.

94. Schwab J, Brown R, Anderle S, Sclievert P. Superantigen can reactivate bacterial cell wall-induced arthritis. *J Immunol* 1993, **150**, 4151-4159.

95. Choi BY, Lafferty JA, Clements JR, Todd JK, Gelfand E, Kappler J, Marrack P, Kotzin B. Selective expansion of T cells expressing V beta 2 in toxic shock syndrome. *J Exp Med* 1990, **172**, 981-984.

96. Conrad B, Weldman E, Trucco G, Rudert WA, Behboo R, Ricordl C, Finegold D, Trucco M. Evidence for superantigen involvement in insulin-dependent diabetes mellitus aetiology. *Nature* 1994, **371**, 351-355.

97. Ohmen J, Barnes P, Grisso C, Bloom B, Modlin R. Evidence for a superantigen in human tuberculosis. *Immunity* 1994, **1**, 35-43.

98. Abe J, Kotzin BL, Jujo K, Melish ME, Glode MP, Kohsaka T, Leung DY. Selective expansion of T cells expressing T-cell receptor variable regions V beta 2 and V beta 8 in Kawasaki disease. *Proc Nat Acad Sci USA* 1992, **89**, 4066-4070.

99. Posnett DN, Schmelkin I, Burton DA, August A, McGrath H, Mayer LF. T cell receptor V gene usage, Increases in Vbeta8+ T cells in Crohn's disease. *J Clin Invest* 1990, **85**, 1770-1776.

100. Tamura N, Holroyd KJ, Banks T, Kirby M, Okayama H, Crystal RG. Diversity in junctional sequences associated with the common human V gamma 9 and V delta 2 gene segments in normal blood and lung compared with the limited diversity in a granulomatous disease. *J Exp Med* 1990, **172**, 169-181.

101. Stuart PM, Woodward JG. *Yersinia enterocolitica* produces superantigenic activity. *J Immunol* 1992, **148**, 225-229.

102. Miyoshi-Akiyama T, Imanishi K, Uchiyama T. Purification and partial characterization of a product from *Yersinia pseudotuberculosis* with the ability to activate human T cells. *Infect Immun* 1993, **61**, 3922-3927.

103. Cole KL, Seymour GJ, Powell RN. Phenotypic and functional analyses of T cells extracted from chronically inflamed human periodontal tissues. *J Periodontol* 1987, **58**, 569.

104. Fleischer B. Superantigens. *Curr Opin Immunol* 1992, **4**, 392-395.

105. Bowness P, Moss PA, Tranter H, Bell JI, McMichael AJ. *Clostridium perfringens* enterotoxin is a superantigen reactive with human T cell receptors V beta 6.9 and V beta 22. *J Exp Med* 1992, **176**, 893-896.

106. Lahesmaa R, Shanafelt MC, Allsup A, Soderberg C, Anzola J, Freitas V, Turck C, Steinman L, Peltz G. Preferantial usage of T cell antigen receptor V region gene segment V beta 5.1 by *Borrelia burgdorferi* antigen-reactive T cell clones isolated from a patient with lyme dieases. *J Immunol* 1993, **150**, 4125-4135.

107. Matis LA. The molecular basis of T-cell specificity. *Ann Rev Immunol* 1990, **8**, 65-82.

108. Moss PAH, Rosenberg WMC, Bell JI. The human T cell receptor in health and disease. *Ann Rev Immunol* 1992, **10**, 71-96.

109. Zadeh HH, Slots J, Karimzadeh K, Kreutzer DL. A. *actinomycetemcomitans*-stimulated T cells express dominance of a limited number of TCR Vβ regions, akin to superantigens. *J Dent Res* 1995, **74**, 125.

110. DerSarkissian C, Wager KA, Kreutzer DL, Slots J, Zadeh HH. Superantigenic properties of *Porphyromonas gingivalis*, dominant expression of a limited number of TCR Vβ regions by in vitro stimulated T cells. *Int Congress Immunol* 1995, 721 (Abstract # 4276).

111. Karimzadeh K, Kreutzer DL, Zadeh HH. Dominant expression of T cell receptor Vβ regions among isolated gingival T cells suggests local stimulation by superantigens. *J Dent Res* 1995, **74**, 62.

112. Zadeh HH, Kreutzer DL. Evidence for the involvement of superantigens in periodontal diseases, skewed expression of T cell receptor variable regions by gingival T cells. *Oral Microbiol Immunol* 1996, **11**, 88-95.

113. Vandenbark AA, Chou YK, Bourdette DN, Whitham R, Hashim GA, Offner H. T cell receptor peptide therapy for autoimmune disease. *J Autoimmunity* 1992, **5 Suppl. A**, 83-92.

114. Kingsley G, Panayi GS. Intervention with immunomodulatory agents, T cell vaccination. *Baillieres Clin Rheumatol* 1992, **6**, 435-454.

updates in periodontics

just published

⇨ **Oral Health Care for those with HIV Infection and Other Special Needs**

⇨ **Innovations and Developments in Non-Invasive Orofacial Health Care**

⇨ **Medical and Dental Aspects of Anaerobes**

Diseases of the Periodontium

Edited by
H.N. Newman, *Institute of Dental Surgery, London,England*
T.D. Rees, *Baylor College of Dentistry, Dallas, Texas, USA*
D.F. Kinane, *University of Glasgow, Glasgow, Scotland*

ISBN 0-905927-93-1   301+v pages   Hardback

The diseases of the periodontium constitute an important part of oral medicine. Yet is is easy to forget that the periodontium is subject to a range of diseases as wide as that of any other part of the body. The diseases of the periodontium have received little attention.This volume establishes a working classification, primarily for the forms of chronic inflammatory periodontal disease and reviews the pathologies to which periodontal tissues are subject.

Contents

Classification of periodontal diseases H. N. Newman
Chronic inflammatory periodontal diseases - genetic and immune factors S. J. Challacombe
Systemic disorders and chronic inflammatory periodontal disease T. D. Rees
Specific periodontal infections P. R. Morgan
Drugs and the periodontium T. D. Rees
Periodontal neoplasia D. M. Walker
Haematological disorders and the periodontium D . F . K inane
Dermatology, autoimmune disease and the periodontium D. M. Williams
Periodontal cysts and epulides W. H. Binnie
Cementum disorders and osteodystrophies J . M. Wright

Medical and Dental Aspects of Anaerobes

Edited by

B.I. Duerden, *University of Wales College of Medicine, Cardiff,* W.G. Wade, *University of Bristol,* J.S. Brazier, *University Hospital of Wales,* A. Eley, *University of Sheffield Medical School,* B. Wren, *St. Bartholomew's Medical College, London,* and M.J. Hudson, *Centre for Applied Microbiology and Research, Porton Down*

ISBN 0-905927-59-1   436 + vi pages   Hardback

The activity and effects of anaerobic bacteria are of special interest to medical and dental microbiology. The contents of this volume are based on peer reviewed papers assembled from the Eighth Biennial International Symposium of the Society for Anaerobic Microbiology jointly with the Oral Microbiology and Immunology Group. Topics addressed ranged from anaerobes as causes of clinical infection, through their role in the normal flora of man and animals and the impact of antibiotics (both beneficial and damaging), to molecular studies opening up new understanding of the taxonomy of anaerobes and providing new approaches to clinical diagnosis.

Contents

• Difficult and Uncultivable Anaerobes in Periodontal Disease

• **16 chapters** on: *Eubacterium, Propionibacterium,* Spirochaetes, unculturable micro-organisms, RNA sequences, *Bacteroides gracilis, Porphyronomas gingivalis,* black pigmented anaerobes, temperate bacteriophages, DNA probes, lethal photosensitisation, anaerobic cocci, *Peptostreptococcus micros.*

• Anaerobic Intestinal Ecosystems

• **7 chapters** on: Microbial ecology and metabolism, probiotics, H_2 disposal, dietary oligosaccharides, intestinal recolonisation, cyst-like structure, *Serpulina hyodysenteriae*

• Ecology and Epidemiology of *Clostridium difficile*

• **18 chapters** on: *Clostridium difficile,* infection, and associated disease, chronic care facilities, associated diarrhoea, laboratory response, ELISA kits, surveillance, rapid detection by PCR, purification of toxins, adherence to mammalian cells, isolation, sporulation, isolation rates, typing methods, chemotaxis, *Bacteroides vulgatus, Bacteroides fragilis.*

• Antibiotics, Anaerobes and Clinical Infections

• **20 chapters** on: antimicrobials, oral infections, 5-nitroimidazole resistance, *B. ureolyticus,* vancomycin, E test, *Prevotella bivia,* spyramycin gel, outer membrane analysis, plasmids in *B. ureolyticus,* morphological characteristics, animal model pathogenecity, recurrent tonsillitis, eye infections, chronic malodorous cellulitis, intra-uterine fusobacteria infection, gram-positive rods in mixed wound infections , *Anaerobiospirillum succiniciproducens,* genital microplasmas, the Oxoid Anaerogen system

• DNA Technology and Anaerobes

• **10 chapters** on: molecular variations of toxins, *C. perfringens,* gram-negative anaerobes, DNA probes, conjugative transposon, molecular cloning, multilocus enzyme electrophoresis, typing fusobacteria, SDS-PAGE, *Bilophila wadsworthia*

Oral Health Care
for those with
HIV Infection and Other Special Needs

Edited by
Stephen R Porter and Crispian Scully, *Eastman Dental Institute for Oral Healthcare Sciences, London, England*

ISBN 0-905927-64-8   220 + vi pages   Published June 1995   Hardback

This volume presents an up-to-date synopsis of the practical oral healthcare for patients with HIV infection and others with special needs. It is based on the experiences of a range of international specialists. It will prove valuable to all members of the healthcare team.

Contents

Introduction
HIV disease: Overview
HIV infection epidemiology and overview of oral and dental problems
HIV-associated oral fungal and bacterial infections
HIV: Viral infections

HIV disease: Gingival and periodontal aspects
HIV disease: Oral neoplasms
HIV-associated salivary gland disease
Oral health care for HIV-positive individuals
Viral hepatitis
Infection control
Congenital coagulopathies

Innovations and Developments in
Non-Invasive Orofacial Health Care

Edited by
Stephen R Porter and Crispian Scully, *Eastman Dental Institute for Oral Healthcare Sciences, London, England*

ISBN 0-905927-84-2   220 + vi pages   Published June 1995   Hardtback

These chapters review the contemporary management of orofacial disease. The contributors are leaders in their clinical fields. This volume therefore provides an invaluable guide for the management of orofacial disease pain, vesicular bullous oral mucosal disease and oral malignancy

Pain
Neuralgia
Idiopathic facial pain
Burning mouth syndrome
The non-surgical management of temporomandibular joint dysfunction
Aspects of placebo and psychological therapy in orofacial pain

Malignancy
Epidemiological considerations of oral malignancy
Chemoprevention and medical theory of oral malignancy and premalignancy

Photodynamic therapy and laser therapy
Mucositis related to cancer therapy
Xerostomia and radiotherapy for malignancy
Post-operative restoration after surgical therapy of oral malignancy

Vesiculoerosive Disorders
Recurrent aphthous stomatitis
Lichen planus and lichenoid lesions
Bullous diseases

Mucosal Infections
Viral infections
Fungal Infections
Chemical plaque control

Order form

To: Science Reviews Ltd., 41-43 Green Lane, Northwood, Middlesex HA6 3AE England
Phone: +44 (0)1923 823 586 Fax: +44 (0)1923 825 066 e-mail srl@scitech.demon.co.uk
in the USA
Henchek & Associates, 68 East Wacker Place, Suite 800 Chicago, IL 60601 Fax 312 324 7719

Please despatch

.....copy(ies) of *Diseases of the Periodontium* at £30/$57 each ....

.....copy(ies) of *Oral Health Care for those with HIV Infection
               and Other Special Needs* at £35/$66.60 each ....

.....copy(ies) of *Medical and Dental Aspects of Anaerobes* at £60/$123 each ....

.....copy(ies) of *Innovations and Developments in
               Non-Invasive Orofacial Health Care* at £35/$66.60 each ....

                                                                    Total ....

Name...

Address...
....

Check enclosed □/ invoice my institution / I wish to pay by Mastercard □ / Visa □ /
Eurocard □ /American Express □

Card number..

Expiry Date..

Name on card...

Signed... Date..

                                    Please tick where appropriate